Grammatically
CORRECT 2ND EDITION

THE ESSENTIAL GUIDE TO SPELLING, STYLE, USAGE, GRAMMAR, AND PUNCTUATION

REVISED & UPDATED

WRITER'S DIGEST
BOOKS

WritersDigest.com
Cincinnati, Ohio

Anne Stilman

For more resources for writers, visit www.writersdigest.com/books.

To receive a free weekly e-mail newsletter delivering tips and updates about writing and about Writer's Digest products, register directly at http://newsletters.fwpublications.com.

17 16 15   8 7

Distributed in Canada by Fraser Direct, 100 Armstrong Avenue, Georgetown, Ontario, Canada L7G 5S4, Tel: (905) 877-4411. Distributed in the U.K. and Europe by David & Charles, Brunel House, Newton Abbot, Devon, TQ12 4PU, England, Tel: (+44) 1626-323200, Fax: (+44) 1626-323319, E-mail: postmaster@davidandcharles.co.uk. Distributed in Australia by Capricorn Link, P.O. Box 704, Windsor, NSW 2756 Australia, Tel: (02) 4577-3555.

Library of Congress Cataloging-in-Publication Data

Grammatically correct : the essential guide to spelling, style, usage, grammar, and punctuation / by Anne Stilman. -- 2nd ed.

p. cm.

Includes index.

ISBN 978-1-58297-616-7 (alk. paper)

1. English language--Grammar--Handbooks, manuals, etc. 2. English language--Rhetoric--Handbooks, manuals, etc. 3. English language--Usage--Handbooks, manuals, etc. I. Title.

PE1112.S748 2010

428.2--dc22

2010001925

Edited by Nicole Klungle and Scott Francis
Designed by Claudean Wheeler
Production coordinated by Mark Griffin

To the memory of my mother, Ruth

CONTENTS

Preface

IN THE YEARS SINCE I WROTE the first edition of this book, the English language has not changed a great deal, but much else has. Back in the mid-1990s, the World Wide Web was just poising to take off and "Google" was not yet a verb. If you needed an answer to something, your options were to haul out the family encyclopedia—which if you were lucky was no more than a decade out of date—or head to the library. Got a question today, on grammar or anything else? Type in a key word, click on "Search," and choose from the ocean of hits that come up.

Reference books today, therefore, must compete against an instant, no-cost, and unimaginably vast resource when it comes to providing information. And yet, their very limitation can be a plus as well. While online searches are unmatched when it comes to looking up quick facts, they are not always the ideal route when there is a need to process, assimilate, and apply what is retrieved. Apart from the fact that the volume of information can be overwhelming, searches often yield fragments of answers that must be pieced together to gain a proper understanding; and the Web's egalitarianism, in so many ways a strength, means *caveat emptor* when it comes to accuracy.

In the first edition, my strategy for squeezing yet another writer's reference book into an admittedly already crowded field was to try to steer a middle course between too little and too much: providing enough detail to give a sufficient understanding of an idea while avoiding scholarly explanations. That approach continues to hold here. Obviously no single book on this subject can meet everyone's needs, but many lie too close to either end of the spectrum to be fully helpful. At the low end are those that are outright superficial, stating flat do's and don'ts without providing a sense of proportion, and leaving readers confused or unsatisfied. Those at the high end, however, may cover topics with such thoroughness as to be overwhelming. Aspiring writers may wish to know with certainty when to say *I* and when *me*, when to use *which* and when *that*, when to apply the semicolon and when the colon. But many of them wish to know all this without having it explained through intimidating terminology and academic rules.

With this type of reader in mind, I have put together a reference that steers clear of jargon and theory, focusing instead on practical strategies and intuitive explanations. Some specialized terminology is unavoidable, but in no case is a discussion presented solely in terms of grammatical constructs. Explanations are designed to get to the heart of a concept and provide a sufficient sense of *when* and *how* to use it, along with examples that show what ambiguities or misinterpretations might result if the rules are not followed. In cases where there is more than one acceptable way to do something, my approach is not to prescribe one over another but simply to describe the options.

As before, I've sought to liven up what can be a somewhat dusty subject by excerpting passages from very quotable literary works, both classic and modern. Academic explanations of how to use a certain punctuation mark or stylistic technique are all very well, but a "real-life" illustration can be a lot more convincing—and engaging. My thanks to all those authors, both past and present, whose work I have cited. To further improve the usability of this book, some sections provide test-yourself exercises that readers can work through before checking the answers or suggested revisions. Such a hands-on approach is often the most effective way of getting knowledge to stick, as it gives learners a chance to recognize and correct their own errors.

While the basic structure of the book remains the same as in the first edition, I have revisited the explanations and examples, freshening up those that seemed dated, and have added several new topics. The content has been slightly rearranged and is organized as follows. Part 1 deals with aspects of individual words: spelling in a broad sense (hard-to-spell words, frequently confused homonyms, spelling variations, and hyphenation); the complexity and irregularity of English vocabulary (words that are frequently confused with others or are used in the wrong way, or that are often muddled in their derivative forms); and how the typography aspects of capitalization, italics, and boldface can be used to add emphasis or other special meanings. Part 2 tackles the bugbear of punctuation, describing the role of each mark in achieving clarity and affecting tone, and showing how misuses can lead to ambiguity. Part 3 looks at a number of grammar issues that frequently present difficulty: agreement of subject and verb, parallel structure, positioning of modifiers, use of tenses, use of pronouns, and active versus passive voice; it also provides a brief review of some conventions that are sometimes taken too seriously. (Note: in the first edition, this part was simply titled "Grammar," but has here been renamed to avoid the implication that the other parts in this book are *not* on grammar. Topics such as the use of punctuation marks and the correct formation of negative and plural words are certainly aspects of grammar as well.) And finally, Part 4 moves on to the more nebulous area of style issues, ranging from sentence length and reading level to avoiding a biased tone.

For all the directives and conventions presented here, a perspective to keep in mind is that knowing the rules of the language does not mean applying them rigidly and unthinkingly. For one thing, these rules are not carved in stone—a glance at any style guide of another era would show how significantly attitudes to language can and do change. More importantly, writing is a combination of science and art. The guidelines outlined in this handbook are concerned with the former: they are the tools you need in order to be able to express your ideas unambiguously and elegantly. To go beyond mere correctness, however, you must know when to accommodate your style to the expectations of your audience; when to bend a convention to capture a certain effect; when to go with common idiom instead of the rule book. Anyone armed with a keyboard can write. Good writing is achieved by those who understand innovation, creativity, and the needs of their readers.

Part 1

The Building Blocks: Word by Word

This chapter deals with the most basic elements of writing—individual words. Elsewhere, the focus is on how to clarify or emphasize them (Part 2, Punctuation), how to combine them grammatically (Part 3, Structure and Syntax), and how to organize sentences logically and fluidly (Part 4, Style). In comparison to that, how much room for error can there be with a single word? Plenty, as it happens. English being what it is, "basic" is not synonymous with "foolproof," and slip-ups can happen in a number of ways.

The discussion here is divided into three main sections. **Spelling Issues** covers common misspellings, spelling variations, commonly confused homonyms, and hyphenation. **Vocabulary Quirks and Challenges** reviews words that are commonly confused or misused, or that take nonstandard plural or negative forms. The final section, **Using Type Style for Effect**, looks at some aspects of the physical presentation of words that can have an impact on meaning or tone: uppercase versus lowercase letters, and the uses of italic and bold type.

Spelling Issues

TO CALL ENGLISH SPELLING eccentric would be putting it mildly. The Germanic/ Latin/Greek/Scandinavian/French etc. roots don't help, nor does the absence of a central authority to insist on standard form, as *L'Académie Française* does for French. Some of today's peculiarities lie in the fact that words from centuries ago have kept their original spelling although the pronunciation has moved on (think Monty Python's English kiniggits). For that matter, given the spectrum of accents today, a strong argument against modern attempts to make the written language more phonetic is that no one spelling convention could reflect the variety of English pronunciation that exists around the world. Would a Jamaican and an East Ender be likely to reach consensus? Another argument, of course, is that spelling is often connected to the origins of a word, and these clues to meaning would be lost if the letters signified nothing more than semantic-free sounds.

Free spirits and text messagers aside, most people agree that standardized spelling is a good thing, with teachers and employers being particularly firm on this point. Fortunately for the orthographically challenged, today's technology provides tools that can catch and correct the bloopers before the writer hits "Print" or (worse) "Send."

The problem is, though, bloopers will sometimes still slip through. Relying on spell-checkers exclusively is risky because the English language just has too many twists. Many programs lack the sophistication to detect misuse of homonyms (would yours amend *Their maybe moor then won weigh two rite sum words?*), and if used unthinkingly can even introduce errors (witness the concert program that promised a performance of Beethoven's *Erotica* symphony). Some will recognize only one form of a word that can be spelled two ways, and will annoyingly try to "correct" already valid spellings. An overly liberal dictionary may accept spelling variants that many readers would view as barbarisms. And, of course—unthinkable as it may be to some—not all writing is done on a word processor.

Hence the need for basic spelling skills remains. This chapter covers the topic in a broad sense, including aspects such as acceptable variations and appropriate use of hyphenation. The information presented here won't turn a poor speller into a good one, but it can help alert the reasonably competent speller to some common pitfalls. No one is expected to know the spelling of every word, but it is important to have an eye for when something doesn't look quite right and the common sense to check if there's any doubt.

FREQUENTLY MISPELLED WORDS

TEST YOUR KNOWLEDGE

The following list presents eighty words that many people get wrong. See how many you can correct without referring to a dictionary. If you caught the frequently misspelled word in the heading above, you're off to a good start.

abcess	diptheria	infinitesmal	perjorative
accessable	disasterous	innoculate	permissable
accomodate	ecstacy	jacknifed	perogative
aquisition	embarassment	knowledgable	perseverence
asterix	eminant	langour	playwrite
auxilary	epitomy	liason	pronounciation
barbituate	explaination	loathesome	quadriped
bellweather	fallable	maintainance	rasberry
boundry	Farenheit	manouver	relevent
calender	Febuary	millenium	respondant
cemetary	flourescent	minature	sacreligious
committment	forgiveable	mischievious	seperate
compatable	fuschia	neccesary	silouette
concensus	geneology	noticable	sympatico
concience	goverment	occurance	tempermental
conjested	gutteral	opthamologist	threshhold
consise	hankerchief	overlayed	underly
contraversial	hemorrage	paraphenalia	vengence
desireable	hierarchial	parliment	vigilent
diaphram	idiosyncracy	passtime	wierd

ANSWERS

ab[s]cess	dip[h]theria	infinites[i]mal	perjorative
access[i]able	disasterous	in~~n~~oculate	permiss[i]able
accom[m]odate	ecsta[s]~~c~~y	jack[k]nifed	per[r]ogative
a[c]quisition	embar[r]assment	knowledg[e]able	persever[a]ence
asteri~~x~~[sk]	emin[e]ant	lang~~ou~~[uo]r	playwri~~te~~[ght]
auxil[i]ary	epitom~~y~~[e]	lia[i]son	pron~~o~~unciation
barbitu[r]ate	explaination	loathesome	quadr[u]iped
bellweather	fall[i]able	maintain[e]ance	ra[p]~~s~~berry
bound[a]ry	Far[h]enheit	man~~ou~~[e]uver	relev[a]ent
calend[a]er	Feb[r]uary	mill[n]enium	respond[e]ant
cemet[e]ary	fl~~ou~~[uo]rescent	min[i]ature	sacre~~l~~[i e]igious
committment	forgiveable	mischievious	sep[a]erate
compat[i]able	fus~~ch~~[chs]ia	nec[s]~~c~~esary	sil[h]ouette
con~~c~~[s]ensus	gene[a]ology	notic[e]able	sympatico[i]
con[s]cience	gover[n]ment	occurr[e]ance	temper[a]mental
con~~j~~[g]ested	gutt[u]eral	opthamologist[h l]	threshhold
con[c]sise	han[d]kerchief	overlay[i]ed	under~~ly~~[ie]
contra[o]versial	hemor[h]rage	paraph[r]enalia	vengence[a]
desireable	hierarch[c]ial	parliment[a]	vigil[a]ent
diaphr[g]am	idiosyncra[s]~~c~~y	passtime	w~~i~~[ei]erd

Two of these words use different spellings in Britain and some other Commonwealth countries: *haemorrhage* and *manoeuvre*. For more on this, see American/British differences on page 12.

The preceding may possibly have taught you some spellings you didn't know, but obviously no such exercise could be comprehensive. Its larger aim is to demonstrate just how capricious and counterintuitive English spelling can be, and thereby drive home the importance of looking things up when necessary rather than trusting your memory or judgment. The words presented here are outright difficult to spell, or—more insidiously—are so frequently misspelled that the wrong version has become almost conventional. There is no shame in having to look up tricky words repeatedly: don't risk leaving in an error just because you're *almost* sure something is right, and it's too much trouble to check.

The majority of spelling errors fall into predictable categories. Keep these categories in mind as you write so as to be particularly alert for high-risk words.

Interchanging *a* and *e*; particularly *-ant/-ent* and *-ance/-ence* endings

calendar, cemetery, separate
eminent, relevant, respondent, vigilant
occurrence, perseverance

The sounds are the same, and there's no rule that will tell you which letter is correct for a given word. (Some words in fact may go either way: for example, *dependant* or *dependent*; *descendant* or *descendent*.)

Interchanging *-able* and *-ible* endings

accessible, compatible, fallible, permissible

Like *-ant* and *-ent*, these sounds are indistinguishable to the ear. The more common ending is *-able*, so writers are more likely to err when the ending should be *-ible*. (Some words can go either way: for example, *extendable* and *extendible* both appear in some dictionaries.)

Interchanging soft *c* and *s*, and soft *g* and *j*

consensus, concise, ecstasy, idiosyncrasy, congested

Watch out for these identical-sounding letters. (A few words can go either way: for example, *supercede* or *supersede*, *offence* or *offense*, *defence* or *defense*, *jibe* or *gibe*.)

An international note here: U.S. dictionaries may consider *practice/practise* and *licence/license* to be simple variants, but in U.K. style these spellings indicate different functions, with *s* used for the verb and *c* for the noun. Thus, to *practise* medicine but open a medical *practice*; to *license* someone but issue a *licence*. For more on this topic, see American/British differences on page 12.

Omitting a silent letter

abscess, acquisition, diaphragm, Fahrenheit, February, handkerchief, hemorrhage (or haemorrhage), parliament, raspberry, silhouette, vengeance

Often a letter whose omission wouldn't change the pronunciation is mistakenly left out. (Note that it is certainly correct to pronounce the *r* in *February*, but most speakers do not, and many dictionaries accept the *r*-less pronunciation as an alternative.)

Misapplying double consonants

accommodate, commitment, embarrassment, jackknifed, millennium, necessary, threshold

Words with double consonants are often troublesome. Errors include doubling the wrong letter, wrongly doubling more than one, and doubling just one letter when the word contains two sets of doubles. Another common mistake is to drop a repeated letter if the word is a compound in which the last letter of the first part and the first letter of the second part happen to be the same (*jackknifed, misspelling*). Conversely, writers sometimes mistake a word for a compound, and double a letter that they shouldn't (*threshold* is not a combination of *thresh* and *hold*).

Spelling words the way they're (mis)pronounced

asterisk, auxiliary, barbiturate, boundary, diphtheria, government, hierarchical, infinitesimal, miniature, mischievous, ophthalmologist, paraphernalia, pejorative, prerogative, temperamental

It must be admitted that some of these words, if not precisely tongue-twisters, do not trip off the tongue. Errors in speech can range from minor slips in enunciation to outright gaffes. Writers may then spell these words the way they say them, not realizing that both are wrong.

Spelling a derivative the same as its root word

disastrous, explanation, maintenance, pronunciation

When one word derives from another, it's *often* the case that the spelling of the root word still holds—but not always. Be aware of the exceptions. (Incidentally, ever notice how many speakers mispronounce the word *pronunciation*?)

Keeping—or not keeping—the final *-e* of a root word

desirable, forgivable, knowledgeable, loathsome, noticeable

For some words, the final *-e* is kept and for some it isn't—and writers often guess wrong. Note in the discussion on American/British differences on page 12 how some words can go either way.

Giving an unfamiliar word the spelling of a more familiar one

bellwether, guttural, pastime, playwright, sacrilegious, simpatico

When a relatively uncommon word sounds like a better-known one (*weather, gutter, pass, write, religious, sympathy*), the spelling of the more familiar word may be mistakenly adopted.

Not recognizing exceptions to familiar letter sequences

controversial, epitome, fuchsia, genealogy, inoculate, overlaid, quadruped, underlie, weird

The prefixes in *contradictory* and *contraindication* may contain an *a*, those in *quadriceps* and *quadrilateral* an *i*, and the suffixes in *mythology* and *ethnology* an *o*—but some words do things a little differently. *School* and *schooner* contain an *sch* sequence, while *chs* doesn't come up very often. Most words that end with an *e* or an *i* sound take a *y*, so exceptions such as *epitome* and *underlie* often get overlooked. Familiar words such as *innocuous, innocent,* and *innovate* contain a double *n*, so *inoculate* often picks up an extra one. Since the past tense form of most words ends in *ed*, exceptions such as *laid* are often missed. And "*i* before *e*, except after *c*" usually holds true—but not always.

Confusion over unusual letter sequences

conscience, fluorescent, languor, liaison, maneuver (or manoeuvre)

Writers can be understandably thrown by words that contain *uo* or *ae* sequences instead of the more familiar *ou* and *ea*. And some words just seem like phonetic outliers—three vowels in a row in *liaison*, or *con* and *science* coming together in a perplexing way to form *conscience*.

Typos

Before leaving the topic of misspellings, a word on **typos**, defined as spelling errors that result from an accidental slip of the finger on the keyboard rather than ignorance of the correct form. Some words are more susceptible to being accidentally mis-typed than others, so when proofing your work, be extra alert for the following:

Transposition of letters to create a similar word

Watch out for scared cows, audit trials, casual factors, martial harmony, complaint pupils and the like—words that differ from another only by two transposed letters. Note that such errors are often not picked up by a spell-checker!

Omission of one occurrence of a repeated letter

> A number of challenging activites have been planned for the day.
>
> Graphic design, typsetting, and proofreading services offered at a reasonable price.

Did you spot the errors in *activities* and *typesetting*? They are easy to miss on a quick read, because the missing letters (*i* and *e*, respectively) are present in another position in the word. Double-check any such words very carefully.

"Word stutter"

> A common type of slip to to make when typing is to repeat short words such as *the* or *is*.

Even a sharp eye can easily miss the typo in the above sentence. Spell-checkers are usually programmed to pick up on repeated words, a useful feature (although slightly annoying when it flags valid combinations such as *had had* or *that that*).

On a final note, when you are proofing your work, check to see if you have left any extra spaces between words or omitted the space between sentences. Such typos are not spelling mistakes, but nonetheless need to be rectified. A grammar checker should pick up this type of error.

SPELLING VARIATIONS

> The Russian Revolution...simmered for years and suddenly erupted when the serfs finally realized that the Czar and the Tsar were the same person.
>
> —Woody Allen, *A Brief, Yet Helpful, Guide to Civil Disobedience*

To the exasperation of copy editors, English contains many words that can be correctly spelled more than one way. Two dictionaries may present the same word differently, and the same dictionary may present alternatives. The main reasons for this, discussed below, are national variations and the degree to which a dictionary is either *prescriptive* (prescribing how to properly spell the word) or *descriptive* (describing how the word is commonly spelled). When alternative spellings exist, sometimes the choice is up to the individual, other times not. It is important to have a solid awareness of spelling variations for the following reasons:

- If you are contracted or employed to write some sort of commercial publication, such as a technical manual for a software producer, marketing material for a bank, or an informational brochure for a government office, you are usually expected to abide by a particular style guide. Organizations generally want their publications to have a uniform look and feel, which includes words always being spelled the same way. For example, a U.S.-based multinational corporation with a branch in the United Kingdom might specify that all printed materials that go to the public—including those materials produced by British writers—follow the conventions of American spelling.

- If your writing is your own—that is, something you are doing not for an employer or client but as a personal project that will bear your name—you will still be expected to abide by the style guide of the publishing house that is producing your work. Not all publishers require that writers go with a particular dictionary, but many do. If you disregard their specifications, it may well mean seeing your text come back heavily revised by the copy editor.

- Just because a variant spelling appears in a dictionary doesn't necessarily mean it's appropriate. If the dictionary you are using allows for unconventional spellings, consider what effect these might have on the tone of your writing. Some dictionaries endorse spellings that would send most copy editors lunging for their virtual red pencils. More on this below.

American/British differences

Some of the variant spellings in the English language are due to the differing styles of the United States and Britain. For staunch upholders of one tradition or the other, the "right" way to spell something will be unambiguous; however, in many parts of the world the path is murkier. (Canadians in particular, with geographical proximity to one country and historical ties to the other, have a hybrid style that borrows from both.)

The following describes several categories of differences between American and British spellings. In *general*—there are many exceptions—American style is to remove letters not necessary for pronunciation, while British style is to retain traditional spellings, which are often less phonetic. Note that spell-checkers can be set to a specific national style of English, so that any word that does not match that style—even if spelled correctly for another country—will be flagged as an error.

Ending some words in *or* versus *our*: American style is *or*, British style is *our*.

humor / humour   honor / honour   endeavor / endeavour

Note that even with British style, certain derivative words such as *humorous, honorarium,* and *laborious* do not take the *u*.

Ending some words in *er* versus *re*: American style is *er*, British style is *re*.

center / centre   fiber / fibre   theater / theatre

Ending some words in *ize* versus *ise*: American style is *ize* (or *yze*), British style is *ise* (or *yse*).

analyze / analyse   organize / organise
paralyze / paralyse   realize / realise

Creating past tense with *ed* versus *t*: There are a few past-tense constructions that take the standard *ed* in American style but take *t* in British style.

burned / burnt   dreamed / dreamt
learned / learnt   spoiled / spoilt

Using single versus double consonants in derivatives: For some words whose roots end in *l, p, s,* or *t*, American style leaves the consonant single before the suffix; British style doubles it.

benefited / benefitted   focusing / focussing
canceled / cancelled   grueling / gruelling
kidnaped / kidnapped   worshiping / worshipping
counselor / counsellor   traveler / traveller

Dropping versus retaining the *e* of a root word: For some words whose roots end in *e*, American style is to drop the *e* before a suffix; British style is to retain it.

acknowledgment / acknowledgement   aging / ageing
usable / useable   judgment / judgement

Using *ae* or *oe* versus *e*: American style is to drop the extra vowel; British style is to keep it.

anesthetic / anaesthetic   estrogen / oestrogen
encyclopedia / encyclopaedia   fetus / foetus
medieval / mediaeval   maneuver / manoeuvre

Using more phonetic versus more traditional spellings: American style is often to simplify spelling, whether by dropping silent endings or by using more phonetic constructions; British style is to retain traditional spellings.

catalog / catalogue	omelet / omelette	program / programme
check / cheque	draft / draught	plow / plough

Miscellaneous differences: Many words differ in ways that do not fit any of the above categories: *pajamas/pyjamas, tire/tyre, jail/gaol, jewelry/jewellery, aluminum/ aluminium*, etc. (The last two have different pronunciations as well.)

* * *

A question that might arise for writers striving for consistency is, must one go exclusively one way or the other? If you have committed yourself to doubling the *l* in *cancelled*, need you also use *re* endings? Unless you are expected to abide rigidly by a particular style guide, using different styles for different words is usually acceptable as long as you spell each individual word consistently. Do, however, treat all words in the same category alike—for example, if you are spelling *valour* with a *u*, do the same for *flavour*.

Regardless of your style choice, always use the original spelling for proper nouns (names of specific entities). For example, even if using American style, be sure the British political party appears as *Labour*, not *Labor;* if using British style, be sure the complex in New York City appears as the *Rockefeller Center*, not *Centre*.

Moving beyond spelling, there are many words that just outright differ between North American and British English: *truck* versus *lorry, gasoline* versus *petrol, potato chips* versus *crisps*, etc. Every English-speaking country has vocabulary that is unique within its borders, and the variants can be impossible for a non-native to anticipate. If you are attempting, say, to set a novel in a country not your own, it would be highly advisable to have a native of that part of the world look your manuscript over for any gaffes. For example, it would not be convincing to have an American character describe red hair as *ginger* or to speak of *hiring* a car instead of *renting* it.

Other spelling variations

Spelling variants can exist for reasons unrelated to national differences. Sometimes this is because a word is a relatively recent import that had to be transliterated from another alphabet, but often there seems no explanation other than the fact that English has a less-than-tidy history. Some examples, distinguished mainly by their sheer capriciousness:

adviser / advisor	gelatin / gelatine
artifact / artefact	mustache / moustache
bandanna / bandana	orangutan / orangoutan
calif / caliph	phony / phoney
cantaloupe / cantaloup	pygmy / pigmy
dietitian / dietician	raccoon / racoon
dissension / dissention	sulfur / sulphur
enroll / enrol	woolen / woollen
fulfill / fulfil	yogurt / yoghurt

The existence of variant spellings raises the question, how do you decide which way to go? The answer is—it depends. If you are writing to the specifications of a style guide, you don't have to make any decisions: typically, you are simply told which dictionary to use as your authority, and if it gives two or more variants of a word, to use the first. There is a great deal of sense to this approach, as it saves you from having to come up with your own rules.

If you have been given free rein, make sure you spell the same word consistently throughout: don't switch halfway through or go back and forth. It is also advisable to maintain consistency across similar categories of words; for example, if you are spelling *fulfill* with a double *l*, do the same with *enroll*. This isn't critical, but it can make your writing look more polished to a discerning reader.

There is also the matter of tone. Dictionaries can be roughly categorized as either prescriptive or descriptive, a distinction that corresponds to conservative versus liberal. The former act as guardians of the language, upholding conventional rules of spelling and usage and adding new entries with caution. Descriptive dictionaries, on the other hand, take the attitude that their job is not to decree but to record how language is being used in the real world, whether supported by tradition or not. They are thus more flexible in incorporating unconventional spellings and definitions, as well as slang and jargon. Hence, whether a certain spelling is considered an error or an acceptable variant may depend on what source is being used.

Both approaches have validity. On the one hand, without the maintenance of standards, the clarity of the language would degenerate. On the other hand, language is a fluid entity that changes over time—just consider how quaint certain terms now seem that were in standard usage a few decades ago. However, a concern held by some writers (this author included) is that descriptive dictionaries sometimes pander to ignorance, and if enough people are misspelling or misusing a word a certain way, the lexicographers will obligingly include that misuse in their next edition. Arguments over this issue could be made either way, since of course even today's prescriptive dictionaries contain entries that were once controversial. The main message to take away is that the presence of a term in a dictionary does not mean that it will be seen as fully legitimate by all audiences.

The widely respected but most definitely not prescriptive *Merriam Webster's Collegiate Dictionary* presents the following as acceptable variants:

alright for *all right*	*nerve-wracking* for *nerve-racking*
accidently for *accidentally*	*nickle* for *nickel*
donut for *doughnut*	*restauranteur* for *restaurateur*
dumfounded for *dumbfounded*	*revery* for *reverie*
loadstone for *lodestone*	*sherbert* for *sherbet*
miniscule for *minuscule*	*straightlaced* for *straitlaced*

In several of these cases, it could be argued that meaning is lost by going with the variants. For example, *doughnut* derives from *dough*; *dumbfounded* from *dumb* (speechless); *lodestone* from *lode* (course), not *load*; and *straitlaced* from *strait* (narrow, constricted, or strict), not *straight*. In other cases, the variant spelling changes the actual pronunciation (*restauranteur*, *sherbert*). As a writer, you must determine your own comfort level. But do remember that even if you can justify an unconventional spelling to your client or publisher by pointing to a source, you run the risk of some readers simply assuming an error on your part; they aren't likely to turn to the dictionary to see if it would vindicate you. It is usually better practice to go with the more standard form of the word.

Transliterations

A special category of alternate spellings is names of people, places, or other entities that have their origin in languages other than English. If the language of origin uses an alphabet other than the Latin one, the transliteration is not the original spelling in any case. For example, the following may be spelled more than one way:

Chassid (member of a Jewish sect), Hassid, or Hasid
Hindustani (language in India) or Hindostani
Mao Tse-Tung (Chinese leader) or Mao Zedong
Tchaikovsky (Russian composer) or Tschaikovsky

A good strategy is to do a Web search on both variants and go with whichever one gives the most hits, since this is a case where a "majority rules" strategy is reasonable.

FREQUENTLY CONFUSED HOMONYMS

A word may be spelled impeccably as far as the spell-checker is concerned—but still be wrong. English is replete with **homonyms**, words that are pronounced the same way but are spelled differently and mean different things. The majority of these present no problem; few adults, for example, would write *brake* for *break* or *see* for *sea*. Certain words, however, get confused with their homonyms systematically. Often the cause is that one of the homonyms is less common than the other, and a writer puts down the more familiar spelling without realizing that it has a different meaning from the word that was intended.

TEST YOUR KNOWLEDGE

Which word in each of the following sentences is incorrect?

1. He was sweating, his hands trembled, and his face twitched occasionally with a nervous tick.
2. Okay, you've peaked my interest: why *are* you wearing a Spiderman suit to work?
3. In her fiancé's case, two months' salary would buy a diamond of about one-sixteenth of a caret.
4. Breaking a long report into discreet sections makes it more digestible.
5. I might have born the news better if it hadn't come on a day when everything was already going wrong.
6. He's been pedaling that idea to investors for years, but no takers.
7. The debate couldn't precede until the security guards had evicted the hecklers.
8. If any of my hoard of admirers come by while I'm out, tell them I'll be back shortly.
9. What a shame, they really should of won that one.
10. What's the rational for going with this particular design?
11. Tall vases of chrysanthemums had been placed on either side of the alter.

12. It didn't auger well that on their first date she told him she had recently broken off her fourth engagement.

13. Who would have thought that such a small thing could have such a big affect?

14. Even when things looked darkest, she refused to loose hope.

15. If you could have only one of these, which one would you chose?

16. In George Orwell's *Animal Farm*, the animals rise up and throw off the yolk of their abusive human master.

17. So far, all attempts to diffuse the tension had proven futile.

18. The stationary supplies consisted of just a package of paper and a few pens.

19. It's a lot easier to give advise than to take it.

20. Professional singers must warm up their vocal chords before they perform, in order to prevent injury.

21. After the broadcast, more then five hundred listeners called the station to protest.

22. Forget what the others are telling you: stand your ground and stick to your principals.

23. According to the survey completed by the managers, employees are happiest and most productive in a cubical environment.

24. Giving the staff free reign did in fact improve productivity.

25. No one is suppose to know anything about this, so keep quiet.

26. The deluxe model comes with air conditioning, cruise control, duel airbags, and leather seats.

27. The council for the defendant contended that this was tantamount to paying twice for the same offense.

28. When a migraine came on, her head would feel as though it were gripped in a vice.

29. The security encryption feature is designed to give users piece of mind when performing online transactions.

30. He was a no-nonsense type: anyone in his class who didn't tow the line was soon set straight.

31. Registration fees may be waved for low-income students.

32. We design, make, and install quality curtains that will compliment your furniture and impress your guests.

33. When they finally broke down the door, a grizzly scene met their eyes.

34. By the end of the session, he felt as if he'd been put through the ringer.

35. When you upload a photo, a palate of colors will automatically appear.

36. I was loathe to interfere, but I felt I must.

37. Her lawsuit claimed that there had been a breech of contract.

38. It was hard to say exactly how it happened; one thing just lead to another.

39. He poured over the accounts, trying to figure out where the error could be.

40. Readers of a book will often skip the forward, although they may come back to read it later.

ANSWERS

1. a nervous **tick**: should be *tic*—a periodic spasm of the facial muscles. Nothing to do with small bloodsucking arachnids.

2. **peaked** my interest: should be *piqued*—intrigued or excited. *Peak* means to be at the maximum (interest has peaked, and will probably soon decline).

3. one-sixteenth of a **caret**: should be *carat*—a unit of weight for jewels. A *caret* is a small wedge-shaped mark (^) used by proofreaders to indicate where text should be inserted. Also do not confuse *carat* with *karat*, a measure of the amount of pure gold in an alloy. And none of the above should be confused with a certain orange-colored root vegetable.

4. **discreet** sections: should be *discrete*—individually distinct. Unless the sections are particularly good at keeping a confidence.

5. **born** the news better: should be *borne*—handled, coped with. This word is the past participle of *to bear*, and in this context has nothing to do with being born. Another usage, however, is related to birth: *to bear children* is to bring them into being (she had borne two children).

6. **pedaling** that idea: should be *peddling*—going about trying to sell something. A vendor on a bicycle, of course, could do both at the same time.

7. The debate couldn't **precede**: should be *proceed*—continue. *Precede* means to go before (he politely stood aside to let her precede him into the boardroom). Note that the pronunciation is slightly different.

8. **hoard** of admirers: should be *horde*—large group of people. *Hoard* is an accumulation of items.

9. **should of** won: should be *should have*—often contracted in speech to *should've*, which the ear detects as *should of*. Fine in speech, not in writing.

10. What's the **rational**: should be *rationale*—justification or underlying reason. Pronounced with emphasis on the last syllable. *Rational* (rhymes with *national*) means logical and reasonable (let's try to discuss this in a rational way).

11. either side of the **alter**: should be *altar*—the raised structure in a place of worship. *Alter* means to change something. (So, how many of you thought the trick word was "chrysanthemums"?)

12. didn't **auger** well: should be *augur*—bode, portend. An *auger* is a carpenter's tool for boring holes.

13. a big **affect**: should be *effect*—a consequence or result. *Affect* (pronounced differently) means to influence or act upon. One is a verb, the other a noun: thus, when you *affect* something, you have an *effect* on it.

    The above definitions are the most common meanings of these words, and are the ones that are most likely to be confused. However, just to complicate things further, there are other, less common usages for each word as well. *Effect* may also be used as a verb, meaning to accomplish, bring about, cause to occur (the committee tried to effect a change). *Affect* can mean to fancy something, usually in a pretentious way (affect Eastern dress), to cultivate a style (affect a bored demeanor), to put on deceptively (affect an English accent), or to stir emotionally (such a sight must affect any who see it). As a noun, with the emphasis on the first syllable, it refers to emotions (the patient exhibited a complete lack of affect).

14. **loose** hope: should be *lose*—be deprived of, fail to keep. Rhymes with *shoes*. *Loose* (rhymes with *moose*) is to release or make less tight.

15. which one would you **chose**: should be *choose*—the present tense of the verb. Rhymes with *shoes*. *Chose* (rhymes with *rose*) is the past tense of *choose*. The similar spellings but different pronunciations in this pair of words and the pair in the previous example may account for some of the confusion around both of them.

16. throw off the **yolk**: should be *yoke*—bondage or servitude. No eggs are involved.

17. **diffuse** the tension: should be *defuse*—to reduce tension, have a calming effect. To *diffuse* something is to scatter or spread it out so that it is less concentrated.

18. **stationary** supplies: should be *stationery*—writing materials. Of course, paper and pens are characteristically stationary—not moving. A helpful mnemonic: station<u>e</u>ry includes <u>e</u>nvelopes.

19. give **advise**: should be *advice*—the noun. The last syllable rhymes with *ice*. *Advise* (last syllable rhymes with *wise*) is the verb. When you advise someone, you are giving advice.

20. **vocal chords**: should be *vocal cords*—structures within the larynx that enable speech. *Chords* are harmonious combinations of musical tones. This very common error is likely due to the association that both words have with sound.

21. more **then** five hundred: should be *than*—a conjunction used when comparing two things (she's younger than I am; easier said than done). *Then* means "at that time."

22. stick to your **principals**: should be *principles*—code of conduct. Stick to your principals only if you hang out with headmasters.

    Principle and *principal*, both of which have multiple meanings, are confused frequently. The first can also be used to mean a fundamental law (the principle of relativity), an underlying phenomenon that accounts for something (the principle of the steam engine), or the essence or fundamentals of a situation (in principle, this action should be possible). The second has several meanings that all relate in some way to being first or primary. As a noun, it can refer to the head administrator of a school (go straight to the principal's office), a main player (he's suspected of being one of the principals), or the main sum of money owing on a loan (the amount includes both interest and principal). As an adjective, it describes something that is prominent (she plays a principal role) or important or pressing (our principal concern is safety). A helpful mnemonic: the princi<u>pal</u> is your <u>pal</u>. (Right.) Once you have this connection in place, think whether the meaning of the word you want has anything to do with "firstness." If it does, the ending will be *pal*; if it doesn't, the ending will be *ple*.

23. a **cubical** environment: should be *cubicle*—a small partitioned work-space with no walls, sometimes presided over by a pointy-haired boss. *Cubical* means shaped like a cube, with six equal square sides.

24. **free reign**: should be *free rein*—that is, not hauling on someone's reins to exert control (figuratively speaking). *Reign* means to rule as a sovereign.

25. No one is **suppose to**: should be *supposed to*—with a *d* on the end. The *d* is often not sounded in speech, but it must be present in writing.

26. **duel** airbags: should be *dual*—two, one on each side. *Duel* also has to do with two, but in a somewhat more antagonistic sense.

27. **council** for the defendant: should be *counsel*—lawyer, legal adviser. As a verb, *counsel* means to advise or consult with, so a *counselor* is one who counsels (a camp counselor, a guidance counselor, a marital coun-selor). *Council* is an administrative or legislative group that deliberates or governs, so a *councilor* is one who is a member of a council (a town councilor, a school board councilor).

28. gripped in a **vice**: should be *vise*—a tool for clenching something strongly. Unrelated to moral depravity.

29. **piece of mind**: should be *peace of mind*—being at ease. This expres-sion presumably gets confused with giving someone *a piece of your mind*, which is not typically an action associated with tranquility.

30. **tow the line**: should be *toe the line*—conform to expected behavior (as in positioning one's toes behind a prescribed line). Not the same action as hauling a barge.

31. fees may be **waved**: should be *waived*—refrain from claiming, voluntarily forgo something to which one is entitled. Flapping the fees up and down in front of the students would be to little purpose.

32. **compliment** your furniture: should be *complement*—go well with, set off to advantage, enhance. Not telling the furniture how good it's looking.

    The word *complement* derives from *complete*, so a good mnemonic is to remember the connection between these two words. Thus, one can have a full complement (a complete set) of cutlery, or assign some comple-mentary (additional) course readings along with the main text. A *com-pliment* is a courteous, admiring, or flattering comment. One can offer compliments (best wishes, regards) of the season, write a complimentary (favorable) review, exchange complimentary (mutually esteeming) remarks, or offer complimentary (free as a courtesy) drinks. This last use is also frequently bungled, as in "Our breakfast special includes limitless refills and a complementary newspaper."

33. a **grizzly** scene: should be *grisly*—gruesome, ghastly. Unless the scene contained a large aggressive bear.

34. put through the **ringer**: should be *wringer*—a device for wringing something out, squeezing it dry. The phrase *put through the wringer* means to feel pressured and exhausted by an ordeal, and does not involve any bell clappers. (Also note that a wish to *ring* someone's neck would mean a desire to put a circlet around it.)

35. a **palate** of colors: should be *palette*—a range of colors (also the board on which an artist holds and mixes pigments). *Palate* refers to the roof of the mouth or to the sense of taste.

36. **loathe** to interfere: should be *loath*—reluctant. *Loathe* means to hate, despise. The pronunciation is slightly different: *loath* rhymes with *oath*, while *loathe* ends in the softer *th* as in *smooth*.

37. **breech** of contract: should be *breach*—violation. This word derives from *break*. Thus, a breach of honor, breaching a standard, a breach in a wall, or a breach in continuity. *Breech* refers to the bottom or back end of something: the breech (rear) of a gun, a breech birth (feet or rear end first), or (archaically) a pair of pants.

38. one thing just **lead** to another: should be *led*—past tense of the verb "to lead." This very common error likely results from a confusion with the metal *lead*, which is pronounced like *led*.

39. He **poured** over the accounts: should be *pored*—examined intently. Pouring anything over one's reading matter is unlikely to help its legibility.

40. skip the **forward**: should be *foreword*—the words that appear at the front (the fore). Nothing to do with the direction of movement or with being too familiar. If this is the very first word to appear in your piece of writing, it's one you want to get right!

Note that several of the pairs of words above are not strict homonyms: advice/advise, affect/effect, choose/chose, loath/loathe, loose/lose, of/have, precede/proceed, rational/rationale, then/than. Often, people who make these errors get the word right when speaking; they just have the spelling wrong.

A word on variants: some dictionaries permit *grizzly* and *loathe* as acceptable alternatives for *grisly* and *loath*, but enough readers would consider these incorrect that writers are advised to stick with the traditional spellings. See the discussion of prescriptive versus descriptive dictionaries on page 11.

HYPHENATION

I worked with [William Shawn, longtime editor of *The New Yorker* magazine] from 1939 until 1987, often from the initial proposal of an idea (he grasped ideas with the speed of light) through the cherished phone call of acceptance and through galley and page proofs. These sessions were mostly brief and businesslike: a word here, a nuance there, a fact to be further clarified. But there is one evening in the late forties that is indelibly impressed on my mind. I had written a long report on a visit to the Argentina of Juan Perón. The narrative ended with Señor Perón unexpectedly introducing me, as he opened elegant French doors in the Presidential palace in Buenos Aires, to Evita Perón. I wrote that I took her hand and found it "stone cold." Shawn and I were going over the proof. The time was around 10 P.M. He became agitated.

" 'Stone cold,' " he said, "requires a hyphen."

I became agitated. "Put a hyphen there and you spoil the ending," I said. "That hyphen would be ruinous."

"Perhaps you had better sit outside my office and cool off," he said. "I'll go on with my other work."

I took a seat outside his office. From time to time, he would stick his head out and say, "Have you changed your mind?"

"No hyphen," I replied. "Absolutely no hyphen." I was quite worked up over the hyphen.

Sometime around two-thirty in the morning, Shawn said, wearily, "All right. No hyphen. But you are wrong."

We remained dear friends, hyphen or no hyphen, to the end.

—Philip Hamburger, "Remembering Mr. Shawn,"
The New Yorker, December 28, 1992

Spelling a word correctly sometimes involves more than just getting the right letters in the right order. A word is considered to be misspelled if it ought to contain a hyphen and doesn't, or conversely, if it ought *not* to contain one and *does*. This section looks at the hyphen as a component of spelling. (For a discussion of its role as a mark of punctuation, turn to page 137.) Its functions in spelling are the following:

- Linking words that make up a compound, where necessary
- Linking a prefix or suffix to the main word, where necessary
- Linking the words of a spelled-out number

Hyphenation of compound words

A **compound** consists of two or more words that come together to express a single concept. It may be a noun, a verb, or an adjective. Some compounds are written as two separate words (**open compounds**), some run the words together (**closed compounds**), and some link them by a hyphen (**hyphenated compounds**). There are no strict rules governing this. Verbs are more likely to be open than are adjectives or nouns (*break through* a barrier but achieve a *breakthrough*, *show off* one's skills but act like a *show-off*, *hand out* money but ask for a *handout*, *walk in* to a room but visit a *walk-in* clinic). Some compound verbs do however take a hyphen (*court-martial*, *spoon-feed*, *freeze-dry*).

For all the other uses of the hyphen discussed in this book, there are reasonably firm rules as to when to include it and when not to, but compounds are a moving target. There is a historical trend for compounds that start out as open or hyphenated to close up over time, presumably because the combination of words becomes familiar enough that running them together no longer seems jarring. (When the *Shorter Oxford English Dictionary* came out with an updated edition in 2007, no fewer than 16,000 entries lost their hyphens.) Commonplace words such as *database*, *crybaby*, *lowlife*, and *bellboy* began their lives as two words or hyphenated, but do not raise an eyebrow (eye brow?) today. Don't try looking for logic or predictability in this matter: just determine what is current usage and go with that.

TEST YOUR KNOWLEDGE

By convention, which of the compounds shown below should be left open, which closed up, and which hyphenated? (The non-bolded words are included to provide grammatical context.)

a **clear cut** decision / a **clear headed** view   [adjectives]
feeling **light hearted** / feeling **light headed**   [adjectives]
a **long term** plan / a **long time** companion   [adjectives]
an **off color** joke / an **off hand** remark   [adjectives]
a **stand by** ticket / a **stand up** comedian   [adjectives]
a **two fold** increase / a **two way** street   [adjectives]
a **water logged** boat / a **water resistant** watch   [adjectives]
train as a **fire eater** / get caught in a **fire fight**   [nouns]
have a **half brother** / be shaped like a **half moon**   [nouns]
review a **life cycle** / reach for a **life line**   [nouns]
watch a **light show** / define a **light year**   [nouns]
attach a **side car** / experience a **side effect**   [nouns]
act as a **stand in** / be at a **stand still**   [nouns]
set a **time frame** / call a **time out**   [nouns]
back check a hockey player / **back slide** from grace   [verbs]
check over a résumé / **check mate** an opponent   [verbs]
cross breed cattle / **cross fertilize** crops   [verbs]
hand feed a pet / **hand write** a letter   [verbs]
hand pick a successor / **hand over** some money   [verbs]
spot light a problem / **spot check** a document   [verbs]
touch type a letter / **touch up** some rough spots   [verbs]

ANSWERS

Adjectives	**Nouns**	**Verbs**
clear-cut / clearheaded	fire-eater / firefight	back-check / backslide
lighthearted / light-headed	half brother / half-moon	check over / checkmate
long-term / longtime	life cycle / lifeline	crossbreed / cross-fertilize
off-color / offhand	light show / light-year	hand-feed / handwrite
standby / stand-up	sidecar / side effect	hand-pick / hand over
twofold / two-way	stand-in / standstill	spotlight / spot-check
waterlogged / water-resistant	timeframe / time-out	touch-type / touch up

The above exercise illustrates how capricious the formation of compound words can be, and should convince you that the grammatical form will not always tell you which way to go. If ever you're not certain how a particular compound should appear, don't attempt to reason it through: check the dictionary. However, be aware that different dictionaries may give different answers (indeed, yours may vary on some of the items above), and it will often be the case that more than one style is acceptable. This is particularly true for compound words that are relatively new to the language. Before a consensus is reached, all three forms may be considered acceptable. For example, *hard copy*, *hard-copy*, and *hardcopy* all appear as both noun and adjective.

Since the language is constantly evolving, not every compound will appear in the dictionary, and you will sometimes have to make your own decisions. If the combination you want does not have its own dictionary entry, you may usually assume it should be written as two words.

A few special cases

Idioms and expressions

Many idioms and expressions take hyphens (*she's such a stick-in-the-mud, he's a Johnny-come-lately, the place was just a hole-in-the-wall*), but this isn't invariable (*the deal sounded like a pig in a poke; she was his partner in crime; the beach was just a hop, skip, and jump from the hotel*). Always check; a good dictionary includes multi-word phrases. Again: if a phrase does not have its own listing, assume it does not take hyphens.

Commonly mis-hyphenated compounds

There are some compound words and phrases that are often mistakenly given hyphens. The following lists a few of these common errors. Note in particular that Latin phrases *never* take hyphens.

No	Yes
more-or-less	more or less
on-going	ongoing
under-way	under way
a-priori	a priori
ad-hoc	ad hoc
bona-fide	bona fide
post-hoc	post hoc
vice-versa	vice versa

Compounds with single letters

If the first part of a compound is a single letter, the compound is hyphenated or open, never closed.

A-frame	T-bone
A-list	T-shirt
B movie	T square
D-Day	U-turn
F distribution	V neck
G-string	x-ray
H-bomb	y-coordinate
I beam	z-axis

An exception is *e-mail*, often acceptably written as *email*, as the standalone *e* loses its significance (short for *electronic*) and comes to be treated as simply the first letter of the word.

Compound adjectives

In the case of compound adjectives, there is an extra complexity to the hyphen situation. If a compound adjective has its own entry in the dictionary, it should always be written as it is shown there—either hyphenated or closed—regardless of its position in the sentence. (See the examples on page 26.) That is, the combination is considered a word in its own right, and the way it appears in the dictionary is its proper and invariable spelling. However, other than these permanent compounds, an almost limitless variety of words can be strung together in a given sentence to collectively form an adjective. These context-dependent compounds (yes, that was an example of one!) typically are linked by a hyphen if they precede the noun they are modifying, but not if they follow the noun. This is covered in detail on page 140, under the discussion of the use of the hyphen as a punctuation mark.

Hyphenation with prefixes and suffixes

There is no single rule here that covers all situations. Some words that contain a prefix or a suffix *never* take a hyphen, some *may* take one, some *should* take one, and some *must* take one.

Never hyphenate

The majority of cases fall into the first category: that is, the prefix or suffix simply merges with the word it modifies. For example, you would never use a hyphen in words such as *unsaid*, *illogical*, *playing*, *added*, or *countable*.

Optionally hyphenate

There are some cases where a hyphen may be a matter of choice. For example, both versions of the following words are legitimate:

anti-hero / antihero	non-aggressive / nonaggressive
bi-annual / biannual	pre-mixed / premixed
co-ordinate / coordinate	semi-private / semiprivate
co-operate / cooperate	sub-optimal / suboptimal
infra-red / infrared	ultra-violet / ultraviolet

There is a trend to view such hyphens as superfluous, and most scientific, technical, and government publications will omit them. Putting them in does no harm, but the words would read just as clearly and unambiguously without them. If you are using a style guide, follow its rules. If you are making your own decisions, be consistent: don't randomly use hyphens with some prefixes and suffixes and not with others.

Best to hyphenate

In a number of situations, a hyphen is strongly recommended. It is a good idea to use one in the following circumstances:

When the combination of root word and prefix/suffix is unusual

There is no need to hyphenate standard words such as *premeditation, worldwide,* or *clockwise.* However, terms such as *prewedding arrangements,* a *communitywide effort,* or *his place could use some improvement furniturewise* would look a bit odd. Such (relatively) unique constructions would read better as *pre-wedding, community-wide,* and *furniture-wise.* That is, include a hyphen if the combination of the root word and its prefix or suffix is not standard and might look peculiar as a single word. A hyphen prevents a momentary "huh?" as the reader encounters a never-before-seen juxtaposition, and allows the meaning to be instantly grasped. For example:

> Penny and his colleagues....wanted to calculate the probability that, purely by chance, two molecules would yield the same family tree, if evolution wasn't true. So they tried to imagine all possible trees that could terminate in eleven descendants. It's a surprisingly large number. Even if you limit yourself to 'binary trees' (that is, trees with branches that only bifurcate—no tri-furcating or higher-furcating), the total number of possible trees is more than 34 million.
>
> —Richard Dawkins, *The Greatest Show on Earth: The Evidence for Evolution*

When the word would have a different meaning without a hyphen

Compare the following two sentences:

> The team announced today that their star pitcher has resigned.

> The team announced today that their star pitcher has re-signed.

The meanings are different, to say the least. Similarly, if referring to the *re-creation* of an event, *re-covering* a sofa, or *un-ionized* molecules, include a hyphen so that readers won't momentarily puzzle over who's out having a good time, who stole the furniture, or whether the molecules have any work grievances.

When the word might be difficult to read if it didn't have a hyphen

Consider the words *coworker*, *coinventor*, *reprepped*, *tristimulus*, and *doable*. On a quick scan, a reader might process the first syllables of these words as being *cow*, *coin*, *rep*, *trist*, and *doab*! Naturally anyone with a competent grasp of the language would quickly see what was meant, but writing these words as *co-worker*, *co-inventor*, *re-prepped*, *tri-stimulus*, and *do-able* makes the reading process a little easier.

When the addition of a prefix or suffix creates an awkward repetition of letters

Consider the following words:

Acceptable	Better
intraarterial	intra-arterial
preengineered	pre-engineered
deemphasize	de-emphasize
antiinflammatory	anti-inflammatory
multiitem	multi-item
shelllike	shell-like
nonnative	non-native
multititled	multi-titled

The double *a*'s, *e*'s, *i*'s, *n*'s, and triple *l*'s don't help readability, while one practically has to squint at *multititled* to make out that it's a word at all.

Mandatory to hyphenate

Finally, there are a number of situations where a hyphen is required. Always include one in the following cases:

When the root word is capitalized

> pre-Columbian
> sub-Arctic

un-American
post-Reformation
Buddha-like
Canada-wide

When the root word is a numeral

pre-1900
under-18's

With certain prefixes and suffixes
Usually the need for a hyphen depends on the root word, but there are a few specific prefixes and suffixes that always demand them, regardless of what follows. Some common ones are the prefixes *all-*, *ex-*, *self-*, and *quasi-* and the suffixes *-elect*, *-odd*, and *-free*.

all-encompassing	ex-employee	self-esteem	quasi-legal
all-knowing	ex-husband	self-care	quasi-socialist
all-embracing	ex-girlfriend	self-doubts	quasi-realistic

president-elect	twenty-odd students	salt-free
chairman-elect	thirty-odd dollars	jargon-free
bride-elect	forty-odd couples	smoke-free

Hyphenation of numbers
Include a hyphen when spelling out (1) any two-word integer from twenty-one to ninety-nine, or (2) a fraction.

Numeral	Word
29	twenty-nine
162	one hundred sixty-two
1/3	one-third
4¾	four and three-quarters

With a fraction that includes a two-word number, hyphenate just the two-word number. Do not add another hyphen, or it may become unclear just what numbers are linked with what.

Numeral	No	Yes
1/25	one-twenty-fifth	one twenty-fifth
65/100	sixty-five-hundredths	sixty-five hundredths

Vocabulary Quirks and Challenges

GIVEN THE MIND-BOGGLING size and complexity of English vocabulary, some slips on the part of users are almost inevitable. There are words that sound similar to each other, words that have almost—but not quite—the same meaning as each other, and words that take unexpected plural or negative forms. This section reviews some common errors.

FREQUENTLY MISUSED WORDS

> After a long life, with one great adventure at its heart, many pleasures and pitfalls, [my copy editor] Helene died at the age of 93. Hopefully, she died in her sleep. Helene would have killed me for that last sentence.
>
> —Dorothy Gallagher, "What My Copy Editor Taught Me,"
> *New York Times Book Review*, September 26, 2008

Homonyms (discussed on page 17, in the section on spelling) aren't the only words that cause trouble. The following exercise presents words that are all too often wrongly substituted for others or are used in the wrong sense. Note that unlike confused homonyms, where the wrong word at least *sounds* right, the errors presented here would be evident in speech as well as in writing.

TEST YOUR KNOWLEDGE

Each of the following sentences contains a word that is used incorrectly (although a few are arguably acceptable). What should appear in its place?

1. Temperatures have been below seasonal for the past week, but should rise tomorrow.

2. The successful applicant will have exceptionable writing skills and previous experience in writing grant proposals.
3. Dignitaries from around the country gathered to mark the historical event.
4. I think he lost the game purposefully, but I can't prove it.
5. Participants praised the retreat as being informative and enervating.
6. After a day in the fields, he would sit down to dinner with a vociferous appetite.
7. The enormity of the dataset increases the likelihood of the findings being valid.
8. His most recent book, entitled *Teach Your Baby to Count in Hexadecimal*, is sure to be a hit with parents.
9. His essays always had to be heavily edited in order to be comprehensive.
10. The memo seemed to infer that layoffs were imminent.
11. In another twenty years, seniors will comprise almost 25 percent of the population.
12. If the study is ongoing (e.g., neither still in the planning stages nor yet completed), describe its activities in the present tense.
13. Budget cuts will almost certainly mean that larger numbers of vulnerable children will fall between the cracks.
14. Her ideas are light-years ahead of her time.
15. The noise was literally enough to raise the dead.
16. Errors like grammar mistakes make a résumé look bad.
17. If you're going to Antarctica, don't forget to bring some warm socks.
18. Be assured that your child will be provided with healthy meals.
19. Hopefully, the problem will resolve on its own.
20. The team is stronger than ever, and may decimate last year's record.
21. Daylight savings time is less popular with farmers than it is with city dwellers.
22. If less than thirty people register, the workshop will be cancelled.
23. Copying a large amount of files from one drive to another may cause the system to crash.
24. If you're that tired, go lay down for a while.
25. We expect to transition to the new schedule by the first quarter of next year.
26. If the problem still persists, call your service representative.
27. Order now and receive a free gift!

28. She isn't the quickest worker, but she approaches every task with care and diligency.
29. They decided to go on the trip, irregardless of the cost.
30. The photographs of the oil-coated birds were heartwrenching.

ANSWERS

The misused words in this exercise arise from a number of causes, categorized below.

Confusing a word with one that sounds similar. In sentences 1 to 9, an appropriate word was replaced by one that, while not a homonym, has some overlap in sound.

1. temperatures have been below **seasonal**: should be *seasonable*—typical of or suitable for the time of year. *Seasonal* means occurring or available only at a particular time of year (seasonal employment, seasonal fruits, seasonal music). This distinction is ignored by a lamentably high percentage of weather announcers.
2. **exceptionable** writing skills: should be *exceptional*—extraordinarily good. *Exceptionable* means the exact opposite: offensive or objectionable (something to which one would take exception).
3. **historical** event: should be *historic*—an important and significant event. *Historical* describes anything that happened in the past, whether significant or not (historical society, historical background).
4. he lost the game **purposefully**: should be *purposely*—on purpose, done with volition. *Purposefully* means to not only do something intentionally, but to do it with determination and/or with a specific goal in mind (she purposefully kept steering the conversation back to the money he owed her).
5. informative and **enervating**: should be *energizing*—increasing one's energy, invigorating. *Enervate* means the exact opposite: to debilitate, weaken, or drain energy.
6. a **vociferous** appetite: should be *voracious*—ravenous, having a huge appetite. *Vociferous* means loud, strident, clamorous (there were vociferous objections to the proposal).
7. the **enormity** of the dataset: should be *enormousness*—huge size. *Enormity* means great wickedness or monstrosity (the enormity of the regime's crimes). Some dictionaries do permit this word to mean immenseness,

but many readers will consider it incorrect. There are plenty of other synonyms to indicate size that are noncontroversial.

8. his book **entitled**: should be *titled*—the title given to a work. *Entitled* should be reserved to refer to a right or a claim (this ticket entitles the bearer to one free soda) or an overly high opinion of one's deservingness (she acts like she's entitled to everything).

9. heavily edited in order to be **comprehensive**: should be *comprehensible*—understandable, intelligible. *Comprehensive* means including all necessary details or information (the list is as comprehensive as it need be).

Confusing a word with one that has an associated meaning. In sentences 10 to 13, the appropriate word was replaced by one that does not sound similar but has a conceptual connection.

10. the memo seemed to **infer**: should be *imply*—hint, say indirectly. *Infer* means to guess, surmise, or conclude something without being told it explicitly (I think I inferred what she meant). Thus, the speaker (or writer) implies; the listener (or reader) infers. Some dictionaries permit the use of *infer* as a synonym for *imply*, but enough readers would consider this incorrect that it is advisable to make the distinction.

11. seniors will **comprise**: should be *constitute* or *compose*—make up. *Comprise* means to contain or include (her collection comprises old playbills and stage memorabilia). The parts constitute the whole; the whole comprises the parts. Again, some dictionaries permit the use of *comprise* as a synonym for *constitute*, but in formal writing it is better to make the distinction.

12. if the study is ongoing (**e.g.**, . . .): should be *i.e.*—abbreviation of the Latin term *id est*, which means "that is." *E.g.* is the abbreviation of *exempli gratia*, Latin for "for example." Memorizing the Latin is not necessary, but understanding the distinction is: while both these terms are used when elaborating on a preceding statement, *i.e.* restates what is there, while *e.g.* provides an illustration—the implication being that other scenarios are possible as well. In the problem sentence above, the information in parentheses covers all scenarios, so it is not an example.

   Confusing *i.e.* and *e.g.* can convey misleading information. Compare the following two sentences: "Both treatments brought about significant improvements in health care utilization; i.e., decreases in emergency room visits and in-patient hospitalization" versus "Both treatments brought about significant improvements in health care utilization; e.g., decreases in emergency room visits and in-patient hospitalization." The first indicates that ER visits and hospitalization were the only two measures of health care utilization being looked at, while the second indicates that these were just two possible measures, and that others, not mentioned, were looked at as well. The distinction is important.

13. vulnerable children will **fall between the cracks**: should be *fall through the cracks*—to be overlooked or failed by a system designed to protect. Think about it. If there are cracks in a safety net, wouldn't you *want* to fall between them?

Attributing the wrong definition to a word: In sentences 14 to 21, the problem is not a matter of confusing two words but of simply misusing the one chosen. Some of these misuses are acceptable in speech, but all should be avoided in formal writing.

14. **light-years** ahead of her time: should be *many years* (or just *years*). A light-year isn't a unit of time; it's the distance that light travels in one year, about 5.8 trillion miles (the star Alpha Centauri is about 4.3 light-years from our solar system).

15. **literally** enough to raise the dead: should be *virtually* or *practically*. *Literally* means—literally! It should not be applied to figurative expressions, and using it as in this example, or saying such things as a flustered executive literally lost his head, or children watching a circus act were literally bursting with excitement, would raise some rather unsettling images. An appropriate use of *literally* is when you are referring to something normally metaphorical that is happening in reality (bugs were literally coming out of the woodwork; these skates are literally cutting edge) or when you want to emphasize that something that might appear to be an exaggeration is in fact accurate (the book contains literally thousands of useful tips; it took literally a split second for the gasoline to catch on fire).

16. errors **like** grammar mistakes: should be *such as*—meaning that spelling mistakes are among the things that make a résumé look bad. *Like* means

"similar to" (he got a bike just like his brother's), so the example sentence seems to say that it is errors that *resemble* spelling mistakes that are the problem, not spelling mistakes themselves. In speech, where the context usually makes *like* unambiguous, the word is commonly and harmlessly misused, but stricter standards must apply in formal writing.

17. **bring** some warm socks: should be *take*—transport away from where one is currently located. *Bring* means to transport toward a location. Thus, it would be correct to say *If you're coming to Antarctica, don't forget to bring me some warm socks*—assuming the speaker is already there—or *If you're going to Antarctica, please bring me back a souvenir snow globe*. Similarly, one would *take the dog out for a walk*, but tell an expected guest to *feel free to bring your dog*. Usually, no misunderstanding results from substituting *bring* for *take*, but the words do indicate different perspectives. For example, *I took all the chairs to the new house* puts the focus on the removal of the chairs from their former location, whereas *I brought all the chairs to the new house* puts it on the chairs' arrival.

18. **healthy** meals: should be *healthful*—supportive of good health. Another appropriate word would be *wholesome*. Strictly speaking, the word *healthy* refers to the health of the noun it is modifying—and it's not the health of the meal that's of concern, but that of the person eating it. (Although one would obviously prefer to avoid diseased food.) Some authorities permit its use as shown above, and it's commonly used this way in speech. In formal writing, however, it is better to use one of the other words.

19. **hopefully**, the problem will resolve: should be *we hope, with any luck, it's to be hoped that*, etc. Strictly speaking, *hopefully* means full of hope (she turned hopefully to the job ads; he looked hopefully at the day's receipts). Certainly, the use shown in the example above is very common in speech, and some authorities feel it should be viewed as legitimate since (1) it doesn't present any ambiguity, and (2) alternatives such as *it is to be hoped that* sound rather stiff. In formal writing, however, it is advisable to avoid this usage—at least for now. Another few years may see it gain full acceptability.

20. **decimate** last year's record: should be *smash* or *obliterate*. *Decimate* should not be used to mean total destruction. Strictly speaking, it means to

destroy one-tenth; more generally, to destroy a significant portion of (the herd was decimated by disease).

21. **daylight savings time**: should be *daylight saving time*. Yes, the light is saved (in a sense), but it is not sitting in a bank account and earning interest.

Using a word ungrammatically. In sentences 22 to 25, the problem word is not misunderstood but is used in a way that is grammatically inappropriate.

22. **less** than thirty people: should be *fewer*—not as many individual entities. *Less* should be used only to refer to a smaller quantity of a single entity (my recipe calls for less sugar; the other route takes less time).

   No copy editor can stand in a supermarket express checkout line without wincing over the inevitable "10 items or less."

23. a large **amount** of files: should be *number*—the quantity of individual entities. Same distinction as *less* versus *fewer*. *Amount* should be used only to refer to how much there is of a singular entity (there's a huge amount of work still to do; what amount of salt does this take).

24. go **lay** down: should be *lie*—the act of being in a horizontal position, literally or figuratively (I really need to lie down; he decided to lie low for a while; the clouds seemed to lie right over the treetops; the wallet was lying there in plain view). *Lay* is a transitive verb meaning to set something down (just lay that box on the table; lay your head on my shoulder).

   The confusion around these words carries into all their verb forms. The past tense of *lie* is *lay* (I lay on the sofa until I felt better; he lay low until the storm blew over), not *laid* as many people believe; and the past participle is *lain* (after I had lain there for a while, I got up), not *laid*. The past tense of *lay* is *laid* (I laid the box on the table; she laid her head on the pillow), not *lay* as many people believe; and its past participle is also *laid* (she insisted that she had laid the forms in their usual place), not *lain*. Got all that? There will be a test.

25. we expect to **transition**: should be *make the transition*. There is a regrettable tendency in some genres of communication, business writing in particular, to puff up text by forcing nouns into verb roles (verbing a noun, as this phenomenon is known as in the editing trade). Architect a solution, dialogue with customers, incentivize your employees . . .

the list is long. In fairness, some words that once served only as nouns have evolved to take on new roles; a section on this topic in Strunk and White's classic 1935 handbook *The Elements of Style* looks askance at the now-respectable *hosted, chaired,* and *debuted.* However, if a use has not gained official status, it is best to go with what the dictionary says.

A note on one particular word, in this case not arising from corporate-think: *disrespect,* as in "Several of the teachers spoke of their students openly disrespecting them." While *respect* can be used as either a noun or a verb, *disrespect* is a noun only. Although this term (often presenting as *diss*) is widely used, it is not standard English and should not appear in formal writing.

Including redundancies. Keep in mind that some words carry inherent meanings that should not be repeated with additional words elsewhere in the sentence.

26. if the problem **still persists**: Anything that is persisting is, by defini-tion, still happening. Other common examples of this type of error are the use of *reaffirm* (should be limited to the *second* repetition of a statement—the first repetition is simply affirming), or repeating a word already contained in an abbreviation, such as *ATM machine* or *PIN number.*

27. receive a **free gift**: As opposed to . . . ? If you're puzzling over this one, look up the definition of *gift.* Similarly, avoid such combinations as *new innovation, foreign imports, unexpected surprise, mutual cooperation,* and *very unique.*

Using a word that isn't. The only problem with the last sentences is that they contain words that don't exist. Despite their ubiquity in speech and print, these words appear in no dictionary.

28. care and **diligency**: should be *diligence.* This error possibly arises from an association with similar-meaning words—*assiduity, alacrity, industry.*

29. **irregardless** of the cost: should be *regardless.* This error likely arises from a confusion with the similar word *irrespective.* The suffix *-less* is all this word needs to make it negative.

30. the photographs were **heartwrenching**: should be *heartrending.* This extremely common error—made regularly by members of the media,

> who should know better—presumably arises from a confusion with the similar word *gut-wrenching*. Keep your internal organs straight!

PLURAL FORMATIONS

Tree, trees. Girl, girls. House, houses. Life would be simpler if all plurals followed the rule of adding *s* to the singular. Unfortunately, the outliers are rampant, and quirky plurals present yet another stumbling block to writers wrestling their way through the exceptions that dot the English language. (A personal favorite *Far Side* cartoon: a learned-looking octopus at a podium addressing a roomful of its peers, with the caption: "Fellow octopi, or octopuses . . . octopi? Dang, it's hard to start a speech with this crowd.") One reason for the irregularities is that many words have been borrowed from other languages, and for some, the plural in the original language has remained the correct form in English as well. To complicate matters even further, some nouns have two acceptable plurals, and one form may be considered more appropriate than the other in certain genres of writing. In a number of cases, the different plural forms actually have different meanings.

This section reviews the rules that govern irregular plurals, and discusses exceptions and variations. Also see the discussion of unusual plurals and singulars under Agreement Between Subject and Verb on page 208.

With compound words where the principal noun is followed by a modifier, the pluralizing *s* goes after the noun

Note that this holds whether the compound is open or hyphenated, and in some cases even when it is closed.

mother-in-law	mothers-in-law
court-martial	courts-martial
attorney general	attorneys general
rule of thumb	rules of thumb
right of way	rights of way
passerby	passersby

Compounds ending in *-ful* usually take the *s* at the end: *roomfuls, mouthfuls.* Some, however, can go either way: *spoonsful* or *spoonfuls, bucketsful* or *bucketfuls, handsful or handfuls.*

If there is no clear principal noun, the plural applies to the entire compound: *hand-me-downs, pick-me-ups, will-o'-the-wisps.*

If you feel that a correct plural sounds too stuffy, rather than ignore the rule and make an error (mother-in-laws, attorney generals), try to recast the sentence so that the need for a plural is avoided.

Words ending in a sibilant sound—*s, sh,* soft *ch, x,* or *z*—add *es*

lens	lenses	fox	foxes
bass	basses	topaz	topazes
rash	rashes	the Jones family	the Joneses
speech	speeches	the Katz family	the Katzes
match	matches	the March family	the Marches

Note that these plurals are *not* formed by adding an apostrophe. For a discussion of the very few types of plurals that do take an apostrophe, see page 204, in the chapter on punctuation.

In a few cases, the final *z* or *s* must be or may be doubled before the *es*: for example, *quiz, quizzes; bus, buses,* or *busses.*

Words ending in *is* change to *es*

basis	bases
crisis	crises
hypothesis	hypotheses
thesis	theses
parenthesis	parentheses

These words do not add an additional *es* as do other words ending in *s*. That is, do *not* pluralize them as *hypothesises* or *thesises.*

Words ending in a consonant followed by *y* change to *ies*

twenty	twenties
harpy	harpies
family	families
brandy	brandies

If the *y* is preceded by a vowel, it usually does not change: for example, *galleys, donkeys. Money,* however, may become *monies* or *moneys.* Note that proper nouns always keep the *y*: the *Kennedys,* the *Applebys,* the *Emmys,* the *Tonys.*

With words ending in *f* or *fe*, some change to *ves*, others add *s*

chief	chiefs
roof	roofs
knife	knives
life	lives
leaf	leaves

Note though that the plural of *still life* is *still lifes*, not *lives*; and the hockey team is not the *Toronto Maple Leaves*!

A number may go either way:

hoof	hoofs or hooves
dwarf	dwarfs or dwarves

While *dwarf* can go either way, the astronomical term is *white dwarfs*, not *dwarves*.

With words ending in *o*, some add *s*, others add *es*

portfolio	portfolios
stereo	stereos
contralto	contraltos
potato	potatoes
tomato	tomatoes

A number may go either way:

ghetto	ghettos or ghettoes
banjo	banjos or banjoes
zero	zeros or zeroes

The general rule is that the *e* is included if the *o* is preceded by a consonant and is not included if the *o* is preceded by a vowel, but there are enough exceptions that it's best to check. Be aware that dictionaries may differ.

Some words of Italian origin that end in *o* change to *i*, but may alternatively add *s*

concerto	concerti or concertos
basso	bassi or bassos

The choice may depend on the formality of the writing.

Latin words ending in *us* change to *i*

alumnus	alumni
stimulus	stimuli
locus	loci

For some—not all—it is acceptable to add *es* instead:

focus	foci or focuses
fungus	fungi or funguses
nucleus	nuclei or nucleuses
radius	radii or radiuses

In cases where both forms are legitimate, the Latin plural is preferred in more formal writing.

Latin words ending in *um* change to *a*

bacterium	bacteria
medium	media
datum	data

For some—not all—it is acceptable to add *s* instead:

millennium	millennia or millenniums
memorandum	memoranda or memorandums
symposium	symposia or symposiums
honorarium	honoraria or honorariums

In cases where both forms are legitimate, the Latin plural is preferred in formal writing. Note however that for some Latin words the English plural has become the standard. For example, pluralizing *museum* and *auditorium* as *musea* and *auditoria* would look far more pretentious than correct.

Latin words ending in *a* add an *e*

alumna	alumnae
larva	larvae
alga	algae

For some—not all—it is acceptable to add *s* instead:

vertebra	vertebrae or vertebras
persona	personae or personas
antenna	antennae or antennas

Use *antennas* for TV and radio aerials, but *antennae* for insects. Use *personas* for the demeanors put on for others (she assumes different personas for different occasions), but *personae* for fictional characters (as in *dramatis personae*). In cases where both forms are legitimate, the Latin plural is preferred in scientific and academic writing.

Latin-derived words ending in *x* either change to *ices* or add *es*

appendix	appendices or appendixes
index	indices or indexes
matrix	matrices or matrixes
cortex	cortices or cortexes

It is usual to use *indices* if referring to indicators (several indices are used to measure economic progress) and *indexes* for the plural of a back-of-the-book index. For all these words, use the Latin plural in scientific and academic writing.

Greek words ending in *on* change to *a*

criterion	criteria
phenomenon	phenomena

If *phenomenon* is being used to mean a remarkable person rather than an observable event, it is pluralized with an *s* (those young musicians are phenomenons).

Many French words that end in *eau* may add either *x* or *s*

beau	beaux or beaus
chateau	chateaux or chateaus
milieu	milieu or milieus

Use the French plural in more formal writing.

Hebrew words add *im* (for masculine nouns) or *oth* (for feminine nouns)

In a number of cases, it is acceptable to add *s* instead.

kibbutz	kibbutzim
Ashkenazi	Ashkenazim
Sephardi	Sephardim
cherub	cherubim or cherubs
seraph	seraphim or seraphs

mitzvah	mitzvoth or mitzvahs
matzo	matzoth or matzos

Use *cherubs* to refer to appealing children (those kids are perfect cherubs), and *cherubim* to refer to biblical angels in art or literature.

Some English words take unpredictable plural forms; and some are the same in both singular and plural form

one mouse	two mice
one foot	two feet
one ox	two oxen
one goose	two geese
one man	two men
one child	two children
one moose	two moose
one deer	two deer
one aircraft	two aircraft
one series	two series
one sweepstakes	two sweepstakes

Native speakers easily handle these plurals along with the more predictable ones. For those learning English as a second language, there is little to do but roll the eyes, tear at the hair, and grimly memorize each one.

NEGATIVE FORMATIONS

> I was furling my wieldy umbrella for the coat check when I saw her standing alone in a corner. She was a descript person, a woman in a state of total array. Her hair was kempt, her clothing shevelled, and she moved in a gainly way. I wanted desperately to meet her, but I knew I'd have to make bones about it since I was travelling cognito.
>
> —Jack Winter, "How I Met My Wife,"
> *The New Yorker*, July 25, 1994

Unreliable. Irreversible. Disloyal. Indecisive. Impractical. Atypical. Counterintuitive. Illiterate. Abnormal. Deactivate. Misremember. Antiracism. Non-addictive. Maladjusted. Shoeless. Cholesterol-free. Just as not every plural is formed by adding *s* to the singular, not every negative is formed by adding *un-*. One of the challenges of the English language is the variety of add-ons that can be united with base words to create their opposites. Sometimes the reason for using a given prefix or suffix has to do with the meaning; sometimes with the form or the etymological root of the base word. The result of all this variation is that negative words present yet another pitfall and are the source of many common errors.

Varied as they are, negative prefixes and suffixes aren't utterly arbitrary. Their meanings are (more or less) as follows:

PREFIX OR SUFFIX	MEANING	EXAMPLES
non-	Not possessing a certain trait. This prefix is merely descriptive and usually does not carry an unfavorable connotation.	nonprofit, noncommercial, nonhuman, nonreligious, non-American
	Of no significance	nonissue, nonevent
un-	The opposite of, sometimes with an unfavorable connotation. The most common prefixes for conveying this meaning are *un-* and *in-*, but there are variants: *il-* for some words starting with *l*; *im-* for some words starting with *b*, *m*, or *p*; and *ir-* for some words starting with *r*. However, many words that begin with these letters take the more common prefixes instead.	unaltered, unenforced, unseen, unqualified, un-American
in-		inhuman, inattentive, inability, incapable
il-		illegal, illegitimate
im-		imbalance, immobile, implausible
ir-		irreligious, irrefutable, irrevocable
dis-	The explicit reverse of (i.e., not merely the absence of the positive aspect)	disqualified, disrespectful, disagreement, disadvantage, discontented
de-		de-emphasize, de-escalate, deforestation, decompose
counter-	In an opposite manner to	counterpressure, counterclockwise, countercurrent
	In opposition or resistance to	countermove, counterespionage

	Possessing opposite traits to	antimatter, Antichrist, anti-hero
anti-	Combating or protecting against	antimissile, antiaircraft, antitoxin, antidepressant, antifreeze
	Hostile to	antimonarchist, antivivisectionist, anti-Semitic
a-	Without, lacking, devoid of	achromatic, asexual, aseptic
an-	(*a-* before a consonant; *an-* before a vowel or the letter *h*)	anaerobic, anhedonia
-less		witless, peerless, motionless, classless
e-	Deprived of something that had existed	emasculated, edentate (lacking teeth)
de-		dehumanized, demagnetized
de-	Excluding or taking away	declassify, decontaminate, dehumidify, deinstitutionalize, deboned
dis-		disbar, disarm, disenfranchise
dys-	Abnormal or impaired	dyslexic, dysfunctional, dyspeptic
mis-	Bad, wrong, or inadequate	mistranslate, misuse, misshapen, misperceive, misfortune
mal-		malformed, malfunctioning, malnourished, maladroit
-free	Unencumbered with; not containing something undesirable. This suffix carries an actively positive connotation.	crime-free, smoke-free, frost-free, caffeine-free

There is clearly a great deal of overlap, which is why it is necessary to check the dictionary if you are not certain which negative form a word should take. If no official negative construction for a word is provided, it is usually most appropriate to prefix it with either *non-* for a neutral negative meaning or *un-* for an unfavorable one, sometimes adding a hyphen if the combination looks a bit shaky (see discussion of this on page 30).

To complicate matters further, in some cases a negative prefix differs for different forms of a word: *incomplete* but *uncompleted, unrepressed* but *irrepressible, undisputed* but *indisputable*. And while some base words have more than one acceptable negative construction *(uncommunicative* or *noncommunicative, mistreated* or *maltreated*), be aware that many readers would view certain variants as incorrect. For example, you would be advised to go with *infeasible* rather than *unfeasible* and *antihero* rather than *nonhero*, even though these variants are accepted by some authorities. (See the discussion of prescriptive and descriptive dictionaries on page 11.)

In a few cases, different add-ons to the same base word imply significantly different meanings. A couple going for fertility treatments may think of themselves as *childless*, while one quite content with each other's company would be *child-free*.

Some common misuses of negative prefixes are illustrated below.

TEST YOUR KNOWLEDGE

Correct the following sentences.

1. She was disinterested in the lecture and quickly tuned out.
2. Children's pajamas should be made of inflammable material.
3. Statistical analysis found the findings to be insignificant.
4. Many of the inmates came from highly nonfunctional families.
5. Science is immoral; it is what humans do with scientific findings that has ethical significance.
6. If the pegs don't fit in the holes, check to see if they're nonaligned.
7. The coach stated that he was very unsatisfied with the refereeing.
8. Her office was wildly unorganized.
9. Planting misinformation is a key wartime strategy.
10. She admits to having a very unscientific mind—her strengths are in the arts.

ANSWERS

1. **disinterested** in the lecture: should be *uninterested*—bored by. *Disinterested* means impartial or objective; that is, having no personal stake—interest—in an outcome (they agreed to have their dispute arbitrated by a disinterested third party).
2. **inflammable** material: should be *nonflammable*—not easily ignited. *Inflammable* means flammable! (As in *inflame*.)
3. found the findings to be **insignificant**: should be *nonsignificant*—failing to reach a certain criterion that would indicate that an effect was real, not

occurring by chance. *Insignificant* means trivial, unimportant, inconsequential (she always managed to make him feel small and insignificant).

4. **nonfunctional** families: should be *dysfunctional*—working badly or pathologically. *Nonfunctional* means not working at all (be sure to replace all nonfunctional batteries).

5. science is **immoral**: should be *amoral*—something to which morals, either good or bad, do not apply. *Immoral* means having bad morals (she felt that to take his money would be immoral).

6. check to see if they're **nonaligned**: should be *misaligned*—not in a straight line. *Nonaligned* is a political term—now dated—referring to countries without political alliances to either the Western or the Communist bloc (the nonaligned nations were supportive of the measure).

7. he was very **unsatisfied**: should be *dissatisfied*—unhappy or displeased with. *Unsatisfied* means not having had enough of something (dinner was meager, and he left the table feeling unsatisfied). Although note that someone who is unsatisfied is probably also dissatisfied.

8. her office was wildly **unorganized**: should be *disorganized*—badly organized. *Unorganized* means not organized, in the sense of either not sorted (two years after she moved, her papers were still unorganized) or not forming a labor union (the workers at the largest plant were unorganized).

9. planting **misinformation**: should be *disinformation*—information that is deliberately misleading. *Misinformation* is information that is wrong, but not intentionally so (teenagers often trade misinformation about birth control).

10. **unscientific** mind: should be *nonscientific*—not working in a scientific way. *Unscientific* carries an implication of being actively counter to science (their theories were unscientific, largely based on anecdotal data).

Using Type Style for Effect

"Good night, little girls!
Thank the Lord you are well!"
And now go to sleep!"
Said Miss Clavel.
    And she turned out the light—
    And closed the door—
        And that's all there is—
            There isn't any more.

—Ludwig Bemelmans, *Madeline*

The focus for writers is of course the words themselves, not their physical appearance. Elements of design such as layout, typeface, and font size are the concerns of designers. However, there is no rule against the occasional writer having a bit of fun with these (for the most famous example of all time, see Lewis Carroll's sinuous "Mouse's Tale"). More typically, the aspects of typography of interest to writers are those that can have a direct impact on meaning or tone: capital letters, italic type, and boldface.

USES OF CAPITALIZATION

In this age of tweets, twitters, and instant messaging, it might sometimes be wondered if capital letters will survive into the next generation. Leaving aside such phenomena as *cul8r* and *g2g* (which do have a certain practicality in some circumstances), many online postings are filled with, ah, variants in spelling, punctuation, and grammar that stretch the definition of literacy to the breaking point. A particular casualty of online communication has been the capital letter, whose absence can make an entire posting look like a single run-on sentence.

Capital letters have a wide range of functions that fall into two main categories: conventional uses, such as starting sentences and setting off important entities; and creative uses, for achieving particular tones and emphases.

Conventional uses of capital letters

The more mechanical roles of capitalization are outlined below. In cases where there is more than one "right" approach, your main concern should be consistency.

Starting a sentence

The most common role of capital letters is, of course, to begin each new sentence. The standard function here requires no discussion, but there are a few situations that bear mention.

Sentence within a sentence: If a grammatically complete sentence lies within parentheses as part of a larger sentence, do not capitalize it.

> All sentences must begin with a capital letter (an exception is when a sentence lies within another sentence).

For more details, see the style conventions for parentheses on page 159.

Sentence containing a non-terminal question mark or exclamation point: These marks, normally terminal punctuation marks that signal the end of a sentence, may occasionally be used to break up what is actually a single sentence, in which case what follows usually appears in lowercase.

> The town square was all peace and tranquility when boom! the midday cannon fired.

If either lowercase or uppercase would work, just be consistent.

> How much longer would we have to wait—one hour? two? five?

> How much longer would we have to wait—one hour? Two? Five?

Dialogue sentence broken by nondialogue: Lowercase the first letter of what follows the break if it's a continuation of the same sentence; uppercase it if it begins a new sentence.

> "Go six blocks past the mall," he directed, "and then turn left at the lights."

> "Go six blocks past the mall," he directed. "Then turn left at the lights."

Sentences starting with names that must be lowercased: Although proper nouns are normally capitalized, a few individuals and businesses (high-tech companies are the likeliest) insist on breaking the rules, which can be interpreted as either audacious and cutting-edge or an annoying affectation, depending on one's perception. A writer who starts off a sentence with one of these exceptions is faced with an undeniable conflict: open with a capital letter, thereby not respecting the preference of the name's owner, or with a lowercase letter, thereby breaking the rule of always starting a sentence uppercase? Either way, of course, you'll be in the wrong. The best strategy is to recast the sentence to avoid the problem. If that isn't possible, go with either uppercase or lowercase and hope that your readers will be understanding.

Sentence containing a colon: Practice varies as to whether the text following the colon should begin with upper- or lowercase. For a discussion and illustrations, see the style conventions for the colon on page 116.

Lending weight

Nouns that refer to objects or abstract entities are normally not capitalized, but they may be if there is a reason to do so. Capitalizing a word gives it more importance, and there are several circumstances where capitalization of ordinary nouns is either mandatory or usual—or at least acceptable.

Well-known events or entities: If an otherwise generic word has come to be associated with a unique, well-known event or entity, capitalize it when you are using it in that specific way. For example, you would use *depression* if referring to some current or minor historical economic downturn, but *the Depression* if referring to the period of worldwide hardship in the 1930s. Similarly,

the Crusades	the Holocaust
the Black Death	the Age of Reason
the Pill	the Golden Rule

Many such terms will be noted in the dictionary; others may not have achieved dictionary status, but their capitalization is considered to be a matter of common knowledge.

Titles and identifiers: Capitalize a title or an identifying term when it is part of a name. If the same word is being used generically, do not capitalize it.

Prince Charles, but the prince
Judge Goldberg, but the judge

>the University of Miami, but the university
>New York City, but the city of New York
>American Sign Language, but sign language

In some cases, if a person or entity is considered to be of particular significance, a title may retain its capitalization even when it is not linked with the name. For example, members of Commonwealth countries refer to the British monarch as the Queen. To a Londoner, the downtown business core is the City. The Olympics are the Games to all. To his devotees, Elvis is forever the King.

Organizations, entities, positions, etc.: It may sometimes be appropriate to capitalize certain descriptive or identifying names and terms that are normally lowercase. The decision to capitalize may be made on the basis of convention, policy, expectations of readers, or any other reason that is specific to your circumstances. Whichever way you go, be sure you are consistent.

>the post office *or* the Post Office
>a nursing assistant *or* a Nursing Assistant
>western values *or* Western values
>the board of directors *or* the Board of Directors

Words that derive from proper nouns: When nouns, verbs, or adjectives have their origins in the names of people (real or fictional) or places, they sometimes retain the capitalization, sometimes not. Check the dictionary.

bowdlerize	Faustian bargain
mesmerize	Norfolk jacket
saxophone	Vandyke beard
bloomers	Marxist ideology
french fries	Camembert cheese

Trade names: Names of commercial products need to be capitalized for legal reasons. Be particularly careful with those that are often unthinkingly used as generic words, such as Dumpster, Plexiglas, Scotch tape, Champagne, Thermos, Styrofoam, Masonite, Jell-O, Band-Aid. Refer to the Web or a dictionary (a good one will include trade names) if you're uncertain.

Titles of books, plays, films, songs, etc.: Capitalize the opening word plus all main words. For these, as well as for titles of places or institutions, do not capitalize minor words such as articles, conjunctions, and prepositions. (Style guides may differ on whether all conjunctions and prepositions should be lowercase, or just those shorter than, say, three or four letters.)

> Arms and the Man
> The Princess and the Pea
> Romeo and Juliet
> The Sound of Music

Bibliographic references: Some style guides specify capitalization of every main word of a book title (nouns, pronouns, verbs, adjectives, and adverbs), lowercase for the words that serve to introduce or join main words (articles, conjunctions, and prepositions). Others capitalize only the first word (as well as any proper nouns, of course). In the latter case, for titles that include subtitles, most style guides will say to capitalize the first word of the subtitle as well, but some will say that the subtitle should open with lowercase.

Whether following a style guide or making your own decisions, present every title in your bibliography in the same manner, regardless of how it appears on its own book cover or in someone else's reference list. Either of the following presentations would be acceptable:

> A Dictionary of Modern English Usage, *or* A dictionary of modern English usage
>
> The Chicago Manual of Style *or* The Chicago manual of style
>
> The Elements of Style *or* The elements of style
>
> Eats, Shoots & Leaves: The Zero Tolerance Approach to Punctuation *or*
> Eats, shoots & leaves: The zero tolerance approach to punctuation, *or*
> Eats, shoots & leaves: the zero tolerance approach to punctuation

Abbreviations

Most all-caps abbreviations derive from multiword terms, where the abbreviation consists of the first letter of each word. A few cautions about capitalized abbreviations:

- Note that the article (*a* or *an*) preceding an abbreviation may differ depending on whether the abbreviation is pronounced as letters or as an acronym. If the abbreviation opens with a vowel sound, precede it with *an*, even if the first letter is a consonant. If it opens with a consonant sound, precede it with *a*, even if the first letter is a vowel.

an RCMP officer   a RAM capacity

an NBC program   a NATO meeting

a UV light   an URN publication

- Occasionally, a single word is abbreviated to two capital letters. Be certain in such cases that you capitalize *both* letters.

    Your user ID may be up to 20 characters long. [not Id]

    If that's what you want, it's OK with me. [not Ok]

- If an all-caps abbreviation is pluralized, be sure that the pluralizing *s* appears in lowercase. If you put it in uppercase, it would look like part of the abbreviation itself.

    Invitees are asked to kindly return their RSVPs as soon as possible. [not RSVPS]

    The RNs' shifts were posted by the front desk. [not RNS']

For more on all-caps abbreviations, see the discussions under Period on page 122 and Apostrophe on page 204.

Headings

Nonfiction writing of any significant length generally requires headings of different levels: high-level headings to introduce main sections, lower-level headings to introduce subdivisions of a main section, still lower-level headings to introduce subdivisions of a subdivision, and so on. It is very important that headings of the same level always appear the same way, and that those of different levels be visually distinct. The typography of a heading serves as a visual cue to readers, informing them whether what follows is a subset of what came before, different information on the same level, or a new topic altogether.

One way to achieve this distinctiveness is through capitalization. For example, the highest level headings within a document could be in all-caps text (LEVEL-ONE HEADING), the next level could have all main words capitalized (Level-Two Heading), and the level below that could have only the first word capitalized (Level-three heading). Other strategies are use of different type sizes, bold and/or italic versus regular type, centering versus left-aligned, and more.

If you are capitalizing all main words in a heading, determine how you will treat hyphenated compounds. Some style guides would capitalize the second word of such compounds; others would lowercase it.

The Private Lives of Stand-Up Comedians	The Private Lives of Stand-up Comedians
English Poetry of the Mid-Eighteenth Century	English Poetry of the Mid-eighteenth Century

Lists

If items in a vertical list consist of entire sentences, begin each one with a capital letter, just as you would with any other sentence. If the items are single words or sentence fragments, the choice is yours or your style guide's. Ensure consistency.

Never create a list where some items are full sentences and others not. See Parallel Structure on page 223.

All caps and small caps

If your writing is of an informative nature, such as a brochure or an instruction manual, it may occasionally be appropriate to present particularly important information in ALL-CAPS TEXT. Reserve this, however, for very short strings; preferably no more than a few words. Writers sometimes capitalize entire blocks of important information out of a belief that the larger letters will draw extra attention, but in fact the effect may be the exact opposite—readers may impatiently skip over the all-caps section because it's tiring to wade through. How easy do you find it to skim the following passage?

> AVOID UNNECESSARY USE OF ALL-CAPS TEXT, AS IT TENDS TO BE DIFFICULT TO READ. SINCE THE LETTERS ARE ALL EXACTLY THE SAME HEIGHT AND LACK THE DISTINCTIVE ASCENDERS AND DESCENDERS THAT CHARACTERIZE LOWERCASE LETTERS, ALL-CAPS TEXT OFFERS FEWER VISUAL CUES THAN LOWERCASE TEXT, AND THE READER MUST EXPEND MORE CONCENTRATION IN PROCESSING IT.

Alternative strategies such as using outline boxes or a different color (if feasible) are usually preferable.

SMALL CAPITALS are, as their name makes obvious, characters in the shape of uppercase letters but the size of lowercase letters (those without ascenders or descenders). They come in handy when you want to present text in uppercase letters for reasons of convention rather than emphasis, as they avoid the jarring effect produced by all caps. Instead of jumping off the page at you, a small-caps word or phrase blends in inconspicuously with the surrounding text.

> I dig in the weediest part near the compost heap, lifting the earth and letting it crumble, sieving the worms out with my fingers. The soil is rich, the worms scramble, red ones and pink ones. . . . They're sold like apples in season, VERS 5¢ on the roadside signs, sometimes VERS 10¢, inflation. French class, *vers libre*, I translated it the first time as Free Worms and she thought I was being smart.
>
> —Margaret Atwood, *Surfacing*

By convention, small caps are employed for certain abbreviations: A.M. and P.M.; A.D. and B.C. (or C.E. and B.C.E., for Common Era and Before the Common Era). For design reasons, they are frequently used to make up the opening word or words of an article or chapter. They also have a few specialized applications that may be peculiar to a particular publication or genre: for example, they may be used for the name of each speaker in a magazine interview, for synonyms in a dictionary, or (in combination with initial full caps) for the title and author's name on a book cover. In business and technical writing, small caps are often used instead of full caps for abbreviations and acronyms.

Creative uses of capital letters

Capital letters once played a larger role than they do today. A couple of centuries ago, it was common for most nouns in English to be capitalized.

> I now began to be weary, and seeing nothing to entertain my Curiosity, I returned gently down towards the Creek; and the Sea being full in my View, I saw our Men already got into the Boat, and rowing for Life to the Ship. I was going to hollow after them, although it had been to little purpose, when I observed a huge Creature walking after them in the Sea, as fast as he could: He waded not much deeper than his Knees, and took prodigious strides: But our Men had the start of him half a League, and the Sea thereabouts being full of sharp pointed Rocks, the Monster was not able to overtake the Boat.
>
> —Jonathan Swift, *Gulliver's Travels*

Modern writing is not quite as liberal with capitals, but makes occasional use of them to add humor or irony.

'You mean you missed me?' said Berry hungrily. 'Do you mean you missed me?'

Ann's Conscience, which up till this morning had been standing aside and holding a sort of watching brief, now intruded itself upon the scene.

'I don't want you to think I am always shoving myself forward,' said Conscience frigidly, 'but I should be failing in my duty if I did not point out that you are standing at a Girl's Cross Roads. Everything depends on what reply you make to the very leading question which has just been put to you. . . . whatever you do, let me urge upon you with all the emphasis of which I am capable not to drop your eyes and say "Yes." '

'Yes,' said Ann, dropping her eyes. 'Of course I did.'

—P.G. Wodehouse, *Big Money*

Our chairs were adjoining, and when Mario had finished with me and was ready to take off and shake out that cloth throwover, I never, never failed to have more of Seymour's hair on me than my own. Only once did I put in a complaint about it, and that was a colossal mistake. I said something, in a distinctly ratty tone of voice, about his "damn hair" always jumping all over me. The instant I said it I was sorry, but it was out. He didn't say anything, but he immediately started to *worry* about it. It grew worse as we walked home, crossing streets in silence; he was obviously trying to divine a way of forbidding his hair to jump on his brother in the barbershop. The homestretch on 110th, the long block from Broadway to our building, on the corner of Riverside, was the worst. No one in the family could worry his or her way down that block the way Seymour could if he had Decent Material.

—J.D. Salinger, *Seymour: An Introduction*

In dialogue, entire words or sentences may be put in ALL CAPS in order to indicate shouting or vehemence.

Alice laid her hand upon his arm, and said, in a soothing tone, 'You needn't be so angry about an old rattle.'

'But it *isn't* old!' Tweedledum cried, in a greater fury than ever. 'It's *new*, I tell you—I bought it yesterday—my nice NEW RATTLE!' and his voice rose to a perfect scream.

—Lewis Carroll, *Through the Looking-Glass*

Greenery I leave to the birds and the bees, they have their worries, I have mine. At home who knows the name of what grows from the pavement at the front of our house? It's a tree—and that's it. The kind is of no consequence, who cares what kind, just as long as it doesn't fall down on your head. In the autumn (or is it the spring? Do you know this stuff? I'm pretty sure it's not the winter) there drop from its branches long crescent-shaped pods containing hard little pellets. Okay. Here's a scientific fact about our tree, comes by way of my mother, Sophie Linnaeus: If you shoot those pellets through a straw, you can take somebody's eye out and make him blind for life. (SO NEVER DO IT! NOT EVEN IN JEST! AND IF ANYBODY DOES IT TO YOU, YOU TELL ME INSTANTLY!) And this, more or less, is the sort of botanical knowledge I am equipped with, until that Sunday afternoon. . . .

—Philip Roth, *Portnoy's Complaint*

Writers would be well advised to use this strategy infrequently, however. Don't fall into the error of relying on typographical tricks to infuse excitement or importance into less-than-inspired lines.

USES OF ITALIC TYPE

'I am obliged to tell you what will hurt you, Rosy. But there are things which husband and wife must think of together. I daresay it has occurred to you already that I am short of money.'

Lydgate paused; but Rosamond turned her neck and looked at a vase on the mantelpiece.

'I was not able to pay for all the things we had to get before we were married, and there have been expenses since which I have been obliged to meet. The consequence is, there is a large debt. . . . I took pains to keep it from you while you were not well; but now we must think together about it, and you must help me.'

'What can *I* do, Tertius?' said Rosamond, turning her eyes on him again. That little speech of four words, like so many others in all languages, is capable by varied vocal inflexions of expressing all stages of mind from helpless dimness to exhaustive argumentative perception, from the completest self-devouring fellowship to the most neutral aloofness. Rosamond's thin utterance threw into the words 'What can *I* do!' as much neutrality as they could hold. They fell like a mortal chill on Lydgate's roused tenderness.

—George Eliot, *Middlemarch*

Italic type serves to make text stand out distinctively. It may be employed for stylistic reasons, lending emphasis, irony, or urgency to what it encompasses, or for reasons of convention. Its main uses are the following:

- Highlighting words that have special significance
- Emphasizing a speaker's words

- Indicating unspoken words
- Setting off non-English words
- Setting off terms, titles, and other special text
- Underscoring a point in a quote

Highlighting significant words

Italicizing a word or passage draws attention to it, informing the reader that it holds particular meaningfulness.

> She twisted the dial, right, left, right again, heard the click as the lock yielded, opened the safe—*and it was empty.*

> Given that it was *my* house he was being so generous with, I did not share his enthusiasm about putting up the entire circus troupe and their elephants for the week.

Italics are particularly important when they affect the meaning of what is being said. Consider the nine different interpretations of the following sentence:

He knew she'd never ask him for a loan.

[Other people thought she would]

He *knew* she'd never ask him for a loan.

[He had good reason to know she wouldn't]

He knew *she'd* never ask him for a loan.

[Someone else would be asking him for one]

He knew she'd *never* ask him for a loan.

[She wouldn't do so in a million years]

He knew she'd never *ask* him for a loan.

[She might hint strongly, though]

He knew she'd never ask *him* for a loan.

[She might ask someone else]

He knew she'd never ask him *for* a loan.

[She'd be more likely to offer him one]

He knew she'd never ask him for *a* loan.

[She wouldn't stop at just one]

He knew she'd never ask him for a *loan.*

[She'd prefer an outright gift]

As effective as italic type can be, do not rely on it excessively as a means of injecting excitement or importance. Good writers achieve emphasis through wording and punctuation, not through typographical tricks. Reserve italics for cases where the intended meaning would not be clear without them, or where you feel that a desired emphasis could not be made apparent through wording alone.

Emphasizing a speaker's words

In dialogue, italics are often used to indicate words that a speaker is stressing, saying loudly, or saying with particular significance.

> Come the crucial seventh, the Filmmakers' First Wives Club grew restive, no longer content to belittle their former husbands from afar, and moved in on the baselines and benches, undermining confidence with their heckling. When Myer Gross, for instance, came to bat with two men on base and his teammates shouted, "Go, man. Go," one familiar grating voice floated out over the others. "Hit, Myer. Make your son proud of you, *just this once.*"
>
> —Mordecai Richler, *St. Urbain's Horseman*

> . . . . "Perhaps this will refresh your memory." The District Attorney suddenly thrust a heavy automatic at the quiet figure on the witness stand. "Have you ever seen this before?" Walter Mitty took the gun and examined it expertly. "This is my Webley-Vickers 50.80," he said calmly. . . . "You are a crack shot with any sort of firearms, I believe?" said the District Attorney, insinuatingly. "Objection!" shouted Mitty's attorney. "We have shown that the defendant could not have fired the shot. We have shown that he wore his right arm in a sling on the night of the fourteenth of July." Walter Mitty raised his hand briefly and the bickering attorneys were stilled. "With any known make of gun," he said evenly, "I could have killed Gregory Fitzhurst at three hundred feet *with my left hand.*"
>
> —James Thurber, *The Secret Life of Walter Mitty*

This device should be reserved for fiction. It is usually not appropriate to include italics when quoting a real person's speech in a report or article.

Note that in dialogue just part of a word can be italicized, which is a realistic representation of how people actually speak.

> [Stradlater] asked me if I'd written his goddam composition for him. I told him it was over on his goddam bed. He walked over and read it while he was unbuttoning his

shirt. He stood there, reading it, and sort of stroking his bare chest and stomach, with this very stupid expression on his face. He was mad about himself.

All of a sudden, he said, "For Chris*sake*, Holden. This is about a goddam *base*ball glove."

"So what?" I said. Cold as hell.

"Wuddaya mean *so what*? I told ya it had to be about a goddam *room* or a house or something."

"You said it had to be descriptive. What the hell's the difference if it's about a baseball glove?"

—J.D. Salinger, *The Catcher in the Rye*

Indicating unspoken words

In fiction writing, sometimes italics are used to represent words that are being thought by a character, rather than spoken aloud.

"Yes. Speaking."

"Oh, well then. You wouldn't remember me, Miss—er—Missus Gunn, but I was in Dragett's Bookshop that day last October when you were there autographing your books . . . . Well, I do a lot of writing myself, Miss—uh—Miss Gunn, so I just thought I'll phone you up, like, and I'd be grateful if you'd just tell me how you got started. I mean, I know once you're accepted, you don't need to worry. Anything you write *now*, I mean, will automatically get published—"

Oh, sure. Just bash out any old crap and rake in the millions. I get my plots from the telephone directory.

"I didn't know a soul," Morag said heavily, trying to force politeness and consideration into her voice. "I just kept sending stories out, that's all. When I wrote a novel, I submitted it. The second publisher took it. I was lucky."

"Yes. But how did you actually get a *start*? What did you *do*?"

"I worked like hell, if you really want to know. I've told you. There's no secret. Look, it's awfully early, I'm sorry. I'm afraid I really can't help you."

"Oh, is it early to you? I always rise at six, so as to work at my writing before I prepare the breakfast for my husband, but I guess a successful writer like you wouldn't have to worry about domestic chores—"

Certainly not. I have a butler, a cook, and a house parlour-maid . . . . Loyal slaves.

"Look, I'm awfully sorry, but—"

"Oh well, in that case, I shouldn't have troubled you, I'm sure." Voice filled with rancor.

Slam!

—Margaret Laurence, *The Diviners*

Often, just leaving off quotation marks is sufficient to indicate silent thought (although you must be careful that the words will be obviously distinguished from the narrative). Because of the other purposes served by italics, using them to indicate unspoken words may sometimes appear to give those words an unintended vehemence or significance.

Another use of italics in fiction is for the text of a note or letter that a character is reading or composing: writing within writing, as it were.

> The top letter was placed with its address upwards: it was in Mr. Irwine's handwriting, Arthur saw at once; and below the address was written, "To be delivered as soon as he arrives." Nothing could have been less surprising to him than a letter from Mr. Irwine at that moment: of course, there was something he wished Arthur to know earlier than it was possible for them to see each other. At such a time as that it was quite natural that Irwine should have something pressing to say. Arthur broke the seal with an agreeable anticipation of soon seeing the writer.
>
> *I send this letter to meet you on your arrival, Arthur, because I may then be at Stoniton, whither I am called by the most painful duty it has ever been given me to perform, and it is right that you should know what I have to tell you without delay.*
>
> *I will not attempt to add by one word of reproach to the retribution that is now falling on you: any other words that I could write at this moment must be weak and unmeaning . . .*
>
> —George Eliot, *Adam Bede*

If a word or phrase within all-italics text needs to be emphasized itself, the convention is to place it in regular type.

Setting off non-English words

Words from other languages are set off in italics as a signal that they should not be processed the same way as the rest of the text.

> Here are a few French terms for fans at the Forum:
>
> *Bataille, Escarmouche, Bagarre générale*—The three stages of mindless hockey violence. A *bataille* is generally waged by two players with no outside interference. When a third party joins the fracas, it escalates into an *escarmouche*. This is often the signal for every player on the ice to drop his gloves and go at it; the ensuing obscene spectacle is your basic Pier Six *bagarre générale*.
>
> —Michael Farber and Mike Boone, *The Anglo Guide to Survival in Québec*

'Oh, look!' broke in Gherkins. 'Here's a picture of a man being chopped up in little bits. What does it say about it?'

'I thought you could read Latin.'

'Well, but it's all full of sort of pothooks. What do they mean?'

'They're just contractions,' said Lord Peter patiently. ' "*Solent quoque hujus insulae cultores*"—it is the custom of the dwellers in this island, when they see their parents stricken in years and of no further use, to take them down into the market-place and sell them to the cannibals, who kill them and eat them for food. This they also do with younger persons when they fall into any desperate sickness.'

. . . The viscount was enthralled.

'I *do* like this book,' he said; 'could I buy it out of my pocket-money, please?'

'Another problem for uncles,' thought Lord Peter, rapidly ransacking his recollections of the *Cosmographia* to determine whether any of its illustrations were indelicate; for he knew the duchess to be straitlaced. On consideration, he could only remember one that was dubious, and there was a sporting chance that the duchess might fail to light upon it.

—Dorothy Sayers, *The Learned Adventure of the Dragon's Head*

I was in love with Kiyo Yamada. He would take me back to Osaka with him and we would live in a house with rice paper *shoji* screens and *tatami* mats. He would wear a *yukata*, and I would wear a glorious silk kimono printed with flying cranes and fresh-cut cherry blossoms.

—Ann Ireland, *A Certain Mr. Takahashi*

Note in the above excerpt that "kimono" is not italicized along with the other Japanese words, since this is a word that has been fully incorporated into English.

Unambiguously foreign words should always be italicized, but how do you treat words that are designated as foreign yet exist as entries in English dictionaries? The problem is, there isn't a neat distinction between foreign-derived words that have come to be considered standard English vocabulary and those that haven't. Thus, some authors would italicize words and terms such as *doppelgänger*, *ad hoc*, *ad nauseam*, *a priori*, *per se*, *summa cum laude*, *raison d'être*, *grande dame*, *sangfroid*, and *gonif*, and abbreviations such as *e.g.*, *i.e.*, *et al.*, *ibid.*, *viz.*, and *etc.* Others would not. Dictionaries and style guides will differ on the treatment of these types of words, so if you are not obligated to follow a particular style, make your own decisions. You may do this on a word-by-word basis, rather than resolving, say, to italicize anything in Latin. Note that modern style is inclined to use roman (regular) type for all but the most unusual or exotic words, on the reasoning that italics are necessary only if a word is likely to be unfamiliar.

Note: Never italicize foreign proper nouns—names of people or places.

Setting off special text

Italic type is used to set off a variety of special words. The full range is too broad to cover here; this section reviews only the more common applications. Specialized areas such as scientific, mathematical, and legal writing will all have their own particular designations.

Terminology

In formal writing, a new term is often set off on its first appearance in some typographically distinct way. The usual strategies are to either enclose it in quotation marks (see page 185) or to put it in italic or boldface type. Other, less common options are underlining or using color.

> *Capital goods* are industrial products that are long-lived and expensive, such as heavy machinery and vehicles; *expense items* are industrial products that are cheaper and quickly consumed, such as office supplies and paper products.

After its first occurrence, the term should appear in regular type.

Titles

It is usual to italicize the names of ships and space vehicles, and the titles of books, newspapers, magazines, films, plays, operas, and CDs. For titles of short stories, poems, book chapters, magazine or journal articles, and songs, it is more common to use quotation marks instead. Note, though, that these are conventions, not absolutes. It is acceptable to use either italics or quotation marks for any of the above, or you may sometimes choose to present a title, such as the name of a newspaper or journal, without setting it off in any special way other than initial capital letters.

Style guides differ as to how titles should be presented in bibliographies. For example, one guide may specify that you must italicize titles of books and journals, but not the titles of articles within journals; a second, to italicize everything; a third, to not italicize at all. If you are expected to use a particular guide, follow its specifications; if you are making your own rules, be sure you treat all titles in the bibliography consistently.

Headings

In text that contains various levels of headings, it is very important to clearly distinguish among them. Strategies to achieve this include centering higher-level headings and placing lower-level ones flush left; using different type sizes; using different fonts (the shape of the letters); using all caps, small caps, or initial caps; and using some combination of regular, boldface, and italic type. Typically, boldface type would be used for higher-level headings and italics for lower-level ones; however, there are no specific rules governing this.

Stage directions

In scripts, the names of the speakers and any directions to the actors must be easily differentiable from the rest of the text. The usual convention is to set them in italics, and to enclose the directions in either parentheses or brackets. (Other typographical conventions such as **bold** or SMALL CAPS may be used for characters' names as well.)

Algernon: [T]his isn't your cigarette case. This cigarette case is a present from someone of the name of Cecily, and you said you didn't know anyone of that name.

Jack: Well, if you want to know, Cecily happens to be my aunt.

Algernon: Your aunt!

Jack: Yes. Charming old lady she is, too. Lives at Tunbridge Wells. Just give it back to me, Algy.

Algernon: (Retreating to back of sofa.) But why does she call herself little Cecily if she is your aunt and lives at Tunbridge Wells? *(Reading.)* "From little Cecily with her fondest love.'

Jack: (Moving to sofa and kneeling upon it.) My dear fellow, what on earth is there in that? Some aunts are tall, some aunts are not tall. That is a matter that surely an aunt may be allowed to decide for herself. You seem to think that every aunt should be exactly like your aunt! This is absurd. For Heaven's sake give me back my cigarette case. *(Follows Algernon round the room.)*

—Oscar Wilde, *The Importance of Being Earnest*

Words and letters referred to as such

Either italics or quotation marks may be used to set off words or letters that are being presented *as* words or letters.

> Her *l*'s were dotted and her *t*'s were crossed.

> The Tangierines—approximately 800 residents—say that their island was first settled in 1686 by a certain John Crockett, a Cornishman. There are no records of this, but the evidence of the Tangier Island speech is overwhelming. To English ears, they sound West Country. Most striking of all "sink" is pronounced *zink*. *Mary* and *merry* have a similar pronunciation, though this is common to much of the tidewater district. "Paul" and "ball" sound like *pull* and *bull*. For "creek" they will say *crik*. And they have a special local vocabulary: *spider* for "frying-pan", *bateau* for "skiff" and *curtains* for "blinds".

> —Robert Mccrum, William Cran, and Robert Macneil, *The Story of English*

Underscoring a point in a quote

If you are presenting quoted material, you may wish to highlight a particular word, phrase, or passage, either because you feel it holds some critical significance or because it makes some controversial point from which you want to dissociate yourself. The way to do this is to italicize the relevant text and then, in order to clearly attribute the italics to yourself and not to the original author, follow it with the words *italics mine, italics added,* or *emphasis added,* enclosed within square brackets.

> "Of this woman's life on the plantation I subsequently learned the following circumstances. She was the wife of head man Frank ... second in command to the overseer. His wife—a tidy, trim woman with a pretty figure ... was taken from him by the overseer ... and she had a son by him whose straight features and diluted color ... bear witness to his Yankee descent. I do not know how long Mr. King's occupation of Frank's wife continued, *or how the latter endured the wrong done to him* [italics mine]. This *outrage upon this man's rights* [italics mine] was perfectly notorious among all the slaves; and his hopeful offspring, Renty, allud[ed] to his superior birth on one occasion."

> —Susan Brownmiller, *Against Our Will: Men, Women and Rape*

If italics exist in the original text that you are quoting and you feel they may be misattributed to you, you may choose to add *italics in original*, in brackets. For more on brackets, see page 175.

Style conventions

- If you cannot produce italic type, use underlining instead.

- If an italicized word or phrase is followed immediately by punctuation, the punctuation mark may either be italicized as well or appear in regular font. Ensure consistency.

  > He did *what?*

  > For a woman of ninety, she was quite *au courant:* there was really nothing one could say to shock her.

- Do not italicize parentheses, brackets, or dashes that enclose italicized text, unless the entire passage that comprises these punctuation marks is italicized.

- If a whole passage is italicized for reasons other than emphasis, and you want to emphasize a word within that passage, put that word in regular type.

USES OF BOLDFACE TYPE

Bold type has a few limited applications in non-fiction writing, all of which have to do with commanding attention. A word or phrase placed in bold type will stand out from what surrounds it and thereby gain more of the reader's notice. Consider using bold type to highlight the following:

- Key terms in such documents as manuals or textbooks, particularly if they are followed by a definition.

- Headings, to increase their contrast from body text.

- Critical information that you want to ensure is noticed, such as alerts and warnings. In particular, it is often a good idea to bold the word "not" in a cautionary statement (Do **not** do action X) to ensure that it is not missed on a quick read.

- General emphasis, to put stress on a word. In this role, it plays the same function as that described for italics (see Highlighting significant words on page 60). Italics, however, are generally preferable.

A caution about bold type: don't overdo it. As with all-caps text (page 58), an entire paragraph—or more—presented in bold is more tiring to read than standard type, so if the intention is to get the reader to pay extra attention to the content, using it for long passages may well backfire.

Part 2

Punctuation

> *April 7*—I used the comma wrong. Its *punctuation* . . . .Miss Kinnian says a period is punctuation too, and there are lots of other marks to learn. I told her I thought she meant all the periods had to have tails and be called commas. But she said no.
>
> She said; You, got. to-mix?them!up: She showd? me" how, to mix! them; up, and now! I can. mix (up all? kinds of punctuation—in, my. writing. There" are lots, of rules; to learn? but. Im' get'ting them in my head:
>
> One thing? I, like: about, Dear Miss Kinnian: (thats, the way? it goes; in a business, letter (if I ever go! into business?) is that, she: always; gives me' a reason" when—I ask. She"s a gen'ius! I wish? I cou'd be smart-like-her;
>
> Punctuation, is? fun!
>
> —Daniel Keyes, *Flowers for Algernon*

The word *punctuation* derives from the Latin *punctus*, which means "point." That is, the marks within a sentence *point* to the various meanings of its words, making sense of what might in some cases be confusing. The marks serve two functions: they define how the various elements of a sentence relate to each other, thereby ensuring clear and unambiguous communication, and they help to establish the tone. The first function is largely mechanical and hence more easily learned; the second is subtler. Sometimes the reason for selecting one mark over another has more to do with achieving a certain nuance than with major differences in meaning.

In dialogue, punctuation helps to convey intonation and style of speaking, so that the reader "hears" a character's words the way the writer intended. Subtleties such as pauses, emphases, hesitations, and changes in pitch can all be achieved through the appropriate marks.

Punctuation marks defy easy categorization, because all play more than one role and different marks can be used for similar purposes. This chapter follows the convention of ordering them according to their main or best-known functions, as follows:

- Marks used to separate elements within a sentence—comma, semicolon, and colon

- Marks used to end a sentence—period, question mark, and exclamation point

- Marks used to link related elements—hyphen and slash

- Marks used to set off digressions from the main flow—parentheses and dashes

- Marks used with quoted material—brackets, quotation marks, and ellipses

- A final mark, the apostrophe, is distinct enough not to be grouped with any other. It acts more like a letter than a punctuation mark, serving as part of the inherent spelling of a word.

This ordering has been done with a recognition that the distinctions are not in fact that neat. Take the terminal punctuation marks: periods have functions other than ending a sentence; question marks and exclamation points occasionally appear in the middle of a sentence; a sentence may end in an ellipsis or a dash rather than in any of the above. Similarly, dashes may be used not only like parentheses but also like colons, to separate elements, and sometimes like hyphens, to link elements. Omitted letters and words may, depending on the specifics of what is being done, be indicated by periods, commas, semicolons, apostrophes, hyphens, ellipses, or dashes. Therefore, the section devoted to each mark includes cross-references to other marks that can perform a similar function, and discusses when it is appropriate to select one mark over another. Most sections end with a review of style conventions, including instructions on how to position the mark when it exists alongside another.

Basic Sentence Structure

IN ORDER TO UNDERSTAND the logic behind some rules of punctuation, particularly those pertaining to the comma and the semicolon, it is necessary to understand the basic components of a sentence. Read this section before turning to the review of those marks, because multiple references are made later to the terms defined here.

SUBJECT AND PREDICATE

A grammatically complete sentence includes, at a minimum, two things: a subject and a predicate. The **subject** is any sort of entity—a person, a place, an object, an abstract concept, a pronoun that refers to some entity identified elsewhere, or an action functioning as a noun. The **predicate** gives some information about the subject, either describing a characteristic it possesses or identifying an action that it performs or that is performed upon it. If there is something in the predicate that is affected by the subject's actions, that is called the **object**. Together, a subject and a predicate (whether or not the predicate includes an object) constitute a **clause**.

In the examples below, the subject and predicate are separated by a line.

- Usually, the subject precedes the predicate:

My stocks | evaporated.	Subject is a **common noun**, the general word to identify a person, place, or thing; predicate identifies something done *by* the subject
Her hopes | were crushed.	Subject is a **common noun**; predicate identifies something done *to* the subject

I | rest my case.	Subject is a **pronoun**, a word used in place of a noun; predicate identifies an action done by the subject plus the target of this action, the **object**
Fifi | is no rocket scientist.	Subject is a **proper noun**, a specific identifier for an individual person, place, or thing; predicate describes the subject
Napping | is his favorite activity.	Subject is a **gerund**, an action functioning as a noun; predicate describes the subject
To drive a Zamboni | was his lifelong dream.	Subject is an **infinitive**, an action functioning as a noun; predicate describes the subject
| Curb your enthusiasm.	Where's the subject here? It's invisible, or, more accurately, it's *implied*. This sentence is in the **imperative mood** (see page 257), which directs a command, request, or instruction at the second person, so the implied subject is always the pronoun "you". That is, an imperative statement means *you* | *do X*, but appears simply as *do X*.

- The predicate may precede the subject:

Waddling around the curve came | the speed-walkers.	Predicate describes the subject's action or situation; subject is a noun in all cases
Here comes | the sun.	
On the table lay | an illuminated manuscript.	
Off went | the unicyclists.	
There's | my missing turnip!	

- A clause may contain more than one subject, with the subjects linked by either *and* or *or*. This construction is called a **compound subject**. In the following examples, the two subjects are marked with an <u>underline</u>.

<u>Ashley</u> and <u>Brian</u> | are twins.	Both subjects are proper nouns
<u>Texting</u> and <u>Twittering</u> during class time | will not be tolerated.	Both subjects are gerunds

| Either <u>Saturday</u> or <u>Sunday</u> \| should be a good day for starting the revolution. | Both subjects are proper nouns, and here represent alternatives |

- A predicate that contains more than one item of information is called a **compound predicate**. A compound predicate can express itself in various ways. In the following examples, the pertinent words in the predicate are marked with an <u>underline</u>.

His hair | was <u>green</u> and <u>spiky</u>.	The subject can take more than one description
The cat | <u>walked</u> disdainfully past his basket and <u>hopped up</u> onto the duvet.	The subject can perform more than one action
The music teacher | asked <u>George</u> and <u>me</u> to sing a little less vigorously.	The action can be directed at more than one object
The robbers | made off with only <u>forty dollars</u> and <u>a jar of jam</u>.	The action can affect more than one object

INDEPENDENT AND DEPENDENT CLAUSES

An **independent clause** (also called a **main clause**) is a clause that expresses a complete thought and can stand alone. A grammatically complete sentence can consist of just a single independent clause, as in all the examples above; or of two or more independent clauses; or of an independent clause plus some other words.

Conjunctions are words that link other words or groups of words together and determine how they relate to each other. The words *and, but, or, for, nor, yet,* and *so* are called **coordinating conjunctions**, and are used to join elements of equal grammatical weight. In the examples below, coordinating conjunctions, marked with an <u>underline</u>, are acting to join two independent clauses.

The first car we considered buying got better mileage, <u>but</u> the second was a prettier color.

Where are we going, <u>and</u> why are we in this handbasket?

Your call is important to us, <u>so</u> please stay on the line.

We have to figure out a faster way of cooking these books, <u>or</u> we're going to be here all night.

A **dependent clause** (also called a **subordinate clause**) is a clause that cannot stand alone because something about it implies that there is more to come. On its own, a dependent clause would be left hanging, its meaning incomplete. It must be combined with an independent clause in order to form a complete sentence.

One type of dependent clause is essentially an independent clause with a subordinating word tacked on. Specifically, it opens with a conjunction that indicates a dependent relationship with information elsewhere in the sentence. Such a conjunction is called a **subordinating conjunction**. For example, if you took the independent clause *it was pouring* and added the subordinating conjunction *since*, you would no longer have an independent clause but a sentence fragment that could not stand alone: *since it was pouring*. This fragment could, however, function within a larger sentence: *Since it was pouring, we cancelled the rain dance.*

Some other common subordinating conjunctions are *after, although, as, as if, as soon as, because, before, despite, even if, even though, if, in order that, now that, provided that, rather than, so that, unless, until, when, whenever, whereas,* and *while.* (Note that some of these consist of more than one word.) Unlike coordinating conjunctions, which are not normally placed at the start of a sentence, subordinating conjunctions may appear either at the start or in the middle.

In another type of dependent clause, the subordinating word is the subject itself. For example, if you replace the noun in the independent clause *The fire had died down to embers* with the subordinating pronoun *which*, you no longer have an independent clause but a sentence fragment: *which had died down to embers.* This fragment could, however, function within a larger sentence: *She gazed dreamily into the fire, which had died down to embers.*

PHRASES

A **phrase** consists of a group of related words, but it doesn't qualify as a clause because it does not contain both a subject and a predicate. It may contain both a noun and a verb, but these don't constitute a clause unless they are in a specific relation to each other, as described above.

Like a dependent clause, a phrase cannot stand alone. It must either precede, follow, or lie within an independent clause.

> *Snooping through his e-mail,* she came across something interesting.

> He asked if she had anything more to say, *his smile menacing.*

> The twins, *by the way,* insist they had nothing to do with the shark turning up in the bathtub.

SENTENCE FRAGMENTS

A **sentence fragment** is a group of words that is punctuated as a sentence—that is, it begins with a capital letter and ends with a terminal punctuation mark—but does not meet the criterion of "grammatically complete" as defined above. A dependent clause or a phrase, standing alone, would constitute a sentence fragment. Sentence fragments are technically errors, but they may be used deliberately for emphasis or some other effect.

> It was hopeless to try to teach that old dog new tricks. *Or any tricks, come to think of it.*

> We ended up building the space pod ourselves. *Which, all things considered, turned out for the best.*

> He dumped the contents of the handbag onto the table. *A key ring, a cell phone, a few coins, and a small garter snake.*

This type of construction should be employed with caution, but it is acceptable if it is the best way of capturing a particular nuance. In addition, some fragments can always legitimately stand independently because they don't need anything more to add meaning.

> But I digress.
> Big deal.
> No way.
> Fat chance.
> Over and out.
> Pity!
> If you insist.
> To be sure.

Comma (,)

Anne gave [Davy] such a serious lecture on the sin of stealing plum jam that Davy became conscience stricken and promised with repentant kisses never to do it again.

"Anyhow, there'll be plenty of jam in heaven, that's one comfort," he said complacently.

Anne nipped a smile in the bud.

"Perhaps there will . . . if we want it," she said, "But what makes you think so?"

"Why, it's in the catechism," said Davy.

"Oh, no, there is nothing like *that* in the catechism, Davy."

"But I tell you there is," persisted Davy. "It was in that question Marilla taught me last Sunday. 'Why should we love God?' It says, 'Because He makes preserves, and redeems us.' Preserves is just a holy way of saying jam."

"I must get a drink of water," said Anne hastily. When she came back it cost her some time and trouble to explain to Davy that a certain comma in the said catechism question made a great deal of difference in the meaning.

—L.M. Montgomery, *Anne of Avonlea*

The comma is by far the most-used punctuation mark, typically outnumbering all the others put together. Its role is to function as an interrupter, separating a sentence into distinct units and indicating shifts in direction.

Most of the comma's numerous functions fall into the following categories:

- Separating the main elements of a sentence from each other
- Separating elements in a series
- Setting off dialogue and quotations
- Indicating omitted words

The first of these functions is the broadest and requires the most explanation. Before beginning this section, be sure that you have reviewed Basic Sentence Structure on page 72, since it is necessary to understand the concepts defined there in order to appreciate how the comma works.

A caveat to this entire section: the "rules" laid out here may sometimes be bent, and several places indicate where exceptions would be appropriate. The reference book *The Chicago Manual of Style* offers this sensible advice: "Aside from [the obligatory rules], the use of the comma is mainly a matter of good judgment, with ease of reading the end in view." It is important to understand the rules, however, so that if you bend them you are doing so intentionally rather than out of ignorance.

SEPARATING THE MAIN ELEMENTS OF A SENTENCE

Using the comma properly means knowing both where to put it—and where not to. The underlying logic comes down to two related points: (1) when a string of words focuses on a single idea or on closely related ideas, it should be treated as an indivisible unit and not be broken up; (2) when one idea ends and a new one begins, there should be a signal that the sentence is shifting direction. Following both these rules is important, since breaking up a unit can send just as confusing a signal to the reader as letting discrete units run into each other.

Do not break up an independent clause

In the following examples, each of which contains just one independent clause, the commas are *in*correct and should not appear.

Don't split the subject and predicate:

> Rodney and his brother, were the worst female impersonators we'd ever seen.

Don't split the subject and predicate, even if the predicate comes first:

> Nestled inside the satin-lined box, was a sparkling cubic zirconium.

Don't split the verb part of the predicate from the rest:

> What he likes best about the condominium is, its no-frogs policy.

Don't split two parts of a compound subject:

> Promising to do something, and actually doing it are not quite the same thing.

Don't split two actions in a predicate:

> Lily stomped down to her dungeon, and slammed the door.

Don't split two descriptions in a predicate:

> The meeting was brief, and to the point.

Don't split two objects affected by an action:

> His plan was to double-major in astrophysics, and numerology.

Don't split two recipients of an action:

> She willed her sister, and brother-in-law her prized collection of tea cozies.

Exceptions: Do consider adding a comma if it would help with clarity. Consider the following sentence:

> The instructor gave out a sheet that described his course and explained how the grading would be done.

This sentence abides by the no-comma-within-a-single-independent-clause rule, but the consequence is ambiguity. Did the instructor give out a sheet and explain the grading—or did he give out a sheet that contained a description of the course and an explanation of the grading? That is, does "explained" get attributed to the subject (the instructor both *gave* and *explained*) or to the object (the sheet both *described* and *explained*)? Adding a comma within the predicate would clarify this:

> The instructor gave out a sheet that described his course, and explained how the grading would be done.

> *or:* The instructor gave out a sheet, which described his course and explained how the grading would be done.

(Note the change in pronoun from *that* to *which*, explained on page 92.)

It is also sometimes beneficial to break up a clause that is not ambiguous but is long or complex. Experienced writers have a feel for when a comma would be a good idea even if it is technically incorrect. At least consider putting a comma within a clause if you sense that omitting it would make the sentence more difficult to follow.

Use a comma to separate two independent clauses that are joined by a coordinating conjunction
The comma goes before the conjunction.

> She left the next day before he woke up, so he never got to say goodbye.

> The high tomorrow will be minus thirty-six, but the wind-chill will make it feel like minus thirty-seven.

> The baking soda and vinegar mixture sizzled excitingly, yet I had to admit it wasn't doing much to unclog the drain.

In many cases, omitting this comma would do little harm. However, consider the following two sentences:

> 1. Dustcovers had been placed on the tables and the chairs and all the smaller items had been packed away.

> 2. We settled only the budget items and the work schedules and all technical issues had to be deferred until the next meeting.

Without a comma, it isn't clear at what point these sentences shift direction. Here, the **syntax**—the order in which the words appear—isn't a sufficient cue, because the same coordinating conjunction (*and*) that is used to link the clauses together is also serving to link subelements within a clause. In sentence 1, were dustcovers placed on both the tables and the chairs, and just the smaller items were packed away—or were just the tables covered, and the chairs were packed away along with the smaller items? In sentence 2, were both the budget and the schedules settled and only the technical issues deferred—or was only the budget settled, and both the work schedules and technical issues were deferred? When a sentence contains multiple units of information, a properly placed comma acts to show precisely where one unit ends and the next begins. Depending on the intended meaning, the above sentences should appear in one of the following ways:

> 1. Dustcovers had been placed on the tables, and the chairs and all the smaller items had been packed away.

> *or:* Dustcovers had been placed on the tables and the chairs, and all the smaller items had been packed away.

> 2. We settled only the budget items, and the work schedules and all technical issues had to be deferred until the next meeting.

or: We settled only the budget items and the work schedules, and all technical issues had to be deferred until the next meeting.

The next examples are not ambiguous, but they might cause a fleeting confusion or hesitation on the part of the reader, along the lines of *huh? oh, I see. . . .*

1. They left early for the concert was giving her a headache.
2. The money hadn't arrived yet he was still managing on what he had.

In sentence 1, the independent clauses are *They left early* and *the concert was giving her a headache*; in sentence 2, they are *The money hadn't arrived* and *he was still managing on what he had*. The words *for* and *yet* are acting as coordinating conjunctions between these clauses. However, many words play more than one role, and *for* and *yet* can also act as **prepositions** (words that provide information about such aspects as time, location, and direction). One could, for example, have a sentence such as *They left early for the concert, so there were still good seats when they got there* or *The money hadn't arrived yet, and he was starting to get anxious*. Without a comma to show where the clause ends, a reader might momentarily take these words to be prepositions in the first case as well. A comma prevents this momentary misunderstanding by sending a clear signal that whatever follows will involve a shift of direction:

1. They left early, for the concert was giving her a headache.
2. The money hadn't arrived, yet he was still managing on what he had.

In sum, without a comma, a sentence may become clear only once it is read through to the end; with a comma, the reader is on top of things all along. Readers should never be forced to backtrack in order to grasp the meaning.

Exceptions: As always, use judgment. If both of the independent clauses in a sentence are brief and simple, and there is no risk of ambiguity if a comma is not included, it can be acceptable to omit it. It's never technically wrong to include it, but sometimes you may think it overly formal or cluttering. Let the tone and context of your writing guide your decision as to whether a comma is really needed. For example, it might be omitted in the following:

This decision is final and there will be no discussion.

The food was okay but the music was lousy.

That's my story and I'm sticking to it.

If two independent clauses are not joined by a coordinating conjunction, separate them with something other than a comma

The commas in the following sentences are *in*correct:

> The chairs and coffee tables were worth restoring, the rest was rubbish.

> I think we'll be able to work together, you'd better start being more punctual though.

> You can bake them or fry them or steam them, there are various options.

This type of construction is called a **comma splice** (*splicing* means to unite two things by fastening their ends together), and is an error because it sends a confusing signal. A comma is intended only for "light" separations, and sets up an expectation that whatever follows will be closely related to what came before. Accordingly, the reader isn't anticipating the greater shift in direction that occurs, and may have to backtrack to make sense of the sentence. There are three remedies for sentences that contain comma splices: add a coordinating conjunction, break the independent clauses into two sentences, or use a semicolon instead of a comma. For a discussion of the last option, see page 106.

Exceptions: If a sentence is short and the style is casual, you can get away with a comma splice. It's never technically correct, but you may sometimes decide that a comma "feels" better than the more formal semicolon.

> The critics hated it, the public loved it.

> You made your bed, now lie in it.

> I doubted she would show up, she was so unreliable.

Use a comma to separate an independent clause from an element that precedes it

The comma serves to provide a clear division between an independent clause and some element that comes before it. Such an element, shown in the examples below in italics, may be a dependent clause,

> *If at first you don't succeed*, don't try skydiving.

> *Although I'd love to stay to help clean up*, I just remembered nine urgent appointments.

> *Because the weather was so bad*, the Polar Bear Club held a special mandatory swim.

a phrase,

> *To see the fall colors at their best,* try taking your Blues Brothers shades off.

> *Reading being her obsession,* Katie's first act upon starting her sentence was to find the prison library.

> *Struck by a sudden idea,* he feverishly began to learn Ancient Greek.

> *Too late,* Max realized that cats and budgies were not a good pet combination.

> *Needless to say,* my friend Cassandra's predictions always came true.

or a single word.

> *Therefore,* it just won't be possible to finish building the opera house in time for the first act.

> *Understandably,* she's reluctant to take on the responsibility of escorting a dozen fourteen-year-olds to Las Vegas.

> *Snarling,* she ripped up the crossword puzzle.

> *Sadly,* his dog didn't live to see him develop the anti-postman device.

Why is a comma needed? Omitting it would do little harm in some of the above sentences, but consider the next ones:

1. Whenever you're ready to eat the pie I'll take it out of the freezer.
2. Whenever you're ready to eat the dining table will be cleared.
3. If you have finished your wine may I pour you some tea?
4. If you have finished your wine waiter will be happy to make a suggestion for a *digestive.*

Just as with two independent clauses, it may not always be immediately obvious from the syntax alone when the direction shifts: that is, when the first clause ends and the next begins. In sentence 1, the verb *eat* is **transitive** (see definition on page 294), meaning that it applies to an object (*pie* in this case), and the dependent clause is not completed until this object is identified. In sentence 2, *eat* is **intransitive** (no object) and the clause ends at that point—but in the absence of a comma, the reader might momentarily expect that the clause will go on to identify what was eaten. This expectation, however, causes the sentence to fall apart, turning its first part into *Whenever you're ready to eat the dining table* (!) and the remainder into a meaningless string. Similarly, *finished* is transitive in sentence 3 (object is *your wine*) but intransitive in sentence 4, leading the reader to momentarily wonder why the diner is polishing off the sommelier. Faced with nonsense syntax, the reader must backtrack, which would be avoided if these sentences read as:

1. *Whenever you're ready to eat the pie*, I'll take it out of the freezer.
2. *Whenever you're ready to eat*, the dining table will be cleared.
3. *If you have finished your wine*, may I pour you some tea?
4. *If you have finished*, your wine waiter will be happy to make a suggestion for a *digestive*.

Exceptions: If an introductory element is short and the sentence would be quite clear without any breaks, you may sometimes make a decision to leave the comma out.

Finally he settled down.

At one o'clock the skies opened.

Naturally I tried to avoid the issue.

When an independent clause is followed by another element, use a comma to separate them only if this element is NOT essential to the meaning of the clause; if the element IS essential to the meaning, do NOT separate them

Unlike the case where an independent clause is preceded by some other text, here the punctuation rules are a bit more complex. An independent clause has only one possible starting point, but its ending has some flexibility, since it can continue past the point where it is already grammatically complete. For example, *She never left the house* is an independent clause, but so is *She never left the house without checking if the burners were on*, which carries a very different meaning.

In the heading above, the term "not essential to the meaning" means that if the words that follow the independent clause were not there, the clause would still mean the same thing. A comma serves as a signal that the independent clause is now complete and the sentence is shifting direction. "Essential to the meaning" means that if the words that follow the independent clause were removed, the clause would no longer be saying the same thing. It would still be grammatically intact—by definition, an independent clause can always stand alone—but the overall meaning of the sentence would have changed.

In the examples below, the phrase (shown in italics) following the independent clause does not do more than add additional information or commentary. Accordingly, a comma is needed for separation.

She got up to leave, *having satisfactorily reduced him to a quivering jelly.*

Change is inevitable, *except from a vending machine.*

They stood by the window, *oblivious to the meteor shower raining past it.*

He leaped up from the exercise machine, *promptly throwing his back out.*

We found her in the washroom, *angrily scrubbing the ketchup off her tiara.*

He pole-vaulted off the stage and over the fence, *leaving his fans howling in frustration.*

In contrast, in the next examples, the phrase completes the meaning of the clause. Here, if the italicized words were removed, the independent clause would still be grammatically intact but some of its meaning would be lost. Accordingly, breaking things up with a comma would be incorrect.

He went to market *to buy a fat pig.*

A new bylaw was passed *to ensure that no cabbage would be boiled within city limits.*

She got an A in the course *by promising to give the instructor her secret recipe for salmon patties.*

They were praised *for their efforts in setting up the downtown bungee-jumping site.*

Meet us at the tractor-pull *at twelve o'clock.*

He ended up in bed *with a bad case of angst.*

We went straight to the "Avoiding Stress in the Workplace" seminar *after the power breakfast.*

When an element that follows an independent clause is a dependent clause rather than a phrase, it usually acts to complete the meaning of the sentence and therefore should not be preceded by a comma. It will still be obvious to the reader where the second clause starts, since its opening word is unambiguously tied to what follows. That is, unlike the coordinating conjunctions *and* and *or*, which could also serve to join subunits within a clause (as illustrated on page 80), subordinating conjunctions only ever appear at the beginning of a dependent clause.

He announced that he was entering politics *because he wanted to spend less time with his family*.

The Nature Worshipping Festival will be held on Saturday *unless it rains*.

She had little income *until the sales of her herring-flavored ice cream took off*.

She waited impatiently *while he finished dancing the schottische*.

Syntax alone may not always be enough to indicate if the second clause is completing the meaning of the first one or adding something separate. Consider the following sentences:

1. Bob was completely ready to leave when Carol showed up.
2. Bob was completely ready to leave, when Carol showed up.
3. Ted didn't like Alice because she was successful and talented.
4. Ted didn't like Alice, because she was successful and talented.

Sentences 1 and 3 each contain a single item of information and therefore do not take
a comma. In the first, Bob is waiting for Carol and his departure is dependent on her
arrival; in the second, Ted likes Alice for reasons other than her success and talent. In
contrast, sentences 2 and 4 each contain two separate items of information. In the
first case, Bob is about to leave (whether on his own or with someone else), and just
then Carol happens to show up. In the second, Ted doesn't like Alice, and the reason is
precisely because she possesses these qualities (and presumably he doesn't).

Use a comma to set off a parenthetical element within an independent clause

A **parenthetical element** is text that is not critical to the basic structure of the
sentence; it interrupts the flow but does not interfere with the meaning. Its defining characteristic is that if it were removed, the remainder of the sentence would
still be grammatically and semantically intact. Some information would be lost or
diminished, but the essential meaning would not be altered.

Parenthetical text may be set off from the rest of the sentence by three types of
punctuation marks: parentheses, em dashes, or commas. Parentheses (discussed on
page 154) are best used when the element is a complete digression and its removal
would have little or no effect on meaning: that is, they de-emphasize. Dashes (discussed on page 162) serve to draw particular attention to the element, making it
stand out; that is, they emphasize. Commas should be used when the element is an
integral part of the sentence but does not call for any special attention. Enclosed

by commas, a parenthetical element just works its way quietly into the sentence, without fanfare.

Consider the following two sentences:

1. Jack thought Melvin should have his head examined.
2. Jack, thought Melvin, should have his head examined.

In sentence 1, someone named Jack is thinking about someone named Melvin; in sentence 2, Melvin is thinking about Jack. What would happen if we removed the words *thought Melvin* in both cases? We would be left with:

Jack should have his head examined.

Sentence 1 is completely changed by the removal of these words: it is no longer referring to the right head. Sentence 2, in contrast, may have *lost* something—the fact that Jack's head-examining need is merely a matter of someone's opinion—but at least it still refers to the same head. In sentence 2, therefore, the words enclosed by commas are parenthetical.

Parenthetical elements may be asides; that is, text that is included simply for emphasis or effect, or as additional commentary:

The meeting was, *to say the least*, a total fiasco.

The committee is, *generally speaking*, reluctant to rock the boat.

The rest, *as they say*, is history.

Some may serve to tie in a point with a preceding sentence:

Her resignation, *therefore*, is inevitable.

We decided, *nevertheless*, to ignore his advice.

Some may contain information that is relevant to the overall point but is parenthetical in the sense that you could take it out without changing the meaning of what is left:

Her workshop on decorating garden gnomes, *she was happy to report*, went very well.

His story of being abducted by giant lizards, *when I stopped to think about it*, made little sense.

The food she had just eaten as a mid-morning snack, *he pointed out*, had been intended to last the week.

In all the above cases, if the parenthetical element is removed, the sentence would be essentially unchanged: *The meeting was a total fiasco; Her resignation is inevitable; His story of being abducted by giant lizards made little sense.*

A caution: when parenthetical text comes in the middle of an independent clause, **do not omit the closing comma**. It is a common error to write sentences such as *The meeting was, to say the least a total fiasco* or *Her resignation, therefore is inevitable.* Just as parentheses always must come in pairs (like this), so must parenthetical commas.

Exceptions: If a parenthetical word or expression doesn't break the continuity of the sentence, it is sometimes acceptable to omit the commas altogether. If you are uncertain whether to include commas, say the sentence aloud, spontaneously, and consider leaving the commas out if it sounds all right without a pause.

> She did in fact pay the loan back.

> The course in my opinion is a joke.

* * *

Contract lawyers take note: in a headline-grabbing case in Canada, an extra comma nearly cost a company an extra $2.13 million. Company A, a major telecommunications provider, had signed a contract to string its cable lines along utility poles administered by Company B for an agreed-upon annual fee of $X per pole. One sentence in the contract read:

> [The agreement] shall continue in force for a period of five years from the date it is made, and thereafter for successive five year terms, unless and until terminated by one year prior notice in writing by either party.

Company A took this to mean that it had a locked-in rate of $X per pole for the first five years, and that renegotiation could take place only after this period of time was up. However, shortly after the deal was signed, Company B announced that it was giving notice of cancellation and intended to renew the contract at a far higher rate per pole. The justification? Based on the rules of punctuation, the presence of a comma after the words *and thereafter for successive five year terms,* in addition to the one before these words, meant that the right to end the contract with one year's notice applied to the first five years as well. That is, since text enclosed by commas is parenthetical and can be taken out without affecting the meaning of the rest of the sentence, the contract could be read as *[The agreement] shall continue in force for a period of five years from the date it is made unless and until terminated by one year prior notice in writing by either party.*

The telecommunications regulatory body sided with Company B, ruling that the significance of the second comma trumped what Company A's lawyers said was the clear intent of the wording since they never would have agreed to a contract that could be cancelled on such short notice.

To the disappointment of copy editors everywhere, the ruling was later overturned.

Use a comma to set off nonrestrictive elements, but not to set off restrictive ones

The topic here has some overlap with earlier ones in that it is concerned with words that can either follow or lie within an independent clause. The focus however is specifically on words that provide information about the subject of the clause. A **restrictive element** is a word or group of words that acts to identify precisely which subject, out of various possible ones, is meant. A **nonrestrictive element**, while it provides information about the subject, does not serve to further identify it; in this case, the assumption is that the subject is already fully identified. (Some authorities call these relationships **defining** and **nondefining**, or **limiting** and **nonlimiting**. The meaning is the same.) Like a parenthetical element, a nonrestrictive element is not critical to the meaning of the sentence, and if it were removed, the meaning of what remained would still be intact. In contrast, if a restrictive element were removed, meaning would be lost.

Restrictive and nonrestrictive elements can be names, words, phrases, or dependent clauses. In the examples below, restrictive descriptors are shown in bold type, while nonrestrictive ones are shown in italics and are either preceded or enclosed by commas, depending on their position in the sentence.

1. The only two people who could tolerate Shirley's singing were her oldest friend, *Allegra*, and her neighbor **Micaela**.
2. The only two people who could tolerate Shirley's singing were her friend **Allegra** and her upstairs neighbor, *Micaela*.

In sentence 1, the name *Allegra* is nonrestrictive, since by definition one can have no more than one *oldest* friend. The inclusion of *Allegra* is adding more information about this friend—her name—but omitting it wouldn't introduce any ambiguity as to which friend is meant. In contrast, *Micaela* serves to identify which neighbor was there: the upstairs one. Saying just *her neighbor* would not be enough, since Shirley can be expected to have more than one neighbor. In sentence 2, Allegra loses the comma (unless Shirley has only one friend in the world), while Micaela picks it up (unless there is more than one upstairs flat). Similarly,

1. Helga showed up at the party with her brother, *Ernie*, and her husband, *Hal*.
2. Helga showed up at the party with her brother **Ernie** and her husband **Hal**.

In sentence 1, Helga apparently has only one brother, and his name happens to be Ernie. She also, quite properly, has only one husband, and his name happens to be Hal. In sentence 2, Helga apparently has more than one brother and has brought along the one named Ernie; on the husband front, she has some explaining to do.

With respect to dependent clauses, sometimes the subordinating word is a pronoun, as described in Basic Sentence Structure on page 72. This type of dependent clause can function as a restrictive or nonrestrictive descriptor, the same way that a word or a phrase can. For example:

1. Canadians **who live in the far North** get to see the midnight sun.
2. Canadians, *who live in a land spanning six time zones*, are often struck by the small size of European countries.
3. The library **where I'd had the most luck in finding what I needed** was closed that day.
4. The library, *where one could usually find peace and quiet*, was hosting a 30-piece brass band that day.

Sentence 1 is referring to a small subset of Canadians (the overwhelming majority live within a hundred miles of the US border); sentence 2 to the entire population. In sentence 3, the clause following "library" is serving to identify which of various possible libraries is meant; in sentence 4, only one library is assumed, and the clause that follows is simply stating something about it.

Does it matter if such commas are present or absent? Usually, text will contain enough context that the intended meaning will come through even if commas are not used correctly. In some cases, however, misuse of commas can cause dissonance. Say a passage describes two people walking along, and indicates whether they are male or female but gives no further identification. Now consider the meaning of the following two identically worded sentences:

1. The man who had lingered behind suddenly quickened his pace.
2. The man, who had lingered behind, suddenly quickened his pace.

In sentence 1, the absence of commas around *who had lingered behind* means that these words are a restrictive clause acting to differentiate the man who lingered from the man who didn't, so the preceding text must have referred to two men. In sentence 2, the presence of commas means that these same words are merely acting to describe the man's action, not to identify him. Here, the preceding text must have referred to a man and a woman; that is, there is only one possible man. If the clause were removed and we were left with just *The man suddenly quickened his pace*, sentence 1 would no longer be identifying which individual speeded up, while sentence 2 would still be referring unambiguously to the same person. The point is this: the commas are correctly absent in the two-man scenario and correctly present in the one-man-one-woman scenario, and doing otherwise in either case might cause momentary confusion on the part of the reader. In each circumstance, the punctuation must be consistent with the meaning.

A comma can be the sole source of information as to whether a clause is restrictive or not. Consider the following:

1. I tried to get the attention of the waiter who was hurrying by with a flaming soufflé.

2. I tried to get the attention of the waiter, who was hurrying by with a flaming soufflé.

What differing information do these two sentences give us? Whether one or more waiters were present. If there is no prior mention in the text of waiters, nor any inherent reason why there should be either one or more than one, the only source of this information is the presence or absence of the comma. In sentence 1, the comma that precedes the clause *who was hurrying by with a flaming soufflé* tells us that there was only one waiter, and incidentally he happened to be passing by with a dishful of fire. Reducing this sentence to *I tried to get the attention of the waiter* would serve to identify this individual just as well. In sentence 2, the absence of a comma tells us that this same clause is serving to identify which of two or more possible waiters is meant: that is, the one with the soufflé, as opposed to the ones who were off in the kitchen, apologizing to customers for dirty forks, or anywhere else.

In the following examples, restrictive clauses are shown in bold type and nonrestrictive ones in italics.

The barber **who gives those great buzz cuts** has moved.

The barber, *who had not missed a day of work in fifteen years*, was in his shop as usual.

The pet shop **where I bought my camel** went out of business last month.

Our next stop was the pet shop, *where we bought a fifty-pound bag of camel treats*.

They headed quickly for shore **when the sea monster appeared**.

They had just settled in comfortably, *when a long tentacle appeared over the side of the boat*.

One last matter before leaving this topic behind. In all the above examples, the pronoun functioning as the subject—*who, when, where*—does not change, regardless of whether the clause is restrictive or nonrestrictive. In one situation, though, the pronoun changes as well. Specifically, *that* is used for a restrictive clause, and *which* is used for a nonrestrictive one.

Compare the following two sentences:

1. When we entered the room, we couldn't stop staring at the painting, which hung over the mantelpiece.
2. When we entered the room, we couldn't stop staring at the painting that hung over the mantelpiece.

These sentences differ in two ways: one has a comma and uses *which*; the other has no comma and uses *that*. How does this affect the meaning? In sentence 1, which is nonrestrictive, the implication is that there is only one painting in the room, and incidentally, it happened to be over the mantelpiece. If this sentence read simply as *we couldn't stop staring at the painting*, it would be missing some information (the location), but would still fully identify what was being stared at. In sentence 2, which is restrictive, the implication is that there is more than one painting in the room; perhaps there are others over the sofa, over the bookcase, etc. Here, saying *we couldn't stop staring at the painting* would not convey the full identifying information.

Other examples are presented below, with restrictive clauses shown in bold type and non-restrictive ones in italic.

The lecture, *which is free to the public*, begins at seven o'clock.

The lecture **that I missed** was apparently the only interesting one of the entire term.

She cut him a huge slice of cake, *which he promptly devoured*.

He grabbed the slice of cake **that was the bigger of the two**.

We bought the bread **that was cheapest**.

We bought the day-old bread, *which was cheapest*.

How critical is it to use *which* and *that* correctly? In most cases, an error will probably not confuse your reader. For example:

> Keep your writing style simple, and avoid words which are obscure or pretentious.

> They went to watch the Super Bowl parade, that was wending its way through the downtown streets.

Although the above sentences are incorrect, it would take a very literal-minded reader to interpret the first to mean that one should eschew all words when writing, and the second to mean that the town was filled with various Super Bowl parades of which one happened to be held downtown. Despite the errors, at least the context allows the intended meaning to come through. However, consider the following:

> After assessing the inventory, they decided that the prints which were heavily water-damaged were probably not worth restoring.

This sentence presents a conflict. The word *which* implies that the clause *which were heavily water-damaged* is nonrestrictive, meaning that all the prints were damaged—but the absence of commas around this clause implies that it is restrictive, and that only certain prints were damaged. So throw out all the prints, or only some? The result is ambiguity, which can be resolved only if the prior text contains information that clarifies which possibility is intended. In the absence of such information, it is not clear if the writer erred in using *which* for *that* or in omitting the commas. Remember the general rule: *which* takes a comma, *that* does not.

A final comment on the "which/that" distinction: it is a North American convention, not a universal one. British writers will happily use *which* for restrictive clauses, and indeed in most cases the meaning will be clear. Disregarding the distinction is not a problem as long as you know to avoid constructions that may be misconstrued.

SEPARATING ELEMENTS IN A SERIES

If a sentence contains a series of elements of equal grammatical weight, these elements must be separated by commas. The elements can be single words, phrases, or clauses.

In a list of three or more elements, separate the elements with commas

Each element up to the second-to-last one *must* be followed by a comma, and the second-to-last one *may* be followed by one: that is, it's a style decision. A comma in this position is called a **serial comma** (also known as a **series comma** or **Oxford comma**), and some writers use it and some don't. If you are writing to certain specifications, check what your style guide says about this comma.

In the following examples, no serial comma is used:

> Her idea of what to take on a camping trip included a nail-polish dryer, an eyelash curler, a vibrating foot massager and twelve changes of clothing.

> His favorite deities are Astarte, Thor and the Flying Spaghetti Monster.

> The woods are lovely, dark and deep. —Robert Frost

Omission of the serial comma does no harm in sentences where the elements are short and their relationships are obvious. In some cases, however, its absence could result in awkwardness or ambiguity. Thus, even if your style is to not use it, you should make an exception in places where it seems necessary. For example:

> Breakfast consisted of orange juice, toast and marmalade and coffee.

Here, "toast and marmalade" is a unit that constitutes the second-to-last element in the series. The absence of a comma, while technically acceptable, makes for a clumsy cadence: *orange juice . . . toast . . . and marmalade . . . and coffee*. This part of the sentence would read better as *orange juice, toast and marmalade, and coffee*.

The next example presents more of a problem:

> The only ones to show up were Erin and Aaron, Pete, Eve and Yves, Gene and Jean and Sidney.

Erin and Aaron clearly came as a couple, as did Eve and Yves, while Pete came on his own. But what about the last three? Did Gene and Jean come as a couple and Sidney is the odd man out, or is the couple Jean and Sidney, with Gene on his own? A correctly positioned comma would clarify this:

> The only ones to show up were Erin and Aaron, Pete, Eve and Yves, Gene and Jean, and Sidney.

> *or*: The only ones to show up were Erin and Aaron, Pete, Eve and Yves, Gene, and Jean and Sidney.

Similarly,

> The panel consisted of three professors, two historians and an economist.

How many people were on the panel: three or six? Being a professor is not mutually exclusive with being a historian or an economist. If the intention is to describe six distinct individuals, a serial comma would clarify this: *three professors, two historians, and an economist.* If the latter two occupations are the professors' specialties, this part of the sentence should appear as *three professors: two historians and an economist.* (See discussion of this role of the colon on page 111.)

Finally, sometimes the length or complexity of the elements in a series calls for the use of the serial comma. For example:

> Teachers need hours outside of class time to plan new curricula, grade tests and papers, meet with parents, consult with specialists about students with academic or behavioral problems, and work one-on-one with children who have special needs.

> The consultants independently ranked each survey item on its relevancy and clarity using a 10-point scale, completed open-ended questions pertaining to the appropriateness of the items, and offered suggestions for the elimination or addition of items.

With no serial comma in these sentences, the reader might have to strain to see where the second-to-last element ends and the last one begins.

In summary, if it is your choice to not use the serial comma, that's fine, but let clarity override consistency if an exception seems necessary.

Put a comma between two adjectives that precede a noun, provided those adjectives are of equal weight

In most cases, commas are needed only when there are at least three items in a series, not if there are just two. For example, you wouldn't put a comma in *The woods are lovely, and dark* or *Teachers need hours outside of class time to plan new curricula, and meet with parents.* You do, however, need to separate two items when those items are adjectives modifying a noun.

> Her bold, innovative rhythms had the audience swaying to the beat.

> The relaxed, laid-back atmosphere was a pleasant change.

> The door opened with a grating, creaking sound.

> A grumpy, tired-looking waiter took our order.

This rule holds only if the adjectives are of equal weight, meaning that they both modify the noun equally. To determine whether they do, use this test: would the sentence still "sound right" if you reversed the adjectives or if you put the word *and* between them? For example, you could say *innovative, bold rhythms* or *bold and innovative rhythms*; a *tired-looking, grumpy waiter* or *a grumpy and tired-looking waiter*.

In contrast, consider the adjectives in the following sentences:

> He went in for a routine physical checkup.

> A purple-clad French skater was next on the ice.

> In my opinion, he's a pompous old bore.

You wouldn't say a *physical routine checkup* or a *routine and physical checkup*; a *French purple-clad skater* or a *purple-clad and French skater*; an *old pompous bore* or a *pompous and old bore*. In all these cases, the second adjective effectively forms a unit with the noun: *a physical checkup, a French skater, an old bore*. Accordingly, the adjective that precedes this unit is treated as if it were the only one: that is, no comma.

Also, do not include a comma between two adjectives when the first one is not directly modifying the noun but rather is combining with the other adjective to form a compound. For example:

> She wore a pale green dress. [*pale* modifies *green*, not *dress*]

> Early spring days are often very cool. [*early* modifies *spring*, not *days*]

In some cases, compound adjectives should be linked by a hyphen. For a discussion of this role of the hyphen, see page 140.

SETTING OFF DIALOGUE AND QUOTATIONS

When a sentence consists entirely of dialogue, punctuate it just as you would any other (with the addition of quotation marks, of course). If it contains both dialogue and non-dialogue components, the dialogue is set off with commas.

If dialogue is preceded by non-dialogue text, put a comma before the opening quotation mark

> The nurse warned, "Patients are going to be hurt by these cutbacks."

> She answered, "Don't be ridiculous."

> He exclaimed, "Of course I didn't!"

It is also acceptable, though less common, to use a colon instead. See Other Uses of the Colon on page 114.

If dialogue is followed by non-dialogue text, put a comma before the closing quotation mark

This applies whether the non-dialogue text comes at the end of the dialogue, breaks it in the middle, or surrounds it.

> "In the six months I've lived here, I've seen only eight rats," she told him reassuringly. [On its own, dialogue would end in a period]

> He shrugged and said, "Please yourself," and walked away. [On its own, dialogue would end in a period]

> "I wouldn't try it," he cautioned, "unless you're quite certain you know what you're doing." [On its own, dialogue would not contain any internal punctuation]

> "If you finish early," she suggested, "how about if we go out for coffee." [On its own, dialogue would contain a comma in the same place]

> "But I never . . . ," he faltered. [On its own, dialogue would end in an ellipsis]

Exceptions: If dialogue ends in a question mark or exclamation point, or if it is broken off by a dash, do not add a comma.

> "Bah!" he said.

> "Are you sure?" she asked.

> "The only thing is—" he began.

Set off non-dialogue quotations with commas only if other rules call for it

Other than dialogue, words may be enclosed by quotation marks because they are cited from some source or because they need to be brought to the reader's attention in a particular way. In these cases, punctuate them exactly as you would if they were not within quotes. For example, use commas if the quoted text is preceded by an introductory element, if it is parenthetical, or if it is part of a series,

> According to the mediator, "a breakthrough is expected tonight."

> As Dickens said, "The law is a ass."

> More and more workers these days are fearful of layoffs, "rightsizing," and pay cuts.

and do not use commas if the quoted text would not take them otherwise.

> A lawyer representing the patients said that the agency "has increasing concerns for the quality of care in psychiatric institutions."

> Critics claimed that the program "would lead to even greater divisiveness."

> The "new, improved" stain remover proved to be not quite that.

For a discussion of quotation marks, turn to page 181.

INDICATING OMITTED WORDS

An **elliptical construction** is a phrasing where one or more words have been dropped because they can be readily inferred. Saying the same thing in fewer words can make writing look less ponderous, more polished.

Sometimes words can be dropped without any ado, and the sentence continues to read clearly without them:

> We were sure that we would win.
> We were sure we would win.

> I looked distrustfully at him, and he looked distrustfully at me.
> I looked distrustfully at him, and he at me.

> She isn't quite as tall as I am.
> She isn't quite as tall as I.

In other cases, however, the sentence would read ungrammatically if you took away the words and did not put anything in their place. One of the ways to indicate that something is missing is to put a comma in the place of the absent words.

> To err is human; to forgive, divine.

> In spring her garden was ablaze with daffodils; in summer, pansies; and in fall, asters.

> His first novel sold six copies and his second, six thousand (admittedly, most to his mother).

OTHER USES OF THE COMMA

Aside from its main functions described above, the comma has a few minor mechanical applications.

Separating numbers

In dates, it is used to separate the day from the year:

World War I was brought to a close on November 11, 1918.

Many of the dreaded "Y2K" failures did not materialize on January 1, 2000.

In numbers greater than three digits, the North American convention is to use a comma as a thousands separator: that is, a mark that separates digits into groups of three. Doing so allows the reader to more easily make sense of a long string of numerals.

The total cost will be $34,459. [easier to read than *$34459*]

The population in the last census was 2,139,897. [easier to read than *2139897*]

Other conventions are to use a narrow space or a period; the latter only if it is a convention to use a comma instead of a period for the decimal separator.

Also use a comma to create a clear separation between numbers that lie next to each other within a sentence. (The examples below would properly take a comma in any case, to separate an independent clause from an adjoining element, but the numerals make this particularly necessary.)

In 2009, 14 candidates ran for the position of school trustee.

Although the final tally was 983, 247 submissions had to be discarded.

Separating repeated words

Whatever it is in here that smells, smells awful.

She finally came in, in a huff.

Whatever he does, he does well.

Separating place names

Miami, Florida

Moose Jaw, Saskatchewan

Semicolon (;)

It was her prose that gained [Mrs Albert Forrester] that body of devoted admirers, fit though few, as with her rare gift of phrase she herself put it that proclaimed her the greatest master of the English language that this century has seen. She admitted herself that it was her style, sonorous yet racy, polished yet eloquent, that was her strong point; and it was only in her prose that she had occasion to exhibit the delicious, but restrained, humour that her readers found so irresistible. It was not a humour of ideas, nor even a humour of words; it was much more subtle than that, it was a humour of punctuation: in a flash of inspiration she had discovered the comic possibilities of the semi-colon, and of this she had made abundant and exquisite use. She was able to place it in such a way that if you were a person of culture with a keen sense of humour, you did not exactly laugh through a horse-collar, but you giggled delightedly, and the greater your culture the more delightedly you giggled. Her friends said that it made every other form of humour coarse and exaggerated. Several writers had tried to imitate her; but in vain: whatever else you might say about Mrs Albert Forrester you were bound to admit that she was able to get every ounce of humour out of the semi-colon and no one else could get within a mile of her.

—W. Somerset Maugham, *The Creative Impulse*

The functions of the semicolon fall into two main categories:

- Separating elements, when a comma would be insufficient or unclear

- Linking elements, as an alternative to joining them with a conjunction or breaking them into two sentences

In the first case, the semicolon is required for clarity. In the second case, it is chosen over other equally clear constructions in order to achieve a certain tone or to emphasize a relationship.

SEPARATING ELEMENTS

The most straightforward role of the semicolon is the same as that of the comma: marking a shift in direction in a sentence. It may be substituted for the comma only in certain circumstances, however. While there is some room for judgment as to when to use it, this should not be taken to mean that it is merely a fancy-looking comma, interchangeable with the latter at the writer's whim. For the most part, its role is subject to predictable and objective guidelines.

Note: Before beginning this section, be sure that you have reviewed Basic Sentence Structure on page 72.

Use a semicolon to separate independent clauses that are linked by an adverb rather than by a coordinating conjunction

Apart from conjunctions, described on page 74, there are certain words and phrases that, while technically classified as adverbs because they modify the actions they are associated with, act like conjunctions in that they indicate a particular relationship between the information they belong with and information that comes before. There are many such adverbs; a list of commonly used ones is shown below.

accordingly	for example	instead	otherwise
afterwards	furthermore	later	preferably
also	hence	likewise	rather
anyway	however	meantime	similarly
as a result	ideally	meanwhile	specifically
besides	in brief	moreover	still
certainly	in conclusion	namely	subsequently
consequently	in contrast	nevertheless	that is to say
conversely	in fact	next	then
currently	in short	nonetheless	therefore
earlier	in particular	notwithstanding	thus
eventually	indeed	on the other hand	to wit
finally	initially	ordinarily	understandably

Any of these can be placed at either the start or the end of an independent clause, set off by commas.

> *However*, the presentation was a calamity.
> The presentation was a calamity, *however*.
>
> *Understandably*, his feelings were hurt.
> His feelings were hurt, *understandably*.
>
> *In fact*, it was my best performance ever.
> It was my best performance ever, *in fact*.

Because they can appear in either position, if you used one of these adverbs to link two clauses and preceded it with a comma, the reader might momentarily mistake it to be the ending of clause #1 rather than the opener of clause #2. This misunderstanding will be cleared up as the sentence continues, but it should be prevented from occurring in the first place. The solution is to use the stronger separation of the semicolon, which—unlike a comma—unambiguously shows that the sentence is shifting direction and a new clause has begun.

> I'd rather have the report by tomorrow; *however*, Monday will do.
>
> I don't think I'd have much to contribute to the meeting; *besides*, I have no interest in the topic.
>
> He finally showed up two hours late; *understandably*, he met with a frosty reception.
>
> She thought she was early; *in fact*, she was the last to arrive.
>
> We waited and waited; *eventually*, we gave up.
>
> No progress was evident; *nevertheless*, they persevered.

Note that such an adverb can carry the exact same meaning as a conjunction:

> The argument was going nowhere, so we decided to drop it. [conjunction preceded by comma]
> The argument was going nowhere; hence, we decided to drop it. [adverb preceded by semicolon]
>
> The apartment was small and dark, but the price was right. [conjunction preceded by comma]
> The apartment was small and dark; however, the price was right. [adverb preceded by semicolon]

There is essentially no difference in meaning between these pairs of sentences. The ones with commas tend to look a bit more casual; the ones with semicolons, a bit more formal. When either way would do, your choice should depend on the tone of your writing. No single style will be the most appropriate for every situation.

Use semicolons to separate elements that are themselves subdivided by commas

Normally, elements in a series are separated by commas (see page 93). If, however, some or all of these elements are themselves divided into subelements, commas wouldn't clearly indicate where one main element ends and the next begins, because they would be indistinguishable from the commas separating the subelements. In such a case, use semicolons instead:

> The toolbox contained 16-gauge, 18-gauge, and 20-gauge nails; quarter-inch, half-inch and three-eighths-inch drill bits; and an assortment of hammers and screwdrivers.

> There are many types of white blood cells, each with a specialized role. Some attack viruses, some bacteria, and some parasites; some destroy invaders directly and some get other parts of the immune system to do so; some have the job of sending out an alarm when a harmful substance enters the body, and others have the job of mopping up the mess after a different set of cells has taken care of the problem.

> With disturbing regularity, the end of the work day found us at the old Monkey Bar, the Dorset Bar, the Warwick Bar, all attached to serviceable and somewhat down-at-heels hotels. Midtown Manhattan used to be full of just such comfortably shabby establishments where career waiters with brilliantined comb-overs and shiny-elbowed jackets might serve marvelously cheap albeit watery drinks, along with free snacks: withered celery sticks; pretzel nuggets accompanying a cheese spread of a color that in nature usually signals "I am an alluring yet highly poisonous tree frog, beware!"; chicken wings kept barely, salmonella-friendly warm in a chafing dish over a Sterno lamp; and a bounty of unironic, faux Asian, pupu platter dough cylinders, pocket, and triangles that were—oh glory!—fried. Dinner and forgetfulness all for ten dollars.

> —David Rakoff, *Fraud*

If only one main element in a series is subdivided into subelements and the remainder are not, you must still put semicolons between all the main elements in the sentence. That is, be consistent: don't use a semicolon in just the one place where it is needed, and commas elsewhere.

No: The competition drew contestants from Georgia and Alabama in the south, New York, New Hampshire, and Connecticut in the northeast; and Oregon in the northwest.

Yes: The competition drew contestants from Georgia and Alabama in the south; New York, New Hampshire, and Connecticut in the northeast; and Oregon in the northwest.

Use semicolons to separate elements in a series if commas might cause a sentence to be misread or otherwise difficult to follow

Even when elements are not subdivided into subelements, commas sometimes would not suffice to mark the divisions between them. For example, consider the following assembly instruction:

Part A attaches to B, C and D attach to E, and F attaches to G.

It would be very easy for a reader to mistake *B, C and D* for a series: that is, to start processing the sentence as *Part A attaches to B, C and D*. (This would be particularly likely if the style does not call for a serial comma.) The rest of the sentence then falls apart: *attach to E, and F attaches to G* (?). A second pass would clear things up, but no sentence should have to be read twice to be understood. Semicolons would prevent any confusion, ensuring that each clause is kept distinct from the others.

Part A attaches to B; C and D attach to E; and F attaches to G.

Optionally use a semicolon instead of a comma to separate independent clauses joined by a conjunction if a comma might not be strong enough

The general rule is that independent clauses linked by a coordinating conjunction are separated with a comma (see page 80). However, if an independent clause contains any internal commas, you may sometimes choose to use a semicolon as the separator instead. As with a series that contains subelements, the purpose is to make it immediately clear to the reader where one main element ends and the next begins. For example:

It is often useful to discuss your research ideas with others before you begin to write, as the questions that arise from the discussion may help clarify things in your own mind. Your consultants may be experts in your field, or they may know nothing of its methods and assumptions; they may be familiar with your particular research project, or they may be completely unacquainted with it; and they may be seasoned investigators or just starting out their own careers.

Similarly, at times you may decide to use a semicolon simply because the elements in a series are *long*. Given that commas perform so many functions, it may not always be immediately apparent what purpose a given comma is serving. Is it separating one main element from the next, separating subunits within a main element, or separating grammatical units within an element, such as an independent clause from a concluding phrase? Divisions that are obvious when sentences are short may become fuzzy with longer constructions, and the reader may sometimes have to pause or backtrack to stay on top. Using the stronger separator of the semicolon makes the divisions stand out better. For example:

> Recruiting participants for the study included screening all subjects to ensure that they had no contraindicating medical conditions; distributing an information sheet that described the protocol to those subjects meeting our inclusion criteria; arranging for eligible subjects to participate in post-treatment discussion groups with the goal of providing feedback to the researchers; and designating a group leader to attend these sessions and coordinate the discussions.

All this sentence is ultimately doing is listing four activities, and if its elements were shorter, commas as separators would work just fine (*Recruiting participants included screening subjects, handing out information, setting up discussion groups, and designating a group leader*). However, because there is so much going on, the divisions between elements are easier to see if semicolons are used instead. Just what constitutes "long" elements will be a matter of judgment; there isn't some magic number that decrees when semicolons become necessary. The only guideline that can be given is to use them if you have reason to think they would make a sentence easier to read.

Finally, even if adjoining elements do not contain any internal commas and are not that long, you may sometimes decide to separate them with semicolons if each one deals with a distinct subject, in order to make this distinctiveness stand out more clearly.

> My criteria are that the building must be no higher than three stories; the main rooms must have lots of light; there must be adequate guest parking; and the neighbors must not be nosy.

Apply this last use of the semicolon with discretion, however. Just as with long elements, it's a judgment call. If commas would work perfectly well, putting semicolons in their place would be inappropriate.

LINKING ELEMENTS

The previous section looked at the uses of the semicolon in promoting clarity. In that role, it is simply used in places where commas would otherwise go, and no other change to the sentence is involved.

This section describes a different role of the semicolon: that of forming elegant alternatives to other sentence constructions. Knowledgeable application of this punctuation mark can serve to tighten up wording, elucidate or emphasize subtle relationships, and add polish to your writing style.

Consider using the semicolon in place of a conjunction

The following sentences all consist of two clauses linked by a coordinating or subordinating conjunction:

> His offer sounded too good to be true, so I didn't believe it.
> [two independent clauses linked by *so*]

> I was starting to worry, for he was now two hours late.
> [two independent clauses linked by *for*]

> We didn't have the heart to continue, as it all seemed so futile.
> [independent clause followed by a dependent clause starting with *as*]

> My favorite plague is hail, whereas my husband's is frogs.
> [independent clause followed by a dependent clause starting with *whereas*]

There is nothing wrong with any of these constructions, and they certainly contain no ambiguity. In each case, however, it would be possible to omit the conjunction, since it could easily be inferred. If this is done, the comma is no longer the right separator, since putting it between two independent clauses would create a comma splice (see page 82). The semicolon is the proper mark instead. In this role, it acts as a sort of stand-in for the missing conjunction, sending a signal to the reader that there is some implicit and self-evident relationship between the clauses it separates.

> His offer sounded too good to be true; I didn't believe it.

> I was starting to worry; he was now two hours late.

> We didn't have the heart to continue; it all seemed so futile.

> My favorite plague is hail; my husband's is frogs.

Apart from shaving off a word, an advantage to omitting the conjunction is that an over-exactitude in spelling everything out can render text a bit ponderous. Writing may come through as subtler, more sophisticated, if it leaves a few blanks for readers to fill in for themselves. (For other strategies, see the discussions of elliptical constructions on page 98 and the suspension hyphen on page 145.)

Of course, omitting conjunctions isn't appropriate in all cases. Sometimes a conjunction couldn't easily be inferred, and a sentence might look puzzling without it.

> She longed to stay till the end of the talk; she had to leave.

The connection between these clauses isn't immediately obvious, so the sentence comes through as mildly confusing. It may be a bit of a strain for the reader to deduce that the missing conjunction must be *yet* or *but*.

In other cases, different conjunctions might be possible, so omitting the intended one might cause a reader to put the wrong interpretation on the sentence.

> The task clearly would be difficult; I would have a day to do it.

Is the missing conjunction here *and? but? since? so?* Is one day plenty of time or not enough time? In the absence of a conjunction, the intention of the second clause could be misconstrued. Other parts of the text might provide enough context to clarify the writer's intentions, but on its own, this sentence is not communicating them.

Consider using the semicolon to unite two sentences

Two adjacent independent clauses can, of course, each stand alone as separate sentences. Often, this is appropriate. However, if the clauses are so closely related in meaning that they are essentially two halves of a whole—that is, they are not merely on the same topic, but the second one completes the first—then separating them to this extent may obscure or downplay their relationship. If your goal is to help the reader pick up on their connection, this may be better achieved by running them together in one sentence, either by adding an appropriate conjunction or by using a semicolon. The semicolon may be the more appropriate choice in cases where the relationship can't be neatly captured in just one word, and where the reader should be able to infer it in any case.

> The early bird gets the worm. The early worm gets eaten.
> The early bird gets the worm; the early worm gets eaten.
> *Implication:* There's a flip side to everything.

Only Leah showed up to help with the move. The others all found excuses to stay away.
Only Leah showed up to help with the move; the others all found excuses to stay away.
Implication: Some friends are more loyal than others.

His old apartment had been a total pigsty. His new one was worse.
His old apartment had been a total pigsty; his new one was worse.
Implication: It's hopeless to get him to improve.

Aside from helping to elucidate relationships, combining sentences this way often makes writing smoother, turning a series of short, choppy sentences into text that flows.

A caution about using the semicolon this way: **don't overdo it**. It's a strong punctuation mark, and sprinkling it too liberally throughout a document will cause it to lose its impact. Even if you can justify each individual use, having semicolons show up in sentence after sentence becomes tedious. Don't make the mistake of trying to make your content look more important by peppering it with fancy punctuation.

STYLE CONVENTIONS

- The usual convention today is to leave just one space after a semicolon, but some style guides specify two. If you are free to choose your own approach, be consistent.

  Dogs have owners; cats have staff.

  or: Dogs have owners; cats . . .

- When a semicolon follows text enclosed by quotation marks, place it *after* the closing quotation mark. (See the style conventions for quotation marks on page 188.)

- If the text immediately preceding a semicolon is italicized, the semicolon may either be italicized as well or appear in regular font. Again, ensure consistency.

Colon (:)

> [The colon] has acquired a special function: that of delivering the goods that have been invoiced in the preceding words.
>
> —H.W. Fowler, *Fowler's Modern English Usage*

The colon acts as a signal of anticipation, drawing the reader's attention to what comes after it. Like the semicolon, in some cases it is required and in others it is used for effect. Its functions fall into the following main categories:

- Introducing the text that follows
- Adding emphasis

Writers are sometimes uncertain about the distinction between the colon and the semicolon. A discussion of their differences and similarities is presented on page 116.

Note: Before beginning this section, be sure that you have reviewed Basic Sentence Structure on page 72.

INTRODUCING WHAT FOLLOWS

A colon is called for when the first part of a sentence is an introduction, a lead-in, or a build-up to the second part.

Use a colon when a sentence contains an implicit question followed by its answer

A sentence can consist, in a sense, of a question and an answer, in that its first part raises an implicit question to which the remaining words provide the response. The colon acts both to indicate what the sentence is doing and to mark where the division between the question and answer occurs.

The text that comes before the colon must be an independent clause; that is, it must be able to stand alone as a complete sentence. The text that follows the colon may be either an independent clause or a sentence fragment.

	IMPLICIT QUESTION	ANSWER
The situation was becoming desperate: supplies were running low, and winter would soon be setting in.	What was desperate about the situation?	Low supplies and imminent winter
One aspect struck him as particularly odd: it was mid-afternoon on a clear, mild day, yet the streets were totally deserted.	What was odd?	Unaccountably deserted streets
There's an issue that we absolutely must address: will our current level of funding be enough?	What's this issue?	Whether funding is sufficient
He guessed what would come next: a torrent of tears and recriminations.	What would come next?	A tantrum
There was a single word that best described her plan: ridiculous.	What's this word?	Ridiculous

Do not put a colon after a sentence fragment. Constructions such as the following are *in*correct:

> The situation was becoming desperate because: supplies were running low, and winter would soon be setting in.

> He guessed that what would come next was: a torrent of tears and recriminations.

> In a word, her plan was: ridiculous.

Note that in the sentences starting with an independent clause, removing the colon would cause the words on either side to bump into each other ungrammatically (*The situation was becoming desperate supplies were running low*; *He guessed what would come next a torrent of tears and recriminations*), but in the examples above, no separator is necessary.

Exceptions: You may put a colon after a sentence fragment if the fragment is one that can stand independently; that is, it does not require anything more to complete its meaning.

> A word of caution: testing has not yet been completed, so any findings must be considered preliminary.

> So far so good: as we had hoped, the results supported our hypothesis.

In addition, it is conventional to use a colon after a single word that is being defined.

> Shin: a device for finding furniture in the dark.

> Poverty: the state of having too much month left at the end of the money.

Use a colon to introduce a list or series

This function is really just a specific case of the one described above. The text before the colon states the nature of the list (the question), and the text after it provides the details (the answer). The colon is required whether the text that follows the lead-in is in paragraph form,

> Any scientific measure must meet two vital criteria: reliability and validity.

> Every student must take the following core courses: English, history, math, and science.

> Two questions remain: how did he do it, and why?

> These are the most urgent staples we need: milk, eggs, flour, and catnip.

or laid out vertically.

> Each camper must bring the following items:
> - a knapsack
> - a flashlight
> - a sleeping bag
> - a canteen
> - a book of ghost stories

Always include a colon when the lead-in to a list contains the words *the following* or *as follows.*

> The system is based upon the following principles: it should be acceptable to both patients and staff, it should be applicable to a wide range of diagnoses, and it should possess a high degree of face validity.

The following tools are needed: a hammer, a Phillips screwdriver, a hacksaw, and a wrench.

The compromise was as follows: we'd each attend one workshop and then cover for the other person.

As before, do *not* use a colon to introduce a list if the lead-in text could not stand alone. The colons below are *in*correct:

She's particularly good at sports such as: tennis, squash, and racquetball.

The next section presents: an overview of our last study, a review of the background literature, and a detailed rationale for our current work.

ADDING EMPHASIS

In addition to the straightforward functions described above, the colon can play the subtler role of clarifying relationships or underscoring a point.

Recommendation: use a colon to make connections clearer

When one unit of information expands on or derives from another, their relationship is more obvious if they are linked with a colon. The colon alerts the reader to the fact that whatever was just said has some special significance, so particular attention should be paid to what follows.

Compare the following two passages:

1. Glancing at the calendar, Morton made a mental note to buy a card that afternoon. He had not forgotten Great-Aunt Alma's birthday in eight years. The one time he had, she had temporarily cut him out of her will.
2. Glancing at the calendar, Morton made a mental note to buy a card that afternoon. He had not forgotten Great-Aunt Alma's birthday in eight years: the one time he had, she had temporarily cut him out of her will.

In passage 1, the reader has no way of anticipating that the information in the second sentence—Morton's keeping track of the birthday—has any particular significance. He's apparently a thoughtful guy who remembers old ladies' birthdays, that's all. But then the next sentence comes along and forces a reinterpretation of this impression. In passage 2, while the reader still won't know Morton's motive until the end, the colon makes it clear that there *is* a motive; that is, there's more to Morton's card-giving than just being a good nephew. Unlike passage 1, the reader

will not have to stop and reconcile the last sentence with its predecessor: the relationship will have been anticipated.

Similarly,

1. Voters approved the controversial amendment by an extremely narrow margin. The
count was 18,278 in favor and 17,916 against.
2. Voters approved the controversial amendment by an extremely narrow margin:
18,278 in favor and 17,916 against.

In the first example, the reader must expend a bit of extra energy figuring out that
the purpose of the figures given in the second sentence is to illustrate the narrow-
ness of the margin. In the second example, the structure makes this connection
instantly obvious.

Optionally use a colon to add emphasis

Judicious use of the colon can serve to make a point more emphatic. If your intention is to draw a contrast between two elements, this contrast may come through
more forcefully if the elements are in immediate juxtaposition, rather than being
placed in different sentences or separated by intervening text.

Compare the two passages below:

1. The next witness testified that she had been fired from her job as a line supervisor.
Her offense was that she had tried to organize the factory's 200 workers, who
earned an average of $90 a week.
2. The next witness testified that she had been fired from her job as a line supervisor.
Her offense: trying to organize the factory's 200 workers, who earned an average of
$90 a week.

The text in both cases is virtually the same, but the message is subtly different. A
contrast exists between the reference to an "offense," which implies some illegal
behavior, and the actual actions of the subject. Assuming the writer is trying to por-
tray the subject's actions in a sympathetic or supportive light, passage 2 achieves
this better. In passage 1, a reader who wasn't paying close attention might get the
impression that the writer as well as the factory owners viewed these actions as a
genuine offense. In passage 2, the colon heightens the contrast, thereby making it
clear that the word *offense* is being used ironically.

Consider the two versions of the next example:

1. Domestic assault cannot be dismissed as merely a symptom of marital problems. It is a criminal activity that is a manifestation of the abuser's inability to deal with frustration and anger.
2. Domestic assault cannot be dismissed as merely a symptom of marital problems: it is a criminal activity that is a manifestation of the abuser's inability to deal with frustration and anger.

Version 1 has less impact than version 2, since the contrast between the key words—the relatively benign "marital problems" versus "criminal activity"—is diminished by putting them in separate sentences. If the goal is to run these two sentences together, would not a semicolon or a dash do as well? The answer is no, for somewhat subtle reasons. The first part of this sentence is acting as a build-up to the second, in that it tells the reader what domestic assault is *not*. The colon then conveys the message that the remainder of the sentence will set you straight as to what it *is*. (Put in the terms given earlier, the implied question is, Well, if domestic assault isn't a marital problem, what is it?, and the answer is, A criminal activity.) Neither the semicolon nor the dash quite captures this idea. The semicolon does not act to draw the reader's attention to what follows it, and while the dash does, it does so for purposes other than answering an implicit question raised in the first part.

Apart from the impact on meaning that the colon can confer, note how it offers some stylistic advantages by allowing you to run choppy sentences together, thereby achieving a better flow, and sometimes allowing you to drop a word or two, thereby making your writing more concise.

OTHER USES OF THE COLON

The colon has a few mechanical applications, as described below.

Separating the numbers in a ratio

4:1

3:2

If you were writing these numbers out as words rather than numerals, you would use the word *to* instead of a colon: *four to one; three to two.*

Separating the hour from the minutes

1:30 a.m.

5:45 p.m.

British style is to use a period instead (1.30; 5.45).

Separating the main title from the subtitle of a book or article

The Fatal Shore: The Epic of Australia's Founding

"Universality and variation in moral judgment: A longitudinal and cross-sectional study"

Separating lead-in text from spoken words in dialogue

The uproar subsided, and I tried again: "Ladies and gentlemen!"

He suddenly turned to her and said: "Why me?"

Similarly, it may be used instead of a comma to introduce a quotation.

Separating low-level subheadings and figure or table identifiers from the text that follows them

The Colon: The colon has a number of functions . . .

Figure 12: Diagram of developmental diversity

Alternatively, a period or a closing parenthesis may be used.

Separating a character's name from his or her lines in scripts and screenplays

Higgins: Come back to business. How much do you propose to pay me for the lessons?

Liza: Oh, I know what's right. A lady friend of mine gets French lessons for eighteen-pence an hour from a real French gentleman. Well, you wouldn't have the face to ask me the same for teaching me my own language as you would for French; so I won't give more than a shilling. Take it or leave it.

Higgins: [walking up and down the room, rattling his keys and his cash in his pockets] You know, Pickering, if you consider a shilling, not as a simple shilling, but as a percentage of this girl's income, it works out as fully equivalent to sixty or seventy guineas from a millionaire.

Pickering: How so?

Higgins: Figure it out. A millionaire has about 150 pounds a day. She earns about half-a-crown.

Liza: [haughtily] Who told you I only—

Higgins: [continuing] She offers me two-fifths of her day's income for a lesson. Two-fifths of a millionaire's income for a day would be somewhere about 60 pounds. It's handsome. By George, it's enormous! It's the biggest offer I ever had.

—George Bernard Shaw, *Pygmalion*

Alternatively, a period may be used, or the character's name may appear on a separate line.

COLON OR SEMICOLON?

Many people are confused by the distinction between the colon and the semicolon, and in fairness, there are a few cases where either mark might do. How do you decide which one to use, then? It depends on context and tone. The colon is a stronger mark, one that increases the emphasis of what is being said. Consider the difference in nuance between the following two sentences:

Time was ticking away; he had to make a decision soon.

Time was ticking away: he had to make a decision soon.

In both examples, the connection between the two items of information is clear, but the second one suggests a bit more urgency to the situation. Thus, the context would determine which mark is the most appropriate.

Note that a choice between these marks could arise only in situations involving their subtler roles—those having to do with emphasizing relationships. In the majority of cases, the roles are distinct, with no overlap. The semicolon is the only mark that is appropriate when you need to separate a series of elements that wouldn't be sufficiently distinguished if commas were used, and the colon is the only mark that is appropriate when you need to separate a lead-in or introductory part of a sentence from what follows.

STYLE CONVENTIONS

- The usual convention today is to leave just one space after a colon, but some style guides specify two. If you are free to choose your own approach, be consistent.

- When a colon follows quoted text, place it *after* the closing quotation mark. (See page 190.)

- If the text immediately preceding a colon is italicized, the colon may either be italicized as well or appear in regular font. Again, ensure consistency.

- With regard to capitalization, style guides differ. Some say to always start the text that follows the colon with a lowercase letter; others say to begin it with uppercase if it's an independent clause and lowercase if it's a sentence fragment. Whichever style you choose, be consistent. However, if you have chosen to go with lowercase, make an exception in the following situations:

  - If you feel the text that follows the colon is important enough to merit the emphasis of capitalization. If the lead-in words are relatively trivial and your real point begins after the colon, you may decide that beginning this part of the sentence with lowercase would inappropriately subsume it.

  - If the colon is introducing a series of sentences of equal weight. For example:

    > Our procedures were as follows: first, we obtained a list of all eligible participants. Second, we contacted all those who lived within a ten-mile radius of the study site, and asked if they would be willing to take part. Third, we mailed out packets, consisting of the questionnaire and a stamped return envelope, to all subjects who agreed to participate.

    The words *Second* and *Third* begin with uppercase, so *first* should be capitalized as well. When it appears in lowercase, the information it introduces does not seem to have equal standing with the other information.

Period (.)

There's not much to be said about the period except that most people don't reach it soon enough.

—William Zinsser, *On Writing Well*

The period has two main functions:

- Ending a sentence
- Indicating abbreviations

ENDING A SENTENCE

Dear John,

I want a man who knows what love is all about. You are generous, kind, thoughtful. People who are not like you admit to being useless and inferior. You have ruined me for other men. I yearn for you. I have no feelings whatsoever when we're apart. I can be forever happy. Will you let me be yours?

Gloria

Dear John,

I want a man who knows what love is. All about you are generous, kind, thoughtful people who are not like you. Admit to being useless and inferior. You have ruined me. For other men I yearn. For you I have no feelings whatsoever. When we're apart I can be forever happy. Will you let me be?

Yours,

Gloria

—Anonymous

The period's basic role in ending a sentence is obvious enough, but there are a few situations that bear mention.

Don't include a period for a parenthesized sentence that lies within another sentence

That is, even if the embedded sentence is grammatically complete and would normally take a period, omit it in this case. The overall sentence may contain only a single period.

> Hospital workers objected that the consultant's advice on business techniques didn't apply in their environment (for example, they felt that telling desperately sick patients to "have a nice day" was inappropriate) and was undermining rather than improving morale.

> The foreign minister said that five more diplomats would be expelled (two had been ordered out of the country the week before), and that a full investigation into the activities at the embassy would be launched.

This also means that parenthesized text within a larger sentence cannot be broken up by a period. If it contains two discrete points, they must be separated by some other punctuation or by a conjunction.

> *No:* We trudged gloomily along the trail (the weather was damp and miserable. We were also being eaten alive by mosquitoes) and looked for a suitable site to pitch the tent.

> *Yes:* We trudged gloomily along the trail (the weather was damp and miserable, and we were being eaten alive by mosquitoes) and looked for a suitable site to pitch the tent.

A stand-alone parenthesized sentence, of course, does take a period. See the section on style conventions for parentheses on page 159.

In dialogue, use a comma rather than a period to end a sentence when more text follows

> "I'm sure no one in the audience noticed when your toupee slid off," she said soothingly.

> "I realize you didn't blow up the house on purpose," he said plaintively. "But it's undeniably rather inconveniencing."

Use a period only when the dialogue ends the sentence.

For other aspects of punctuation in dialogue, see the discussions under Comma, page 96, and Quotation Marks, page 181.

Don't include a period if a sentence ends in another terminal punctuation mark

> They signed their divorce papers right after lunch and then headed off to a matinée of *I Do! I Do!*

> The only Anthony Trollope novel she had ever read was *Can You Forgive Her?*

> She has this annoying habit of ending almost every sentence with "you know what I mean?"

Readers will understand that in cases like this, the question mark or exclamation point applies to just the words at the end, and that the entire sentence is not querying or exclamatory.

Note that if the words for which the other punctuation mark applies are enclosed within parentheses, you *would* put a period at the end of the sentence. See the style conventions for parentheses, on page 159.

If a sentence ends in an abbreviation that includes a period, do not add another period

> If you have any complaints about this product, send them in writing to Porcupine Quill Duvets, Inc.

> The list of student demands included no homework, a better selection of ice cream flavors in the cafeteria, permission to send text messages during exams, etc.

Here, the period that goes with the abbreviation is understood to do double duty as a terminal punctuation mark. Do not use *Inc..* and *etc..* to end these sentences.

If using ellipses within a quotation, add a period after an ellipsis at the end of a sentence

One of the functions of the ellipsis (see page 191) is to indicate the omission of words in quoted text. This punctuation mark consists of three dots (. . .) that individually are indistinguishable from periods, and it can be used at any position in a sentence: the start, middle, or end. If it appears at the end—that is, to indicate that the final words of a quoted sentence have been dropped—then a period must be added to clarify this. The effect is that four dots appear instead of three.

Original quotation: Unlike American crosswords, which are generally straightforward affairs, requiring you merely to fit a word to a definition, the British variety are infinitely more fiendish, demanding mastery of the whole armory of verbal possibilities— puns, anagrams, palindromes, lipograms, and whatever else springs to the deviser's devious mind. British crosswords require you to realize that *carthorse* is an anagram of *orchestra*, that *contaminated* can be made into no *admittance*, that *emigrants* can be transformed into *streaming*, *Cinerama* into *American*, *Old Testament* into *most talented*, and *World Cup team* into (a stroke of genius, this one) *talcum powder*. (How did anyone think of that?) To a British crossword enthusiast, the clue "An important city in Czechoslovakia" instantly suggests Oslo. Why? Look at *Czech*(OSLO)*vakia* again.

—Bill Bryson, *The Mother Tongue: English & How It Got That Way*

Shortened version: Unlike American crosswords . . . the British variety are infinitely more fiendish. . . . British crosswords require you to realize that *carthorse* is an anagram of *orchestra*, that *contaminated* can be made into no *admittance*. . . . To a British crossword enthusiast, the clue "An important city in Czechoslovakia" instantly suggests Oslo. Why? Look at *Czech*(OSLO)*vakia* again.

In lists, be consistent with the use of periods at the end of items

Style guides differ as to whether a period should appear at the end of each item in a vertical list. Thus, a list may appropriately be presented as either of the following:

A patient must meet all the following criteria in order to be included in the study:

1. Aged between 18 and 64 years.	**or:** 1. Aged between 18 and 64 years
2. Diagnosed with LVP syndrome within the past six weeks.	2. Diagnosed with LVP syndrome within the past six weeks
3. A body mass index between 14 and 35 kg/m².	3. A body mass index between 14 and 35 kg/m²
4. Not currently enrolled in any other clinical trial.	4. Not currently enrolled in any other clinical trial

If you are not obliged to follow a particular guide, make your own decision and treat all lists the same way. Some writers choose to include periods if each item on a list is a complete sentence, and omit them if the items consist of single words or sentence fragments. (In the interest of maintaining parallel structure, a list should not contain a mixture of both. For a discussion of parallelism, turn to page 223.)

If list items contain multiple sentences, the individual sentences within the items are naturally separated from each other by periods. In this case, it is preferable to have the last sentence in each item end in a period as well, since it can look odd to have periods after each sentence but the last. Some style guides, however, say to leave off the final period even in this circumstance.

If you ever have a situation where you are avoiding periods as a rule but a particular list item seems to need one, consider adding them for all the other items in that list too, in the interest of uniformity.

INDICATING ABBREVIATIONS

> A girl who weighed many an oz.
> Used language I dare not pronoz.
> For a fellow unkind
> Pulled her chair out behind,
> Just to see, so he said, if she'd boz.
>
> —Anonymous

Words may be shortened in several different ways. **Contractions**, which take apostrophes, act to make words more informal or easier to say. A contraction effectively becomes a new form of the word, and is both written and pronounced differently from the full word. **Abbreviations**, which may take periods, are for purposes of efficiency rather than casualness.

Abbreviations of multiple words are made up of the first letter of each word, or sometimes the first couple of letters. They are pronounced either as the individual letters (NBC, CIA, LSD) or sometimes, if the letters spell out something pronounceable, as an acronym (ANOVA, MCAT, UNICEF).

Abbreviations of single words come in a variety of forms. They may consist of the first few letters of the word (*Avenue—Ave., population—pop., January—Jan.*); its first and last letters (*Mister—Mr., Senior—Sr., foot—ft.*); some combination of the above (*Boulevard—Blvd., Route—Rte., building—bldg.*); or the first letter only (*Fahrenheit—F, North—N, University—U*). Some even include letters that are not in the original word (*number—no., pound—lb., ounce—oz.*). With a few exceptions, single-word abbreviations are pronounced as the entire word.

Some abbreviations must take periods, some optionally take them, and some don't take them. Periods are more likely to be used when an abbreviation is sounded out as letters than when it is an acronym, but this distinction cannot be taken as a rule. In cases where periods are optional, the general trend today is to omit them, but this is by no means universal. The following are some rules and guidelines.

Always use periods

Titles, honorifics: In North America, the convention is to include periods.

Mrs. Robinson	Mr. Bean
Dr. Seuss	Rev. Moon
Martin Luther King, Jr.	St. Peter

In Britain and some other Commonwealth countries, the period is omitted for abbreviations that include the final letter of the word (*Mrs, Mr, Dr*).

Note that the honorific *Ms*—or *Ms.*—is a special case. Many writers spell it with a period, and indeed some style guides say to do so. Presumably this is to make it equivalent to its male counterpart, *Mr.* However, given that the word isn't actually short for anything, leaving the period off is legitimate as well. Either way, ensure consistency.

Initials: Periods are usually although not always included. Some style guides require them to be omitted in bibliographic references.

J.K. Rowling
J.R.R. Tolkien
Franklin D. Roosevelt

Latin abbreviations. Errors in period placement are common here, since writers are often not familiar with the original words and do not know if the abbreviation is based on one word or two.

YES	NO	ORIGIN
e.g.	eg.	two words, *exempli gratia* ("for example")
i.e.	ie.	two words, *id est* ("that is")
et al.	et. al.	two words, but only one abbreviated: *et alia* ("and others")
cf.	c.f.	one word, *confer* ("compare")
viz.	viz	one word, *videlicet* ("namely"; *z* is a medieval contraction for *e-t*)

Miscellaneous: Periods are included in the following abbreviations:

anonymous	anon.	gallon	gal.
born	b.	inch	in.
cash on delivery	c.o.d.	Incorporated	Inc.
continued	cont.	number	no.
died	d.	ounce	oz.
edition (or editor)	ed.	pound	lb.
figure	fig.	versus	vs.

Note that in some cases, omitting the period might cause momentary confusion with a complete word: for example, *cod, no,* or *in.*

Never use periods

Metric measurements:

Periods in the following are always incorrect:

10°C	[not *C.*]
250 km	[not *km.*]
39 cm	[not *cm.*]

U.S. states and Canadian provinces:

Do not include periods in the two-letter postal abbreviation.

Connecticut: CT
Alberta: AB
Washington: WA
Newfoundland: NF

Do however use them in the standard form of abbreviation: Conn., Wash., Alta., Nfld. (Note that for states and provinces with two-word names, the only difference in these two forms of abbreviation will be the period: NJ or N.J., SC or S.C., BC or B.C., NS or N.S.)

Optionally use periods

Style guides differ on whether the following categories of abbreviations should include periods. If you are using a guide, go by its rules; if not, decide for yourself. Whichever way you go, ensure consistency.

Academic degrees:

M.Sc.	MSc
Ph.D.	PhD
R.N.	RN
M.D.	MD

Geographical names:

U.S.A.	USA
U.K.	UK
N.Y.C.	NYC

Time indicators:

A.M., P.M.	AM, PM
B.C., A.D.	BC, AD
B.C.E., C.E.	BCE, CE

OTHER USES OF THE PERIOD

Apart from its two main functions, the period has a number of mechanical applications. The more common of these are described below.

Setting off list numbers

In numbered vertical lists, a period may be placed after each number to mark it off from the text that follows.

> The following topics will be covered this semester:
>
> 1. The history of the world
> 2. The meaning of life
> 3. The origins of the universe
> 4. The applications of the semicolon

Colons, closing parentheses, or hyphens are alternatives. In lists that are presented in paragraph form, the mark used is generally the closing parenthesis. That is, 1) here is the first item, 2) here is the second item, 3) here is the third item. Another style is to enclose the numbers in a set of parentheses, as in (1) here is the first item, (2) here is the second item, etc.

Setting off headings and captions

A period is often used to separate inline subheadings and figure or table identifiers from the text that follows.

> *The period*. The period has the following functions . . .

> Table 6. Short-term and long-term projections

Alternatively, a colon may be used.

Representing a decimal point

> 44.5   596.371

In some parts of the world, a comma is used instead.

Question Mark (?)

THE QUESTION MARK is a terminal punctuation mark that turns a sentence into a query. It may also be used to indicate uncertainty, tentativeness, or incredulity. There are cases where it is necessary, cases where it is optional, and cases where it is inappropriate. It has the following functions:

- Indicating queries
- Indicating rhetorical questions
- Indicating requests
- Indicating uncertainty

INDICATING QUERIES

Use the question mark when posing a direct query

Were there any messages for me?

How does this electric cat brush work?

Just how many crates of mangoes *did* you eat last night, anyway?

Use it to turn a statement into a query

You promise not to tell anyone?

You don't really mean that?

She really said she would?

This way of posing a question is more likely when the speaker is assuming or hoping for a particular answer, as opposed to genuinely seeking information.

In dialogue, both forms of questions are common.

> Of course St John Rivers' name came in frequently in the progress of the tale. When I had done, that name was immediately taken up.
>
> . . ." This St John . . . . You have spoken of him often: do you like him?"
>
> "He was a very good man, sir; I could not help liking him."
>
> "A good man. Does that mean a respectable, well-conducted man of fifty? Or what does it mean?"
>
> "St John was only twenty-nine, sir."
>
> " '*Jeune encore*,' as the French say. Is he a person of low stature, phlegmatic and plain? A person whose goodness consists rather in his guiltlessness of vice, than in his prowess of virtue?"
>
> "He is untiringly active. Great and exalted deeds are what he lives to perform."
>
> "But his brain? That is probably rather soft? He means well: but you shrug your shoulders to hear him talk?"
>
> "He talks little, sir: what he does say is ever to the point. His brain is first-rate, I should think not impressible, but vigorous."
>
> ". . . His manners, I think you said, are not to your taste?—priggish and parsonic?"
>
> "I never mentioned his manners; but, unless I had a very bad taste, they must suit it; they are polished, calm, and gentleman-like."
>
> "His appearance—I forgot what description you gave of his appearance;—a sort of raw curate, half strangled with his white neckcloth, and stilted up on his thick-soled high-lows, eh?"
>
> "St John dresses well. He is a handsome man: tall, fair, with blue eyes, and a Grecian profile."
>
> (*Aside*) "Damn him!"—(*To me*) "Did you like him, Jane?"
>
> "Yes, Mr Rochester, I liked him: but you asked me that before."
>
> —Charlotte Brontë, *Jane Eyre*

Use it for a statement that ends in a word inflected as a query

Just leave me alone, okay?

So you're quitting your job, eh?

Use it for a direct question contained within a statement

He was beginning to wonder, was she truly what she claimed to be?

You must ask yourself, Will I be better off with him or without him?

In this type of sentence, whether or not you capitalize the question portion depends on how much emphasis you wish to give it. Capitalization is allowable, but in most cases would probably give the question more prominence than it needs.

Note that such constructions can also be presented the other way around, with the question coming first. That is, the question mark may appear within the sentence, rather than as the terminal punctuation.

> Was she truly what she claimed to be? he was beginning to wonder.

> Why bother even trying? was the question.

Do not use a question mark for statements that contain indirect questions. For example, the question marks in the following sentences are *in*correct and should be replaced with periods.

> I couldn't help wondering how she had done it?

> They asked us if we'd seen the film yet?

> The tourists invariably asked if the glacier was still advancing?

Note, however, that sometimes such a construction can be turned into a statement that contains a direct question, in which case it does take a question mark. For example:

> I couldn't help wondering, how had she done it?

> They asked us, had we seen the film yet?

Use it to achieve a tentative inflection

In dialogue, you can employ question marks to impart an uncertain, tentative tone to a character's manner of speaking. Some people have a habit of inflecting ordinary statements as questions, almost as if they're chronically expecting to be challenged on what they are saying?

> Muriel said, "Once I was riding Alexander uptown on some errands for George? My company? And I'd had these two cats in the car just the day before? And I didn't think a thing about it, clean forgot to vacuum like I usually do, and all at once I turn around and Alexander's stretched across the seat, flat out."

> —Anne Tyler, *The Accidental Tourist*

INDICATING RHETORICAL QUESTIONS

A rhetorical question—one for which no answer is expected or for which the answer is self-evident—may end in either a question mark or an exclamation point. The context determines which will be most appropriate.

> Coincidence? I think not.

> But when I reminded her of everything I'd done for her, do you think she was grateful?

> My grandmother's chicken soup? Poetry in a pot.

> How was I to know that asking him his age would cause him to flee the room in tears!

> How can we ever thank you enough!

> Breathes there the man, with soul so dead,
> Who never to himself hath said,
> This is my own, my native land!
> Whose heart hath ne'er within him burn'd,
> As home his footsteps he hath turn'd,
> From wandering on a foreign strand!

> —Sir Walter Scott, *The Lay of the Last Minstrel*

In dialogue, it is sometimes realistic to have a speaker's rhetorical question end in a period.

> Look, why don't we just drop the whole thing.

> Well, isn't that just dandy.

Since different inflections in a speaker's voice carry different implications, sometimes the choice of punctuation for a rhetorical question will be determined by the tone you want to achieve.

> So he really said that, did he? [interested or surprised reaction]

> So he really said that, did he. [uninterested or musing reaction]

> So he really said that, did he! [indignant or excited reaction]

You can use a question mark in combination with italics to indicate shock or incredulity.

> He said *what?*

> At your age, you're planning to wear *that?*

INDICATING REQUESTS

For a request that is really a politely phrased order or instruction, decide what tone is intended. A question mark makes the words look more humble; a period, more peremptory. Usually, a period is more appropriate.

> Would you take the garbage out when you leave? [Translation: It would be nice if you would.]

> Would you take the garbage out when you leave. [Translation: Take out the garbage!]

> Would you mind feeding the piranhas?

> Would you be good enough to leave immediately.

> How about if you wash and I dry?

> Would you pass the pickles, please.

> Won't you sit down.

INDICATING UNCERTAINTY

A minor role of the question mark is to indicate uncertainty about dates.

> Joan of Arc, 1412?–1431
> Desiderius Erasmus, 1466?–1536

Similarly, you may choose to follow any tentative statement of fact with a question mark enclosed within parentheses. Obviously, it will not enhance the force of your writing if this device appears often.

STYLE CONVENTIONS

Style conventions for the question mark are the same as those for the exclamation point, and are presented there (page 135).

Exclamation Point (!)

The shortest correspondence in history took place in 1862 between Victor Hugo and his publisher following the release of *Les Misérables*. The day after his novel came out, Hugo, wanting to know how initial sales were going, sent a telegram that read: "?" The first print run had in fact sold out immediately, and the publisher telegraphed back: "!"

The exclamation point (also called the **exclamation mark**) is a terminal punctuation mark that can be used in place of the period to add emphasis or emotion. It turns simple statements into forceful ones, and remarks into exclamations or outbursts. It comes up most commonly in dialogue, but has a role in nondialogue text as well. Its functions are the following:

- Indicating importance or emotion
- Optionally indicating rhetorical questions
- Capturing attention

Almost all of its occurrences fall into the first category; the other two uses do not arise frequently.

INDICATING IMPORTANCE OR EMOTION

In nondialogue, the exclamation point can be used to lend emphasis or grab attention.

Let me know immediately if you do not receive this e-mail!

I found myself turning down the familiar drive—I, who had sworn never to go within ten miles of the place again!

We paused to survey the result. A fine mess he'd made of it!

In dialogue, it can be used to indicate excitement, urgency, vehemence, or astonishment.

"Are you guilty?" said Winston.

"Of course I'm guilty!" cried Parsons with a servile glance at the telescreen. "You don't think the Party would arrest an innocent man, do you?" His frog-like face grew calmer, and even took on a slightly sanctimonious expression. "Thoughtcrime is a dreadful thing, old man," he said sententiously. "It's insidious. It can get hold of you without your even knowing it. Do you know how it got hold of me? In my sleep! Yes, that's a fact. There I was, working away, trying to do my bit—never knew I had any bad stuff in my mind at all. And then I started talking in my sleep. Do you know what they heard me saying?"

He sank his voice, like someone who is obliged for medical reasons to utter an obscenity.

" 'Down with Big Brother!' Yes, I said that! Said it over and over again, it seems. Between you and me, old man, I'm glad they got me before it went any further. Do you know what I'm going to say to them when I go up before the tribunal? 'Thank you,' I'm going to say, 'thank you for saving me before it was too late.' "

—George Orwell, *Nineteen Eighty-Four*

"Oh, Rumpole!" It was an astonishing moment. She Who Must Be Obeyed actually had her arms around me, she was holding me tightly, rather as though I were some rare and precious object and not the old White Elephant that continually got in her way.

"Hilda. Hilda, you're not . . . ?" I looked down at her agitated head. "You weren't worried, were you?"

"Worried? Well, of course I was worried!" She broke away and resumed the Royal Manner. "Having you at home all day would have been impossible!"

—John Mortimer, *Rumpole and the Learned Friends*

Note that exclamation points are by no means compulsory in dialogue every time a speech takes on some emphasis. You may often prefer to let your readers infer a character's emotions from wording or context.

Although the exclamation point normally appears at the end of a sentence, it may occasionally be used as internal punctuation. The text that follows does not have to begin with a capital letter, as it is still part of the same sentence. (This text may, however, be capitalized if it seems appropriate. See the discussion under Conventional uses of capital letters on page 51.)

Mrs Palmer's eye was now caught by the drawings which hung round the room. She got up to examine them.

"Oh! dear, how beautiful these are! Well! how delightful! Do but look, mama, how sweet! I declare they are quite charming; I could look at them for ever." And then sitting down again, she very soon forgot that there were any such things in the room.

—Jane Austen, *Sense and Sensibility*

I took the subway to group . . . and tried to concentrate on how I was going to tell the group what had happened to me. I felt mortified. Two years earlier, I had walked off into the sunset—cured! it's a miracle! she can walk!—and now I was back again, a hopeless cripple.

—Nora Ephron, *Heartburn*

An exclamation of horror broke from the painter's lips as he saw in the dim light the hideous face on the canvas grinning at him.

There was something in its expression that filled him with disgust and loathing. Good heavens! it was Dorian Gray's own face that he was looking at!

—Oscar Wilde, *The Picture of Dorian Gray*

INDICATING RHETORICAL QUESTIONS

It is sometimes appropriate to end a rhetorical question—one for which no answer is expected—in an exclamation point instead of a question mark.

How do you expect me to finish all these chores by noon!

Isn't he adorable!

What on earth did she expect!

See also the examples of rhetorical questions under Question Mark on page 130.

CAPTURING ATTENTION

An unsubtle way of underscoring statements that are unlikely, ironic, or unexpected is to follow them with an exclamation point enclosed in parentheses.

After trying and failing to borrow money, first from his cousin, then from his best friend, and finally from the starving artist upstairs (!), Joe decided there was no alternative but to sell off the private jet.

After nineteen pastries (!), Albert decided he'd had enough.

While this strategy is not illegal, it demands attention a bit too loudly. It is occasionally appropriate, but as a general rule you are better off wording things so that ironies or oddities speak for themselves. Give your readers credit for being able to pick up on these.

CAUTIONS ABOUT THE EXCLAMATION POINT

> An exclamation mark is like laughing at your own jokes.
>
> —F. Scott Fitzgerald

Use this punctuation mark sparingly, or it will lose its effectiveness. Relying on it to infuse excitement or importance into uninspired lines will make your writing look amateurish or—even worse—gratingly like ad copy.

It is permissible to use it in combination with other strategies for indicating emphasis, such as capital letters, boldface, or italic type, but don't overdo this. Usually, a better approach is to use one strategy or the other. It is also inadvisable to use multiple exclamation points to indicate extreme astonishment or excitement (*Could you believe what she said!! The concert was incredible!!!*). Occasionally, this may be effective in drawing the reader's attention more closely to something, but more typically it makes it look as if you're trying too hard.

Some writers fancy using a combination of a question mark and an exclamation point for extra emphasis, usually following a rhetorical question. There is in fact an obscure punctuation mark for this purpose, called an **interrobang** (‽), which merges the two marks into one. More typically, one sees them presented side by side.

> Could anyone have thought it possible?!

> Can you believe what she's done now?!

Combining a question mark and an exclamation point may occasionally be appropriate, but should be kept to a minimum.

STYLE CONVENTIONS

The question mark and exclamation point follow similar rules when it comes to style conventions and so are reviewed together here.

- When a question mark or exclamation point occurs in the middle of a sentence, do *not* follow it with a comma. This holds whether the text preceding the mark is dialogue, unvoiced thought with no surrounding quotation marks, or straight narrative.

    > He said, "Nonsense!" and ambled off.
    >
    > "You don't really mean that?" she asked incredulously.
    >
    > Did he really mean it? she wondered.
    >
    > Now here was a pretty kettle of fish! I said to myself.
    >
    > Who would blink first? was the question.
    >
    > We had barely made it to the door when crash! everything collapsed.

- When a question mark or exclamation point appears at the end of a sentence, do not follow it with a period, even if it applies only to the last words. The context will make it clear to readers whether or not the entire sentence is querying or exclamatory. For illustrations of this, see the discussion under Period on page 120.

- When a question mark or exclamation point follows quoted text, place it *after* the closing quotation mark if it applies to the entire sentence, and *before* if it applies to just the quoted part. For illustrations of this, see the style conventions for Quotation Marks on page 188.

- When a question mark or exclamation point applies only to text enclosed within parentheses, it does not affect the terminal punctuation for the remainder of the sentence. See the style conventions for Parentheses on page 159.

- If the text immediately preceding a question mark or exclamation point is italicized, the punctuation mark may either be italicized as well or appear in regular font. Ensure consistency.

    > Surely you didn't mean *me?*
    >
    > Come here *immediately!*

Hyphen (-)

THIS SECTION LOOKS AT THE HYPHEN as a mark of punctuation, as opposed to a component of spelling. The distinction is that in its punctuation role, the hyphen is not an inherent part of a word or phrase but rather is required only when words are presented in particular combinations or ways. (For a discussion of its spelling role, turn to page 24.)

The functions of the hyphen as a punctuation mark are the following:

- Marking word breaks at the end of a line
- Drawing together words that form a compound adjective
- Acting as a "stand-in" for a repeated word
- Indicating special intonations or pronunciations

INDICATING WORD BREAKS

During a late election Lord
Roehampton strained a vocal cord
From shouting, very loud and high,
To lots and lots of people why
The budget in his own opin-
-Ion should not be allowed to win.

—Hilaire Belloc, *Selected Cautionary Verses*

Knowing where to break a word that's too long to fit on a line was more of an issue in the days of typewriters. (Remember them?) Still, it doesn't hurt for writers in the age of word processors to have at least an awareness of the rules. As any newspaper reader knows, a computer's idea of word breaks can be hilarious—or worse. *Menswear, wee-knight, heat-her, mans-laughter, Pen-elope, Superb-owl, prolife-rated, pots-hot,* and *the-rapist* have all made appearances in print.

The rationale behind breaking words only in certain places is to prevent the reader from having to struggle to make sense of the two parts. Some types of breaks are better to avoid even if a dictionary indicates they are permissible.

Don't break words of one syllable

This holds no matter how long a word is and even if it has more than one phoneme (distinct sound unit).

No	Yes
bar-bed	barbed
thro-ugh	through
school-ed	schooled
scrun-ched	scrunched
he-arth	hearth

Don't break a word if just one letter would be left on a line

By definition, this applies to any three-letter word. For longer words, it applies whether the word has two syllables or more than two.

No	Yes
a-do	ado
i-vy	ivy
i-dea	idea
tax-i	taxi
a-bout	about
e-nough	enough
throat-y	throaty
a-miable	ami-able
i-dentify	iden-tify
epitom-e	epito-me

Break hyphenated compound words at the hyphen

Hyphenated compounds are those where two words are linked by a hyphen as part of the proper spelling. In this situation, let that hyphen do double duty, functioning both as an integral part of the word itself and as an end-of-the-line word breaker. Having two hyphens in a word would look awkward.

No	Yes
by-prod-uct	by-product
dou-ble-edged	double-edged
teeter-tot-ter	teeter-totter

Break closed compound words between the words

Closed compounds are those made up of two words run together. Breaking them between the words is preferable to breaking either of the words themselves, even if those words could be broken if they stood alone.

No	Yes
com-monplace	common-place
quar-terback	quarter-back
mead-owlark	meadow-lark

Similarly, if a word contains a prefix or a suffix, try to break between the prefix/suffix and the root word, rather than breaking either of those components themselves.

No	Yes
su-perscript	super-script
anticli-max	anti-climax
precon-dition	pre-condition
coun-terclockwise or counterclock-wise	counter-clockwise
sis-terhood	sister-hood

Do not break a word if two unrelated words would coincidentally result

Sometimes, breaking a word according to the rules just happens to result in the separate presentation of two completely unrelated words, which might cause momentary puzzlement. To prevent the reader's having to backtrack to make sense of this, avoid breaking words such as the following unless absolutely necessary:

bin-	is-	pick-	prose-
go	sue	led	cute

(In some cases, breaking a word can result in new words that are not entirely unrelated to the original. Following a certain search engine's launch of a service allowing users to navigate close-up views of public places, some observers noted that the name could be read as the imperative "Go-ogle".)

LINKING THE PARTS OF A COMPOUND ADJECTIVE

This role of the hyphen has some complexity to it, because the rules are so varied. There is a main rule, but then there are exceptions, and then there are exceptions to the exceptions. The best way to introduce this function is to lead up to it, so that the rationale behind all the rules is understood.

When a noun is preceded by not one but two words that modify it, there are three possibilities about the relationship between all three words.

> Scenario 1:
> long red braids
> grumpy old man
> shiny new bike

Here, each of the two adjectives independently modifies the noun that follows. (For an explanation of why there is no comma between the adjectives, see page 95.) The reader understands that the reference is to braids that are both long and red, a man who is both grumpy and old, and a bike that is both shiny and new.

> Scenario 2:
> deadly viral infection
> large urban center
> rude civil servant

The words *deadly*, *large*, and *rude* are clearly adjectives, while *infection*, *center*, and *servant* are clearly nouns. What about the words in the middle, though? They are also adjectives—but each one is combining with the noun that follows it to create a **compound noun**, which expresses a single concept. The reader understands that the first word modifies the next two: *deadly* modifies the compound noun *viral infection*, *large* modifies *urban center*, and *rude* modifies *civil servant*.

> Scenario 3:
> civil rights leader
> major league player
> mad cow disease

Here again the first word is an adjective and the third is a noun, but now the middle word in each case is a noun that combines with the adjective that precedes it to create a **compound adjective**. The reader understands that the reference is to a leader in civil rights, not to a "rights leader" with good manners. Similarly, it is the league that is major, not the player, and the cow that is mad, not the disease itself.

None of the above combinations of words should present any confusion or be interpreted as meaning anything other than what they do. But how about the following?

1. stone carving knife
2. new driver legislation
3. blond bearded man
4. thirty odd guests

In examples 1 and 2, is the middle word meant to be combined with the word that follows to create a compound noun, or with the word before to create a compound adjective? That is, a carving knife made of stone, or a sculptor's knife for carving stone? New legislation that applies to all drivers, or legislation that applies only to people who have recently received their licenses? In examples 3 and 4, does the middle word form a compound adjective with the one before, or is it independently modifying the noun that follows? That is, a man with blond hair and a beard, or a man with a blond beard? Somewhere between thirty and forty guests, or thirty eccentrics?

Use hyphens to link the words of a compound adjective that precedes a noun if ambiguity or uncertainty might otherwise result

When two or more words are intended to collectively function as a single adjective, link them with hyphens if they come before the noun they modify *and* if there's any possibility of misinterpreting them. Hyphens make the status of each word immediately clear and make the sentence easier to read overall.

I wouldn't touch that line with a ten-foot pole.

Workers spend too much time wrestling with user-hostile software.

A single 256-byte record allows for 256 single-byte output values.

Come take advantage of this once-in-a-lifetime opportunity to buy a set of silver-plated lint-removal brushes at a not-to-be-believed price!

In some cases, as already demonstrated, the absence of a hyphen could produce misinterpretation or ambiguity.

Ten month old babies were observed in the study.

Did the study look at ten babies, each of whom was one month old—or at an unspecified number of babies, each of whom was ten months old? In the absence of hyphens, we can't tell whether *ten* is modifying *babies* or *months*. This sentence should read as either *Ten month-old babies were observed in the study* or *Ten-month-old babies were observed in the study*.

In other cases, the absence of a hyphen might not render a sentence ambiguous but could cause momentary confusion as the reader started to process things one way and then realized that a word had been misinterpreted.

> The company sponsored events usually attracted a high turnout.

> The office generated paperwork soon became too much for one secretary to handle.

> His girlfriend related problems began to take their toll on his work.

Hyphens would make it clear that *sponsored, generated,* and *related* are functioning as parts of compound adjectives, not as verbs.

Exceptions: A hyphen is not necessary when a compound adjective consists of words that are commonly associated with each other so there is little possibility of ambiguity or misinterpretation. In the earlier examples of *major league player* and *mad cow disease,* hyphens (*major-league player, mad-cow disease*) would serve no purpose. You would certainly not include them in phrases such as *high school student, baby boomer generation,* or *carbon monoxide fumes,* where the first two words make up a very familiar compound. It will sometimes be a judgment call as to whether or not a particular combination calls for a hyphen. The only advice is, include a hyphen if you think the sentence might be harder to follow without it.

Do not link the words of a compound adjective with hyphens when they come after the noun

When a compound adjective comes *after* the noun it modifies, rather than before, it does not take a hyphen, since in this case no ambiguity or misreading could result from omitting it.

> Read the easy-to-follow instructions to work your way through the ninety-step assembly process.

> *But:* The assembly process has ninety steps, and comes with instructions that are easy to follow.

Of course, if the compound inherently takes a hyphen, ensure it is included. (See Hyphenation of compound words on page 25, in the chapter on spelling.) In that case, it is serving not to distinguish the compound from adjoining words but as part of its proper spelling, so it naturally applies regardless of the position of the compound in the sentence.

> The back-to-back workshops were exhausting to sit through.
>
> It's exhausting to sit through workshops that are back-to-back.
>
> The cross-eyed doll seemed to be giving him a baleful look.
>
> The doll was cross-eyed.

Hyphenated compounds appear as their own entries in the dictionary, so it's easy to confirm if a hyphen is needed. If you don't see a compound listed, assume that it does not take a hyphen—although note that dictionaries may differ on what gets hyphenated.

Do not use a hyphen when the first word of a compound adjective is an adverb ending in *ly*

Adjectives are words that modify nouns; **adverbs** are words that modify verbs. Adverbs also modify adjectives, participles (verb forms acting as adjectives), and other adverbs. They are usually easy to recognize, as the majority are formed by taking an adjective and adding *ly* to it (although note that some adjectives, such as *friendly* or *cowardly*, end in *ly* as well).

The words that make up compound adjectives may individually be nouns, adjectives, verbs, participles, or adverbs. For all but the last, hyphens are often necessary because, as demonstrated above, word order alone may not be sufficient to clarify which words are modifying which. An adverb, however, always modifies the word that immediately follows it in a sentence. Since no ambiguity is possible, putting a hyphen after an adverb to link it with the next word would be redundant.

The hyphens in the following examples are *in*correct and should be removed:

They're a highly-motivated team.	[should be *highly motivated*]
She admitted that she had poorly-developed spatial skills.	[should be *poorly developed*]
The clerk showed him selections of beautifully-woven fabric.	[should be *beautifully woven*]
Add two cups of freshly-chopped parsley.	[should be *freshly chopped*]

The no-hyphen rule also applies, of course, when the adverb-adjective compound follows rather than precedes the noun: *The team was highly motivated; The fabric was beautifully woven.*

Exceptions: Do include a hyphen after an *ly* adverb if the compound adjective contains at least two more components and those two are hyphenated. You wouldn't want to have part of a compound using hyphens and part not.

> The engineer emerged with some hastily-drawn-up plans.

> It sounded like a poorly-thought-out strategy.

> He turned in a clumsily-done-up sketch.

Very occasionally, it may not be clear whether the word that follows an adverb is linked with the adverb or with whatever lies on its other side. For example:

> Try as she would, she couldn't get around the maddeningly slow moving van.

Is the reference here to a moving van that is maddeningly slow, or to a plain old van that's moving maddeningly slowly? If the former is intended, a hyphen to combine *maddeningly* with *slow* would make it clear which word gets linked with which.

> Try as she would, she couldn't get around the maddeningly-slow moving van.

In most cases, do use a hyphen for adverbs that do not end in *ly*

The rules are more complex for adverbs that do not have *ly* endings, because such words are the same as their corresponding adjectives and therefore may not be as instantly recognizable as adverbs. Style guides do not all give the same direction on how to handle these situations. Rather than prescribing the "correct" way, this section simply describes the alternatives.

Authorities agree that in most cases, when a "non-*ly*" adverb combines with another word to form a compound adjective modifying a noun, do link the two with a hyphen.

> She counts several well-known authors among her clientele.

> He turned over the still-smoldering log.

> It was clearly an ill-advised plan.

> A fast-talking salesman cornered us.

As before, do not use a hyphen if the compound follows the noun . . .

> The authors were well known.

> The log was still smoldering.

. . . unless the compound takes one as part of its proper spelling.

> The plan was ill-advised.

> The salesman was fast-talking.

There is not a consensus as to whether a hyphen is needed when the modifier is a **comparative** (indicating a degree of intensity) or a **superlative** (indicating one or the other extreme). Some authorities hold that hyphens would *not* appear in the following sentences:

> She's her country's best loved poet.

> He holds the dubious distinction of being the city's least trusted politician.

> The higher ranked players went on to the next level of competition.

> The most criticized questions on the exam were eventually dropped.

> The better fitting dress, unfortunately, was the wrong color.

> The less sophisticated members of the audience applauded wildly between movements.

Others would say to use *best-loved poet, least-trusted politician, higher-ranked players,* etc. Make your own decision on how to handle these constructions, and be consistent.

ACTING AS A STAND-IN FOR A REPEATED WORD

If a word appears more than once in a sentence and each time is linked with a different modifier, it can sound a bit ponderous to repeat it each time. An occasionally useful strategy is to write the whole compound out on its final occurrence only and replace the earlier occurrences of the base word with a hyphen. Consider the sentence:

> His critics both overestimated and underestimated his abilities.

This could appear more efficiently as:

> His critics both over- and underestimated his abilities.

In this role, the hyphen is called a **suspension hyphen**. A suspension hyphen informs the reader that there is something intentionally missing; that *over* is not intended as a complete word in itself but just as the first part of a compound, the remainder of which is about to be identified. It is important to include the hyphen, for omitting it would create momentary confusion as the reader tried to make sense of *His critics both over and*. (Note that use of the suspension hyphen is unrelated to whether or not the word it is standing in for is normally hyphenated. For example, the actual word *overestimate* does not take a hyphen, nor need you put one in *underestimate* to match the one in *over-*.)

Similarly,

> Use either a two-, three-, or four-column layout.

> At one time, scientists were interested in relating endo-, ecto-, and mesomorph builds to personality.

> Referrals were given for both clinic- and hospital-based services.

A caution: Even when applied correctly, the suspension hyphen has the potential of obscuring meaning or making a sentence look awkward. Think carefully before you include it, and don't overuse it.

INDICATING INTONATIONS AND PRONUNCIATIONS

The hyphen has several applications in dialogue that let an author achieve various effects of tone and pronunciation.

Spelling a word out

Hyphens between each of the letters of a word indicate that it is to be pronounced letter-by-letter, rather than as a word.

> ". . . Now, then, where's the first boy?"
>
> "Please, sir, he's cleaning the back parlour window," said the temporary head of the philosophical class.
>
> "So he is, to be sure," rejoined Squeers. "We go upon the practical mode of teaching, Nickleby; the regular education system. C-l-e-a-n, clean, verb active, to make bright, to scour. W-i-n, win, d-e-r, der, winder, a casement. When the boy knows this out of book, he goes and does it. It's just the same principle as the use of the globes. Where's the second boy?"

"Please, sir, he's weeding the garden," replied a small voice.

"To be sure," said Squeers, by no means disconcerted. "So he is. B-o-t, bot, t-i-n, tin, bottin, n-e-y, bottinney, noun substantive, a knowledge of plants. When he has learned that bottinney means a knowledge of plants, he goes and knows 'em. That's our system, Nickleby: What do you think of it?"

"It's a very useful one, at any rate," answered Nicholas significantly.

—Charles Dickens, *Nicholas Nickleby*

A slight pause in the middle of a word, for emphasis

"She sot down," said Joe, "and she got up, and she made a grab at Tickler, and she Ram-paged out. That's what she did," said Joe, slowly clearing the fire between the lower bars with the poker, and looking at it: "she Ram-paged out, Pip."

—Charles Dickens, *Great Expectations*

A drawn-out intonation

"You're having a time, Sherman. What on earth are you doing?"

Without looking up: "I'm taking Marshall for a wa-a-a-a-a-alk."

Walk came out as a groan, because the dachshund attempted a fishtail maneuver and Sherman had to wrap his arm around the dog's midsection.

—Tom Wolfe, *The Bonfire of the Vanities*

A lilting or singsong intonation

"Eddy! Boomer! Where are those [expletive] trainers?" a voice bellows. It is almost noon, and in the final panic of getting ready, laces get broken, tape and cotton are urgently needed, and it's a question we're all asking. In an eminently reasonable, hide-and-seek voice, Robinson calls out, "Oh Ed-dy, Boo-mer, you can come out now. We give up."

—Ken Dryden, *The Game*

Hissed *S*'s or rolled *R*'s

Bilbo seeing what had happened and having nothing better to ask stuck to his question, "What have I got in my pocket?" he said louder.

"S-s-s-s-s," hissed Gollum. "It must give us three guesseses, my preciouss, three guesseses."

"Very well! Guess away!" said Bilbo.

"Handses!" said Gollum.

"Wrong," said Bilbo, who had luckily just taken his hand out again. "Guess again!"

"S-s-s-s-s," said Gollum more upset than ever. He thought of all the things he kept in his own pockets: fishbones, goblins' teeth, wet shells, a bit of bat-wing, a sharp stone to sharpen his fangs on, and other nasty things. He tried to think what other people kept in their pockets.

—J.R.R. Tolkien, *The Hobbit*

[T]he Lady, who rode side-saddle and wore a long, fluttering dress of dazzling green, was lovelier still.

"Good day, t-r-r-avellers," she cried out in a voice as sweet as the sweetest bird's song, trilling her R's delightfully. "Some of you are young pilgrims to walk this rough waste."

"That's as may be, Ma'am," said Puddleglum very stiffly and on his guard.

"We're looking for the ruined city of the giants," said Jill.

"The r-r-ruined city?" said the Lady. "That is a strange place to be seeking . . ."

—C.S. Lewis, *The Silver Chair*

Stuttering, stammering, or teeth-chattering

In the wheelchair was a woman, wearing a deep-crowned, wide-brimmed green felt hat, obscuring her face, and a paisley silk scarf at the throat of a caped loden coat. . . . There was, Roland saw, a huge flint embedded in the mud under the back of the wheel, preventing all attempts at manoeuvre or reversal.

"Can I help?"

"Oh," on a long stressed sigh. "Oh, thank you. I do s-seem to be b-bogged down." The voice was hesitant, old and patrician. "S-such a b-bother. So so h-h-h-*helpless*. If you please—"

"There's a stone. Under the wheel. Wait. Hold on."

—A.S. Byatt, *Possession*

To indicate an actual cutting off of speech, use a dash instead, as described on page 169.

Slash (/)

THE SLASH, also known as the **diagonal**, **slant** or **solidus** (or more esoterically as the *virgule* or *shilling*) is a somewhat nebulous mark. There are a couple of situations where no other punctuation will do, but often it is used as a casual shorthand for more precise modes of expression. Since it runs the risk of being ambiguous, it should be applied with caution. In more formal genres of writing, such as that expected for academic journals, it may be considered too informal or imprecise to be used at all.

The functions of the slash are as follows:

- Indicating "and" or "or" relationships
- Indicating various other relationships between words or numbers
- Separating lines of poetry

INDICATING "AND" OR "OR" RELATIONSHIPS

The slash may be variously used to indicate options, dual roles, and alternatives.

Use it as a symbol for "and"

In this role, it may be used to identify an entity that has more than one characterization or function.

> She liked to describe her position as that of vice-president of finances/baby-sitter.

> The trial/media circus has the city in a frenzy.

> The one room in his tiny apartment had to serve as a bedroom/workshop.

The slash is unique among punctuation marks in that it is sounded out as a word. That is, if you were reading such sentences out loud, you would say, "vice-president of finances slash baby-sitter" and "trial slash media circus," since the significance of the relationship cannot be inferred from the words alone.

Linking words with a hyphen wouldn't carry the same meaning, since the function of the hyphen is to form a new compound word. With a slash, each word retains its independence. If your intention is to form a compound, the hyphen is probably the more appropriate mark.

A more formal way of expressing the type of relationship expressed by the slash is to use the Latin word *cum*, optionally italicized and linked to the other words with hyphens: *a trial-cum-media circus, a bedroom-cum-workshop.*

Use it to connect two distinct entities that are either parts of a whole or closely affiliated

> The audio/video controls are at the back of the console.
>
> Her specialty is obstetrics/gynecology.
>
> Contestants are eligible to win a washer/dryer set, a radio/CD player, and other exciting prizes!

In more formal writing, use the word *and* instead, or link the related words with a hyphen (if appropriate).

Use it as a symbol for "or"

In situations that present two clear alternatives, the slash is often an acceptable substitute.

> The graduate courses are graded pass/fail.
>
> In the second part of the exam, the questions were true/false.
>
> If a player draws an ace, he/she loses a turn.
>
> Dear Sir/Madam:

In more formal writing, use *or* instead. (It should also be noted that many people balk at *he/she*—and hit the roof over *s/he*. For more on this, see the discussion of pronouns under Avoidance of Bias on page 314.)

A common use of the slash is in the combination *and/or*, which is an efficient way of expressing a slightly unwieldy concept. It is useful for scenarios where the possibilities are option *a*, option *b*, or both: that is, *a* and *b* do not necessarily co-exist, but they are not mutually exclusive either.

> The tent offers suitable protection against cold and/or windy conditions.

> Headings may be set in bold type and/or capital letters.

> Ingredients: Sugar, glucose, fructose, palm and/or coconut oil, artificial flavor and color.

Some authorities frown on this quasi-word, viewing it as a lazy substitute for more carefully crafted phrasing; others accept it. In more formal writing, it is usually better to use a few extra words in order to avoid it.

Be on the lookout for possible ambiguity

Since a slash can indicate either "and" or "or," there are situations where it might not be clear which of these conjunctions is intended. In some cases either word will do, so the reader's interpretation doesn't really matter.

> Come to beautiful Mount Avalanche for a weekend of cross-country skiing/alpine skiing.

> The new policy is aimed only at contract employees. Regular full-time/part-time employees will not be affected.

In other cases, its use could result in ambiguity.

> Please do not use the library/study between noon and six.

> The figures/illustrations are not complete.

Are these two separate rooms, or one room with a dual purpose? Two different groups of artwork, or two terms for the same thing? Avoid using the slash as a hasty shorthand when the resulting meaning could be unclear.

INDICATING OTHER RELATIONSHIPS

Apart from indicating "and" and "or" relationships, the slash may be used for the following purposes:

Separating elements that are being compared

> The Toronto/Montreal hockey rivalry had its heyday in the 1960s.

More formal alternative: *The hockey rivalry between Toronto and Montreal*

Separating origins and destinations

The Los Angeles/Sydney flight was fully booked.

More formal alternatives: *The Los Angeles-to-Sydney flight* or *The Los Angeles–Sydney flight*. (See discussion of the en dash on page 163.)

Separating the numerals making up a date

01/01/09
12/10/2010

Indicating a period spanning two calendar years

academic year 2009/10
records from 1955/56

As a shorthand designation for "per"

$5/yard
sixty words/minute
100 km/hour

More formal alternative: *$5 per yard; sixty words per minute.*

Indicating division or fractions

6/3=2	1/2
x/y=z	2/3

SEPARATING LINES OF POETRY

Use the slash to separate lines of a poem or song that are run in with a prose sentence. Leave a space on either side of the slash when using it for this purpose.

"And what about his trademark, the whistle?"

"That was heard by the three people who came quickly on the scene after the East-haven murder. One just heard a whistle, one said it sounded like a hymn and the third, who was a churchwoman, claimed she could identify it precisely, 'Now the Day Is Over.' We kept quiet about that. It could be useful when we get the usual clutch of nutters claiming they're the Whistler. But there seems no doubt that he does whistle."

Dalgliesh said: " 'Now the day is over / Night is drawing nigh / Shadows of the evening / Fall across the sky.' It's a Sunday-school hymn, hardly the kind that gets requested on *Songs of Praise*, I should have thought."

—P.D. James, *Devices and Desires*

For longer excerpts of poetry, set off the lines vertically.

Parentheses ( )

THE FUNCTION OF PARENTHESES is to set off an element that interrupts a flow of thought significantly. The element must be relevant enough to merit being included in the text, but enough of an aside to require being set off distinctly. Content that is appropriate for parentheses is usually an explanation, an amplification, or an example of the topic the sentence is dealing with, or some digression that bears a relationship to the topic but not a tight one. If a digression, it must not be a non sequitur (something with no logical connection to anything previously said): it must have some bearing on what precedes it, and this connection should be evident to the reader. Don't treat parentheses as a way of stashing stray bits of information that don't quite fit in anywhere else.

Digressive elements may be set off with either commas, dashes, or parentheses. How then do you decide when it's appropriate to use each? Sometimes the decision is obvious; sometimes it's more a matter of achieving a particular tone. In general, commas serve to integrate a digressive element unobtrusively, dashes serve to draw particular attention to it, and parentheses serve to *de*-emphasize it, signaling to the reader that the text is temporarily getting off track. These distinctions aren't hard-and-fast, though, and in some cases the effect of parentheses may be to draw more, rather than less, attention to what they enclose. It very much depends on context.

Don't overuse parentheses, as they can be distracting and too many can make your writing look choppy and awkward. If you find yourself sprinkling them around liberally, ask yourself whether all those asides really need to be included.

Parentheses are useful for accomplishing the following:

- Working in digressions
- Making complex text easier to follow
- Setting off minor details

WORKING IN DIGRESSIONS

Parentheses may enclose a digression within a sentence, or they may enclose one or more entire sentences that are a digression from the text around them.

When a parenthesized element is part of a sentence, it has no impact on the structure of the rest of the sentence: it may fit in grammatically, or it may not. The parts that come before and after it are treated as if it weren't there, and must mesh with each other, both grammatically and logically, just as they would if nothing intervened between them. Within a sentence, a parenthesized element may be a single word,

> After considerable pleading, she finally got him to reveal the secret ingredient (sarsaparilla).

a sentence fragment,

> It turned out that they liked the same toppings on pizza (truffles, green peppers, sardines and a dash of coriander), which cemented their relationship.

> The race for second place (first place, of course, was a foregone conclusion) was still wide open.

or there may be more than one parenthesized segment.

> Brian gave the impression of never shutting up. This was not quite true, though, because he *did* stop talking when he slept. But when he finally flipped his cookies (as we politely said in my immediate family) or showed symptoms of schizophrenia (as one of his many psychiatrists put it) or woke up to the real meaning of his life (as he put it) or had a nervous breakdown (as his Ph.D. adviser put it) or became-exhausted-as-a-result-of-being-married-to-that-Jewish-princess-from-New York (as his parents put it)—then he never stopped talking *even* to sleep. He stopped sleeping, in fact. . . .
>
> —Erica Jong, *Fear of Flying*

When parentheses enclose one or more entire sentences, the text following the interrupting element must pick up exactly where the text preceding it left off. The parenthesized sentences may be part of a paragraph,

> As she said these words her foot slipped, and in another moment, splash! she was up to her chin in salt water. Her first idea was that she had somehow fallen into the sea, "and in that case I can go back by railway," she said to herself. (Alice had been to the seaside once in her life, and had come to the general conclusion that, wherever you go on the English coast, you find a number of bathing machines in the sea, some children

digging in the sand with wooden spades, then a row of lodging houses, and behind them a railway station.) However, she soon made out that she was in the pool of tears which she had wept when she was nine feet high.

—Lewis Carroll, *Alice's Adventures in Wonderland*

or an entire paragraph.

In the end, I always want potatoes. Mashed potatoes. Nothing like mashed potatoes when you're feeling blue. Nothing like getting into bed with a bowl of hot mashed potatoes already loaded with butter, and methodically adding a thin cold slice of butter to every forkful. The problem with mashed potatoes, though, is that they require almost as much work as crisp potatoes, and when you're feeling blue the last thing you feel like is hard work. Of course, you can always get someone to make the mashed potatoes for you, but let's face it: the reason you're blue is that there *isn't* anyone to make them for you. As a result, most people do not have nearly enough mashed potatoes in their lives, and when they do, it's almost always at the wrong time.

(You can, of course, train children to mash potatoes, but you should know that Richard Nixon spent most of his childhood making mashed potatoes for his mother and was extremely methodical about getting the lumps out. A few lumps make mashed potatoes more authentic, if you ask me, but that's not the point. The point is that perhaps children should not be trained to mash potatoes.)

For mashed potatoes: Put 1 large (or 2 small) potatoes in a large pot of salted water and bring to a boil. . .

—Nora Ephron, *Heartburn*

There is no specific limit to the length of what may be put in parentheses, but it is inadvisable to set off *too* long a section, as the reader may have forgotten what preceded the digression by the time the closing mark finally appears. If you find yourself setting off anything longer than a paragraph, you should probably rethink your structure.

MAKING COMPLEX TEXT EASIER TO FOLLOW

Parentheses aren't always planned in advance: sometimes their desirability becomes apparent only after you have looked over a first draft. In descriptive (as opposed to creative) writing, if you need to cram in dense amounts of information, you might find that adding parentheses in certain places serves to make the main points easier to follow. Consider using them when you want to work in elements that are important but not central, and you don't want these elements to distract from the primary ones. For example:

> The immune system consists of several organs and of billions of specialized cells, called **white blood cells**. White blood cells are produced in the **bone marrow**, which is a spongy tissue found in the hollow interior of large bones, and move around the body in the bloodstream, alongside the much more numerous **red blood cells**, whose job is to bring oxygen to all the cells of the body. They also travel in the **lymphatic system**, a network of vessels that drains excess fluid from cells and returns it to the bloodstream, and many of them cluster in the **lymph nodes**, small bean-shaped organs located along the lymphatic system.

All true, but there is a fair bit going on in this paragraph. Putting the asides into parentheses makes the information specific to the primary subject, white blood cells, stand out more clearly.

> *Revised:* White blood cells are produced in the **bone marrow** (a spongy tissue found in the hollow interior of large bones) and move around the body in the bloodstream, alongside the much more numerous **red blood cells** (whose job is to bring oxygen to all the cells of the body). They also travel in the **lymphatic system** (a network of vessels that drains excess fluid from cells and returns it to the bloodstream), and many of them cluster in the **lymph nodes** (small bean-shaped organs located along the lymphatic system).

The same reasoning applies for setting off entire sentences. In the following passage, the mention of T cells is relevant but should not distract from the main focus.

> One very important class of white blood cell is the **B cell**. An equally important class, the **T cell**, is not discussed here, since its role in allergic reactions is more complex. The part that T cells play in allergies is discussed in Chapter 3. B cells don't attack invaders themselves. Instead, they produce large, complex protein molecules called **antibodies**, and the antibodies then go after the invader. The antibodies in turn do not destroy the invader themselves, but they latch onto it and help disable it, and send signals to other parts of the immune system to come and finish it off.

> *Revised:* One very important class of white blood cell is the **B cell**. (An equally important class, the **T cell**, is not discussed here, since its role in allergic reactions is more complex. The part that T cells play in allergies is discussed in Chapter 3.) B cells don't attack invaders themselves. Instead, . . .

The next passage, an example of technical writing, contains information that could distract significantly from the main point:

> Error messages are recorded on the local and the host message queues. The local message queue has the same name as the session. To find out the cause of the failure, use the information in both message queues.

Readers—even those who understood the jargon—might have trouble spotting that two of these three sentences are critically related. The main thread here is that there are two message queues (whatever those are!) and the user must apply the information in *both* queues in order to solve a problem. The secondary information is that one of these two message queues is identified in a particular way. Subsuming this secondary information in parentheses would make the relationship between the first and third sentences clearer.

> *Better:* Error messages are recorded on the local and the host message queues. (The local message queue has the same name as the session.) To find out the cause of the failure, use the information in both message queues.

Parentheses can sometimes be employed to make text read more smoothly and concisely. Consider the next example:

> A validity coefficient cannot exceed the square root of the reliability coefficient. For example, if the reliability of a test is .70, the test validity cannot exceed .83. If the validity coefficient exceeds the square root of the reliability coefficient, a sampling error has occurred.

Note the unwieldiness of the third sentence, which repeats the entire contents of the first. It would be nice to avoid this repetition by using a pronoun, but the second sentence prevents this, since it would intervene between the pronoun and its antecedent. (See Referring to the Right Antecedent on page 278.) If this sentence were enclosed in parentheses, however, the third sentence could be constructed as though it came immediately after the first. That is, the second sentence would effectively "not be there" as far as the rest of the text is concerned. Since it is just an example, subsuming it does no harm to the flow.

> *Better:* A validity coefficient cannot exceed the square root of the reliability coefficient. (For example, if the reliability of a test is .70, the test validity cannot exceed .83.) If it does, a sampling error has occurred.

SETTING OFF DETAILS

Parentheses are employed to set off a variety of small details that may need to be worked into a sentence. Some common examples of this type of use are as follows.

Short clarifications

The settlement is 80 kilometers (about 50 miles) from the nearest town.

The one-way fare is $200 (U.S.).

Birth/death dates

Marie Curie (1867–1934) was the first person to be awarded a second Nobel prize.

References

In some academic styles, citations of quoted sources, whether presented as names or numbers, are enclosed in parentheses.

The leading proponents of this theory (Maxwell, 2006; Rosenberg & Terrence, 2008) agree that the process must be sensitive to issues of timing.

Other researchers, however, have found conflicting results (3, 4, 5).

Some style guides specify the use of square brackets or superscript numbers instead. In academic writing, it is almost always necessary to follow the specifications of a particular guide.

Abbreviations

If you are using an abbreviation for a name or term, it is sometimes appropriate on the first occurrence to spell out the full term followed by the abbreviation in parentheses, or (less commonly) vice versa. Once the abbreviation has been defined, it may be used without further explanation.

The Organization of African Unity (OAU) was founded in 1963.

The study compared Transference Focused Psychotherapy (TFP) with Cognitive Behavior Therapy (CBT).

Note: It is not necessary to spell out abbreviations that are assumed to be common knowledge, such as NBC or MBA.

STYLE CONVENTIONS

- Don't leave spaces around the enclosed text (like this). Place the opening and closing marks directly next to the text (like this).

An exception is if you are using parentheses to enclose a symbol, as might occur in some forms of technical writing. For example, (.) and (*) are slightly easier to read than (.) and (*).

• Try to avoid putting parenthetical text within parenthetical text, as the structure may become difficult to follow. If you must do so, make the inner parentheses square brackets instead.

> Subjects from the other two study sites (rural [N=58] and urban [N=60]) were followed for four months.

• It is permissible to use a pair of dashes within parentheses, but think before you do so. The parenthesized text is already an aside, and it can be distracting to have an aside within an aside. See the discussion of this role of dashes on page 172.

• Ensure that parentheses always come in pairs. Particularly with longer elements, writers occasionally forget that text is parenthetical and neglect to close it off.

• When parentheses enclose an entire sentence, put the terminal punctuation mark *inside* the parentheses.

> Dealing with multiple punctuation marks in a single sentence can be tricky. (The positioning of parentheses and periods is a case in point.)

> The shoe was now on the other foot. (Or was it?)

> For weeks afterward, he gave the shop a wide berth. (Evidently, he had learned his lesson!)

• When parentheses enclose just part of a sentence, put the terminal punctuation mark *outside* the parentheses, even if the parenthesized element comes at the end.

> The promotion was unanimously approved (although some members privately had their doubts).

> Do you really think this move is necessary (because if not, we still have time to cancel it)?

> After all, *someone* has to win (ridiculous as the odds are)!

In the case of exclamation points, note that it would actually be somewhat counterproductive to put parenthesized text at the end of the sentence, since the purpose of an exclamation point is to impart excitement or urgency, and the interruption would detract from this. If you ever do construct such a sentence, analyze it carefully. It is likely that recasting it would improve it.

- The following additional conventions must be observed when parentheses enclose text within a sentence:

  - If a comma, semicolon, or colon is needed between what precedes and follows the parentheses, put this mark *after* the closing parenthesis—not before the opening one, and not in both places.

    > The room contained only a sofa (much the worse for wear), a faded armchair, and a carpet (if that stained and threadbare square could be called such); the other furnishings had long since been sold off.

  - Even if the parenthesized element is a complete grammatical sentence, it must not begin with a capital letter, and it must not end with a period. The overall sentence may contain only one period.

    > It was well past the appointed hour (the shops had already closed, and the streetlights were coming on) when she arrived.

    You may however end a parenthesized element in one of the other terminal punctuation marks.

    > Her sour face (did it ever look otherwise?) peered suspiciously around the doorway.

    > Factors that contributed to the success of the group included friendship (we actually enjoyed seeing each other!) and acceptance of criticism.

  - Regardless of what punctuation appears within the parentheses, don't omit the appropriate terminal punctuation mark for the overall sentence. Remember, always treat the rest of the sentence as though the parenthesized element were not there.

    > We actually managed to finish on time (a first!).

    > Can you possibly get the report in by Tuesday (Wednesday would be the absolute latest!)?

    > The reading assignments consisted of three novels and one play (*Who's Afraid of Virginia Woolf?*).

Dashes

DASHES COME IN SEVERAL SIZES, so strictly speaking the term "dash" refers to more than one mark. There is the **en dash**, which is roughly the width of the capital letter *N* in whatever font is being used; the **em dash**, which is the width of the letter *M*; and the **2-em dash** and **3-em dash**, which are the widths of two and three side-by-side *M*'s, respectively. Not every font will follow these specifications literally. The important point is that an en dash is distinctively longer than a hyphen, an em dash is longer than an en dash, a 2-em dash is longer than an em dash, and a 3-em dash is the longest of all.

The em dash is by far the most commonly used of these marks and, except to sticklers such as copy editors and typesetters, is almost always what is meant by the unqualified term "dash." The en dash has its uses but comes up in only a few specialized circumstances, while 2- and 3-em dashes are downright esoteric.

En Dash (–)

THE EN DASH has two primary functions:

- Linking ranges
- Substituting for a hyphen in cases where a hyphen could be unclear

Some style guides specify other, very specialized roles for this punctuation mark; only the main ones are reviewed here.

LINKING RANGES

The main use of the en dash is to serve as a link for such things as ranges of dates, times, and page numbers.

2008–2010	10:30–10:45
pp. 112–116	Elizabeth I, 1533–1603
Chapters 1–8	encyclopedia volumes Q–SC

Also use this mark if giving the birth date of someone who is still alive.

Egbert Clodhopper, 1931–

LINKING WORDS

Normally, the hyphen is the punctuation mark used to link words together. However, as described elsewhere in this book, the hyphen has several roles: it may be used to link compound words (see page 25), to link a prefix or a suffix to a main word (see page 28), and to link words that make up a compound adjective (see page 140). A tricky situation can arise when two of these situations combine: that is, if you need to link two entities that themselves contain hyphens. For example:

> The anti-conscription-pro-conscription debate was turning into a shouting match.

In situations such as this, leave the hyphens that are linking the prefixes to the root words, but use the longer en dash instead of the hyphen to link the compounds to each other.

> The anti-conscription–pro-conscription debate was turning into a shouting match.

A similar problem exists with open compounds (compounds where each word stands alone), because it may look as if only the word closest to the hyphen is linked to what precedes or follows. For example, writing *the ex-prime minister* looks— just a little—like a reference to a minister who is no longer in his prime! Again, the solution is to use an en dash in place of the hyphen.

> the ex–prime minister
> a non–computer expert
> a credit card–sized calculator
> the New York–Tokyo flight

STYLE CONVENTIONS

- Word processing programs allow for the insertion of en dashes; however, if you can't create one, use a hyphen. (No one but a copy editor will actually notice.)

- Do not leave spaces around an en dash. Always have it lie directly against the adjoining text on both sides.

Em Dash (—)

THE EM DASH serves the following functions:

- Marking off an important point or a digression
- Marking a break in structure or turn in content
- Indicating interrupted or scattered speech

MARKING OFF AN IMPORTANT POINT OR A DIGRESSION

A pair of em dashes can be employed in two ways: it can act to draw particular attention to elements that you wish to emphasize, and it lets you veer off in a different direction temporarily and then get back on the original track.

In the first case, dashes may be used to set off such elements as identifying information, descriptions, examples, and lists. In this role, they function much as commas do (see the discussion on page 86). Consider using them instead of commas if you want to emphasize an element,

> Up till now—as far as I know—he's managed to stay out of trouble.

> The board members—with the conspicuous absence of the treasurer—met to discuss the missing funds.

> I may have lacked—I may still be lacking—the knowledge of when it's time to give up and move on.

> We both arrived at the same time, and—here's the interesting part—he said he'd finally heard back about that job application.

or if the element consists of a series of subelements that already contains commas, and surrounding it by more commas might make the punctuation difficult to follow.

> Several of the neighbors—the Walkers, Goldbergs, and Millhouses—started a petition to get rid of the Boylstons' rooster.

> The more subjective measures—the patients' energy levels, health outlooks, and emotional well-being—tended to correlate more highly with the charts than did the objective measures.

In another role, dashes act much like parentheses, enclosing a digression. The difference is that their effect is usually to emphasize the digressing text rather than subsume it. In general, text enclosed by dashes is more integral to the sentence than is text enclosed by parentheses. As with parentheses, the digressive text may or may not be grammatically congruent with the rest. (See Parentheses on page 154.)

> The school nurse had seen what Aunt Petunia's eyes—so sharp when it came to spotting fingerprints on her gleaming walls, and in observing the comings and goings of the neighbours—simply refused to see: that, far from needing extra nourishment, Dudley had reached roughly the size and weight of a young killer whale.
>
> —J.K. Rowling, *Harry Potter and the Goblet of Fire*

> [The hair] was grey at the root, the rest dyed a vivid metallic orange. Dirk pursed his lips and thought very deeply. He didn't need to think hard in order to realise who the hair belonged to—there was only one person who regularly entered the kitchen looking as if her head had been used for extracting metal oxides from industrial wastes—but he did have seriously to consider the implications of the discovery that she had been plastering her hair across the door of his fridge.
>
> It meant that the silently waged conflict between himself and his cleaning lady had escalated to a new and more frightening level. It was now, Dirk reckoned, fully three months since this fridge door had been opened, and each of them was grimly determined not to be the one to open it first. . . .
>
> —Douglas Adams, *The Long Dark Tea-Time of the Soul*

> . . . I am now living, for economy's sake, in a little town in Brittany, inhabited by a select circle of serious English friends, and possessed of the inestimable advantages of a Protestant clergyman and a cheap market.
>
> In this retirement—a Patmos amid the howling ocean of Popery that surrounds us—a letter from England has reached me at last. I find my insignificant existence suddenly remembered by Mr. Franklin Blake. My wealthy relative—would that I could

add my spiritually-wealthy relative!—writes, without even an attempt at disguising that he wants something of me. The whim has seized him to stir up the deplorable scandal of the Moonstone; and I am to help him by writing the account of what I myself witnessed while visiting at Aunt Verinder's house in London. Pecuniary remuneration is offered to me—with the want of feeling peculiar to the rich. . . . My nature is weak. It cost me a hard struggle, before Christian humility conquered sinful pride, and self-denial accepted the cheque.

—Wilkie Collins, *The Moonstone*

Note that the distinctions between using dashes, commas, or parentheses may not always be cut-and-dried, and you may sometimes want to play with the different marks to see which effect looks best.

MARKING A BREAK IN STRUCTURE OR TURN IN CONTENT

Unlike parentheses, which must always come in pairs, dashes come in singles as well. Use a single em dash if your text is going along in one direction, then suddenly veers off in another. That is, you can abruptly end a thought midstream, leave it hanging, and start another thought, all in the same sentence. There must be some logical connectedness between what precedes and follows the dash, but there does not have to be any grammatical connectedness.

This hobbit was a very well-to-do hobbit, and his name was Baggins. The Bagginses have lived in the neighbourhood of The Hill for time out of mind, and people considered them very respectable, not only because most of them were rich, but also because they never had any adventures or did anything unexpected: you could tell what a Baggins would say on any question without the bother of asking him. This is a story of how a Baggins had an adventure, and found himself doing and saying things altogether unexpected. He may have lost the neighbours' respect, but he gained—well, you will see whether he gained anything in the end.

The mother of our particular hobbit—what is a hobbit? I suppose hobbits need some description nowadays. . . .

—J.R.R. Tolkien, *The Hobbit*

"I do appreciate, Mrs Sauskind," continued Dirk, "that the cost of the investigation has strayed somewhat from the original estimate, but I am sure that you will in your turn appreciate that a job which takes seven years to do must clearly be more difficult than one that can be pulled off in an afternoon and must therefore be charged at a higher rate. I have continually to revise my estimate of how difficult the task is in the light of how difficult it has so far proved to be."

The babble from the phone became even more frantic.

"My dear Mrs Sauskind—or may I call you Joyce? Very well then. My dear Mrs Sauskind, let me say this. Do not worry yourself about this bill, do not let it alarm or discomfit you. Do not, I beg you, let it become a source of anxiety to you. Just grit your teeth and pay it."

—Douglas Adams, *Dirk Gently's Holistic Detective Agency*

It is also appropriate to use an em dash when text that appears to be heading for a predictable ending suddenly takes an unexpected turn or otherwise reaches a conclusion worthy of extra emphasis. In this case, all parts of the sentence mesh grammatically. The dash is here not acting to divide grammatically independent structures, but rather to draw special attention to what follows.

She planned the trip for months, got her hands on all the travel information she could find, booked the hotel—and then called the whole thing off.

The room was the picture of order, the mahogany furniture gleamed, not an ornament on the shelves was out of place nor a painting on the wall askew—the only note of discord was the corpse draped over the back of the chesterfield.

At least he hasn't alienated anyone—yet.

. . . In a trice, I remember'd my Poem, writ last Night upon the Tablecloth, and hastily flipp'd 'neath the Capon before the foul Debauch.

I clamber'd out of Bed to seek for it, walkt gently upon the Floor so as not to wake Tunewell again, flipp'd o'er the Tablecloth—and lo! found that my Words were smudged out of the Linen! Bits of Charcoal clung here and there where my Epick's grand Opening Lines had been!

—Erica Jong, *Fanny*

There is some overlap between this role of the dash and that of the colon, another punctuation mark that acts to draw attention to what follows it (see the discussion on page 113). However, a colon is usually most appropriate if the relationship between the opening and concluding parts of the sentence is straightforward, while a dash is appropriate if this relationship contains something unexpected. If either mark would meet your purpose, it is preferable to use the more low-keyed colon, as the dash is stronger and will lose its punch if overused. Reserve it for situations where you want its dramatic impact.

A caution: some people enthusiastically use the dash as their main punctuation mark, applying it wherever any sort of break in a sentence seems to be needed. Such sloppy usage may be acceptable in rough drafts and informal memos, but is completely unacceptable in serious writing.

INDICATING INTERRUPTED OR SCATTERED SPEECH

In dialogue, the em dash serves to indicate broken-off speech. One speaker can interrupt another:

"Listen, I'm serious," I said. "No kidding. Why's it better in the East?"

"It's too involved to go into, for God's sake," old Luce said. "They simply happen to regard sex as both a physical and a spiritual experience. If you think I'm—"

"So do I! So do I regard it as a wuddayacallit—a physical and spiritual experience and all. I really do. But it depends on who the hell I'm doing it with. If I'm doing it with someone I don't even—"

"Not so *loud*, for God's sake, Caulfield. If you can't manage to keep your voice down, let's drop the whole—"

"All right, but listen," I said. I was getting excited and I *was* talking a little too loud. Sometimes I talk a little loud when I get excited.

—J.D. Salinger, *The Catcher in the Rye*

A speaker can stop abruptly without being interrupted:

". . . I took a corkscrew from the shelf:
I went to wake them up myself.
And when I found the door was locked,
I pulled and pushed and kicked and knocked.
And when I found the door was shut,
I tried to turn the handle, but—"
There was a long pause.
"Is that all?" Alice timidly asked.
"That's all," said Humpty Dumpty. "Good-bye."

—Lewis Carroll, *Through the Looking-Glass*

A break can come in the middle of a word:

> "*Tabernac,*" growls Robinson, breaking a skate lace. "Eddy, Eddy, I need a lace!" he shouts.
> "Left or right?" a voice asks.
> "Ri—," he starts, then stops angrily.

—Ken Dryden, The Game

The dash also serves to indicate speech that is scattered or faltering: that is, not interrupted by a second speaker, but by the speaker breaking off a thought and starting another, or talking in disjointed sentence fragments.

> Supper was announced. The move began; and Miss Bates might be heard from that moment without interruption, till her being seated at table and taking up her spoon.
>
> "Jane, Jane, my dear Jane, where are you? Here is your tippet. Mrs. Weston begs you to put on your tippet. She says she is afraid there will be draughts in the passage, though everything has been done—one door nailed up—quantities of matting—my dear Jane, indeed you must. Mr. Churchill, oh! you are too obliging. How well you put it on—so gratified! . . . Well, this is brilliant! I am all amazement! could not have supposed anything—such elegance and profusion! I have seen nothing like it since—Well, where shall we sit? Where shall we sit? Anywhere, so that Jane is not in a draught. Where *I* sit is of no consequence. Oh—do you recommend this side? Well, I am sure, Mr. Churchill—only it seems too good—but just as you please. What you direct in this house cannot be wrong. Dear Jane, how shall we ever recollect half the dishes for grandmamma? Soup too! Bless me—I should not be helped so soon, but it smells most excellent, and I cannot help beginning."

—Jane Austen, Emma

Similarly, it can be used to convey the halting intonation of a speaker searching for the right words when something is not easy to say.

> He had been planning this speech since they left King's Cross. He had been quite unable to imagine how he would say it, or how she would respond.
>
> She said she was listening attentively. The little hand in his curled and crisped. He gripped it.
>
> "We are travelling together," he said. "We decided—you decided—to come. What I do not know is whether you would—whether you would choose—to lodge and manage yourself separately from me after this point—or whether—or whether—you would wish to travel as my wife. It is a late step—It is attended with all sorts of inconvenience, hazard and—embarrassment. I have rooms reserved in Scarborough where a wife could

well—find space. Or I could reserve other rooms—under some false name. Or you may not wish to take this step at all—you may wish to be lodged separately and respectably elsewhere. Forgive this baldness. I am truly trying to discover your wishes. We left in so exalted a state—I wish decisions could arise naturally—but you see how it is."

—A.S. Byatt, *Possession*

Compare the above uses of the dash with those of the ellipsis (page 192).

STYLE CONVENTIONS

- Word processing programs allow for the insertion of em dashes. If you cannot produce one, type two hyphens with no space between them (--).

- The usual convention today is to have the dash lie directly against the words it adjoins, but some style guides specify to leave a space on both sides. Be consistent; don't leave a space on one side of a dash but not on the other.

  Bobby Fischer died in 2008 at the age of 64—the number of squares on a chessboard.

  or: at the age of 64 — the number of squares . . .

  He suspected—no, he knew—that something was up.

  or: He suspected — no, he knew — that something was up.

- Whichever style you choose, do not put a space before a dash that is being used to interrupt dialogue in the middle of a word.

  "But I nev—" she started.

- When a dash is being used to indicate broken-off dialogue, follow it immediately with a closing quotation mark. Do not add a comma.

  "How was I supposed to—" she sputtered indignantly.

- Do not put any other punctuation immediately adjacent to a dash, with the exception of a question mark or exclamation point before a closing dash. Even if the text that is broken by dashes would otherwise take a comma or semicolon, do not include it.

  She shrugged her shoulders, and he went back to arguing with the brick wall.

  She shrugged her shoulders—it was all so futile—and he went back to arguing with the brick wall.

- Text that is enclosed within dashes may contain any punctuation mark other than a period. Parentheses should be avoided if possible, as the construction of an aside within an aside would be awkward.

- Do not employ both a single dash and a pair of dashes in the same sentence, as it would then be unclear which text is enclosed by the pair. The following sentence, for example, presents a challenge:

  > He had a determined goal—to bring together all the parties in the dispute—students, faculty members, and administrators—and get them talking.

2-Em (——) and 3-Em (———) Dashes

THESE PUNCTUATION MARKS do not come up frequently, but writers should at least have an awareness of them.

2-EM DASH

A 2-em dash is used to indicate missing letters within a word. In fiction, the device of dropping letters to conceal names or to sanitize profanities was once more commonly employed than it is today.

> "If J.E. who advertised in the ——shire Herald of last Thursday, possesses the acquirements mentioned; and if she is in a position to give satisfactory references as to character and competency; a situation can be offered her where there is but one pupil, a little girl, under ten years of age; and where the salary is thirty pounds per annum. J.E. is requested to send references, name, and address, and all particulars to the direction: 'Mrs Fairfax, Thornfield, near Millcote, ——shire.' "
>
> —Charlotte Brontë, *Jane Eyre*

> Matters were thus restored to a perfect calm, at which the serjeant, tho' it may seem so contrary to the principles of his profession, testified his approbation. "Why now, that's friendly," said he; "D——n me, I hate to see two people bear ill-will to one another, after they have had a tussel. The only way when friends quarrel, is to see it out fairly in a friendly manner, as a man may call it, either with fist, or sword, or pistol, according as they like, and then let it be all over: for my own part, d——n me if ever I love my friend better than when I am fighting with him. To bear malice is more like a Frenchman than an Englishman."
>
> —Henry Fielding, *Tom Jones*

Such uses now appear rather archaic. One does occasionally see 2-em dashes being used to tame certain words deemed unfit for family newspapers, if the reporter feels obliged to include them in a quote. Another use is in transcribed material, where it is not clear what word the original author intended.

3-EM DASH

A 3-em dash indicates an entire missing word. It too may be used to indicate a missing or unclear word in transcribed material. More commonly, it is used in bibliographies to indicate the repetition of a name, where one author (or the same set of co-authors) has successive works listed.

> Williams, T.R. The structure of the socialization process in Papago Indian society. Social Forces, 36 (1958): 251–256.
>
> ——. A Borneo childhood. New York: Holt, Rinehardt, & Winston, 1969.

STYLE CONVENTIONS

- With a 2-em dash, do not leave any space between it and the remaining letters of the word.

- With a 3-em dash, leave spaces before and after, just as you would with the word it is standing in for.

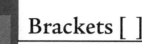

Brackets [ ]

THE TERM "BRACKETS" IS OFTEN USED informally to refer to parentheses but, aside from some minor overlaps, these punctuation marks have quite distinct uses. Brackets have two primary functions:

- Identifying changes to quoted material
- Enclosing digressions within parentheses

Note: This section deals specifically with square brackets [ ]. Other styles are curly brackets { } and angle brackets < >, which are usually reserved for specialized uses in technical and mathematical fields.

IDENTIFYING CHANGES TO QUOTED MATERIAL

Not every word in a piece of writing must be the author's own; it is valid to include properly attributed quotes. In such genres as reportage, obviously, quoting a speaker's words is often the main point. Writers must sometimes make a decision as to whether paraphrasing or direct quotation would be a better strategy, but that is outside the scope of what is covered here.

If you are going with direct quotation, whether from a written or an oral source, there is some room for editorial judgment. Simply changing any of the original wording without indicating that you have done so would make you guilty of misquoting, but it is legitimate to make minor changes *provided you clearly identify which words are your own*. If you simply drop part of a quote, the convention is to indicate the missing words by an ellipsis, discussed on page 191. If you add or alter words, the convention is to enclose them in square brackets.

There is no specific length limit on the text you put in brackets, but it should usually be quite brief: it is, after all, an interruption of someone else's words. If you want to make a lengthy clarification or editorial comment, it would be better to finish the quotation and then add your comments.

Note: Some writers use parentheses instead of brackets for this purpose, but that can be problematic as parentheses play other roles as well. That is, if the original material contained any parentheses of its own, readers might have a hard time distinguishing the original author's digressions from the quoter's insertions. Brackets, in contrast, are unambiguous.

Use brackets to clarify the original material

If a quoted passage is put down absolutely verbatim, sometimes there is something about it that might not be clear to readers. For example, it may include a pronoun— she, his, it, those—that was clear in context but not in the selected fragment being presented. If that's the case, it is best to replace the pronoun with the word or name that the original writer or speaker meant. The need for clarification is particularly likely when quoting from oral sources, as speakers tend to choose their words more casually than writers.

> *Original quotation:* "All my friends said I was a shoo-in for it, but I never even got a nomination," Ms Plotnick said mournfully.
>
> *Revised:* "All my friends said I was a shoo-in for [the Academy Award], but I never . . ."
>
> *or:* "All my friends said I was a shoo-in for it [the Academy Award], but I never . . ."

Note that your own text may either replace or be added to the original wording. (Do, of course, retain the original words if there is anything about them that is important.) If your words are replacing the original, they must mesh grammatically with the remainder of the sentence.

Use brackets to expand on the original material

You may feel that a quote will have more meaning for your readers if you add some relevant information, explanation, or clarification. In this situation, you would not drop or change any of the original wording.

> *Original quotation:* Her library includes all the works of Grass and Day-Lewis.
>
> *Revised:* Her library includes all the works of [German writer Günter] Grass and [British poet laureate Cecil] Day-Lewis.

Original quotation: Researchers believe that the reading of Kana and Kanji characters may tap into different brain processes.

Revised: Researchers believe that the reading of Kana [the Japanese phonetic script] and Kanji [the Japanese logographic script] characters may tap into different brain processes.

Note that the bracketed material may appear either before or after the text it is qualifying, as appropriate. Also, when the text within brackets is a comment or clarification, it does not have to mesh grammatically with the rest of the sentence; it is understood to be independent of it.

Use brackets to work quoted words into a new sentence

If you are working a fragment of a quote into a sentence of your own, you may need to alter it slightly so that it fits grammatically. Consider the following quotation from Fowler's *Modern English Usage:*

A waiter might as well serve one on a dirty plate as a journalist offer such untidy stuff as: *The University of London Press* hopes *to have ready the following additions to* their *series of* . . .

In your own text, this might be presented as:

Another authority, Fowler, admonishes journalists against "[offering] such untidy stuff as: *The University of London Press* hopes *to have ready the following additions to* their *series of* . . ."

Use brackets to shorten a quoted sentence

If you have dropped part of a quotation by using an ellipsis and are picking it up again in the middle of a sentence, you may prefer to present the partial sentence as if it were complete—that is, capitalize it. If you do this, enclose the opening capital letter in brackets to indicate that it did not appear this way in the original. To use another example from Fowler:

It need hardly be said that shortness is a merit in words. There are often reasons why shortness is not possible; much less often there are occasions when length, not short-ness, is desirable. But it is a general truth that the short words are not only handier to use, but more powerful in effect; extra syllables reduce, not increase, vigour.

You could present this quote as follows:

It need hardly be said that shortness is a merit in words. . . . [S]hort words are not only handier to use, but more powerful in effect; extra syllables reduce, not increase, vigour.

Use brackets to draw attention to something in the original material

You may wish to highlight something in a quote, either because you feel it holds particular significance or because it makes some point that you want to dissociate yourself from. One way to do this is to italicize the relevant text and then follow it with the words *italics mine, italics added,* or *emphasis added,* in brackets. For an illustration of this, see Underscoring a point in a quote on page 67.

Under some circumstances, it may suit your purposes better to follow the text with an explicit comment in brackets; obviously, however, this will be more intrusive. Other times, it will be best to simply present the entire quote in an uninterrupted way and have your comments follow.

Use [*sic*] when appropriate

If a quotation contains a misspelling, misused word, or factual error, you may want to make it clear to your readers that it's not *your* slip. The convention is to follow the offending text with the Latin word *sic*, which means "thus" or "so" (essentially, this is saying it appeared thus in the original—I didn't mis-transcribe it!). Traditionally, this word is italicized and enclosed in brackets, although it sometimes appears in regular type and/or in parentheses. It is always in lowercase.

> In his statement, the education minister said: "Grammar standards in our schools today is [*sic*] slipping sadly, and I intend to do something about this."

> An oil sketch by Group of Seven artist Lawren Harris titled *Mts: Emarald* [*sic*] *Lake* depicts a scene of snow-covered mountains above Emerald Lake in British Columbia.

> He won great acclaim in the Battle of Britain in 1941 [*sic*], and after the war went on to a distinguished political career.

The advantage of *sic* is that it provides a relatively unobtrusive way of pointing out errors. However, it must be used with discretion; applying it too enthusiastically can make you look overly earnest or even obnoxious. Don't stoop to adding it just to get in a little jab at an author's ignorance or to draw attention to errors that are irrelevant or trivial. If the error is a misspelling, it may be best to just quietly fix it, unless the blooper is somehow relevant. If the quote is from a country or an era with different rules of spelling or usage, it would be inappropriate to imply that incidences of these are errors.

ENCLOSING DIGRESSIONS WITHIN PARENTHESES

Digressions in text are typically enclosed in parentheses, but what do you do if you need to put a digression within a digression? Placing parentheses inside parentheses could be confusing, as the reader might mistake the closing parenthesis of the nested unit as indicating the close of the whole thing. The convention is to enclose the inner digression in square brackets, since brackets and parentheses are easily distinguished. Examples of this type of construction come up most often in academic or scientific writing. For an illustration, see the style conventions for parentheses on page 159.

Brackets within parentheses may look awkward, so avoid this construction unless absolutely necessary. If possible, try to either recast the sentence or see if commas could be used instead. See the discussion of parenthetical commas on page 86.

OTHER USES OF BRACKETS

Apart from their main functions, brackets have a few roles to play in certain types of specialized writing.

To enclose stage directions

In stage and film scripts, they may be used instead of parentheses to mark off text that is not part of the actors' lines.

To enclose citations

In scholarly writing, they are sometimes used instead of parentheses to mark off reference citations, which may be presented as either names or numerals. For example, the appearance of [1] following a quote or description means that this information is attributable to the first author listed in the reference section. Some style guides specify to cite the author's name and date of publication instead of a numeral: for example, [Leung, 2009].

To enclose a surmised word

If a word in a document is missing or illegible, the publisher or editor may surmise what it should be and fill it in, enclosed in square brackets to clarify that it was not in the original. Note that this situation is far likelier to arise with older, handwritten manuscripts than with modern writing.

By Mrs Hurst and Miss Bingley they were noticed only by a curtsey; and, on their being seated, a pause, awkward as such pauses must always be, succeeded for a few moments. It was first broken by Mrs Annesley, a genteel, agreeable-looking woman, whose [endeavour] to introduce some kind of discourse proved her to be more truly well-bred than either of the others; and between her and Mrs Gardiner, with occasional help from Elizabeth, the conversation was carried on.

—Jane Austen, *Pride and Prejudice*

To enclose grouped numbers

In mathematical equations, various styles of brackets are used to clarify which numbers are grouped with which. Note that here the placement of parentheses and brackets is reversed from what it is with text, with parentheses appearing within brackets.

a = [(b+1)/x] - [(2b/(x+3)]

STYLE CONVENTIONS

- Don't leave spaces around the text enclosed by brackets [like this]. Place the opening and closing marks directly next to the text [like this].

- Unlike parentheses, brackets may be immediately preceded by other punctuation, such as a comma. Simply treat the rest of the quotation as you would if it still contained the original words.

    Original quotation: Well, they may be in their infancy right now, but there's some very exciting work being done on them.

    Revised quotation: Well, [bibliographic visualization tools] may be in their infancy right now, but there's some very exciting work being done on them.

Quotation Marks (" ")

QUOTATION MARKS have several distinct functions:

- Setting off dialogue
- Setting off citations
- Setting off words that are meant in a special way
- Setting off titles

SETTING OFF DIALOGUE

This function is, of course, a very familiar one. In text that includes dialogue, quotation marks serve to set off speech from narrative and one speaker's words from another's. Quotation marks are required at the beginning and end of each speaker's lines.

If a single speaker's words run more than a paragraph, put opening quotation marks at the start of each paragraph but a closing mark only at the end of the last one, since the closing mark is the signal that the speech has ended.

> Frodo sat silent and motionless. Fear seemed to stretch out a vast hand, like a dark cloud rising in the East and looming up to engulf him. "This ring!" he stammered. "How, how on earth did it come to me?"
>
> "Ah!" said Gandalf. "That is a very long story. The beginnings lie back in the Black Years, which only the lore-masters now remember. If I were to tell you all that tale, we should still be sitting here when Spring had passed into Winter.
>
> "But last night I told you of Sauron the Great, the Dark Lord. The rumours that you heard are true: he has indeed arisen again and left his hold in Mirkwood and returned to his ancient fastness in the Dark Tower of Mordor. That name even you hobbits

have heard of, like a shadow on the borders of old stories. Always after a defeat and a respite, the Shadow takes another shape and grows again."

—J.R.R. Tolkien, *The Lord of the Rings*

For a single speaker, dialogue and nondialogue text may be interspersed in the same paragraph.

"Goddamn it, Boogie, I can't leave town during the Stanley Cup Finals." And, with a heavy heart, I went on to show him my two tickets in the reds for the next game in Montreal. *The game that was being played on my wedding night.* If the Canadiens won, it would mean our fourth straight Stanley Cup, and, just this once, I was hoping that they'd lose, so that I could postpone our honeymoon and take in what would surely be the final and winning game. "Do you think she'd mind," I asked, "if, after the dinner, I slipped out for an hour and maybe caught the third period in the Forum?"

"Brides tend to be touchy about things like that," he said.

"Yeah, I guess so. My luck, eh?"

—Mordecai Richler, *Barney's Version*

For multiple speakers, begin a new paragraph each time the speaker changes.

"I just shot my husband," wept Cynthia Freem as she stood over the body of the burly man in the snow.

"How did it happen?" asked Inspector Ford, getting right to the point.

"We were hunting. Quincy loved to hunt, as did I. We got separated momentarily. The bushes were overgrown. I guess I thought he was a woodchuck. I blasted away. It was too late. As I was removing his pelt, I realized we were married."

"Hmm," mused Inspector Ford, glancing at the footprints in the snow. "You must be a very good shot. You managed to plug him right between the eyebrows."

"Oh, no, it was lucky. I'm really quite an amateur at that sort of thing."

—Woody Allen, *Match Wits with Inspector Ford*

This convention may occasionally be broken if the spoken lines are brief and if the effect of the writing would be enhanced by breaking the paragraph only when the scene changes.

"We're going through!" The Commander's voice was like thin ice breaking. He wore his full-dress uniform, with the heavily braided white cap pulled down rakishly over one cold grey eye. "We can't make it, sir. It's spoiling for a hurricane, if you ask me." "I'm not asking you, Lieutenant Berg," said the Commander. "Throw on the power lights!

Rev her up to 8,500! We're going through!" The pounding of the cylinders increased: ta-pocketa-pocketa-pocketa-*pocketa-pocketa*. The Commander stared at the ice forming on the pilot window. He walked over and twisted a row of complicated dials. "Switch on No. 8 auxiliary!" he shouted. "Switch on No. 8 auxiliary!" repeated Lieutenant Berg. "Full strength in No. 3 turret!" shouted the Commander. "Full strength in No. 3 turret!" The crew, bending to their various tasks in the huge, hurtling eight-engined Navy hydroplane, looked at each other and grinned. "The Old Man'll get us through," they said to one another. "The Old Man ain't afraid of Hell!"

"Not so fast! You're driving too fast!" said Mrs. Mitty. "What are you driving so fast for?"

—James Thurber, *The Secret Life of Walter Mitty*

Quotation marks are not used to enclose words that a character is thinking silently rather than saying aloud. Be certain, of course, that you make the status of such words perfectly clear so that the reader does not confuse them with the rest of the narrative. Often, italics are used for this purpose; see description on page 62.

An occasional writer will use artistic license to omit quotation marks around spoken dialogue. The absence of these cues forces readers to focus a little harder to distinguish whether a line is dialogue, narrative, or a character's silent thought; an effort that some will find annoying and others intriguing. This device might sometimes come through as pretentious, but when done well, its spare quality can impart a sense of remoteness, understatement, almost surrealism.

Ruby said, I was watching you in there this morning with him and I've been thinking ever since.

— About him? Ada asked.

— You.

— What about me?

— I've been trying to know what you're thinking. But I can't come to it. So I'll just say out plain what's on my mind. It's that we can do without him. You might think we can't, but we can. We're just starting. I've got a vision in my mind of how that cove needs to be. And I know what needs doing to get there. The crops and animals. Land and buildings. It will take a long time. But I know how to get there. War or peace, there's not a thing we can't do ourselves. You don't need him.

Ada looked at the fire...

— You don't need him, Ruby said.

— I know I don't need him, Ada said. But I think I want him.

— Well that's a whole different thing.

—Charles Frazier, *Cold Mountain*

When quoted material lies within text that itself is enclosed by quotation marks, the inner quotation marks must be distinguished from the outer ones. If the outer marks are double, make the inner ones single, and vice versa. For more detail, see page 189.

> "This is the end of a perfect day, Jeeves. What's that thing of yours about larks?"
>
> "Sir?"
>
> "And, I rather think, snails."
>
> "Oh yes, sir. 'The year's at the spring, the day's at the morn, morning's at seven, the hillside's dew-pearled—' "
>
> "But the larks, Jeeves? The snails? I'm pretty sure larks and snails entered into it."
>
> "I am coming to the larks and snails, sir. 'The lark's on the wing, the snail's on the thorn—' "
>
> "Now you're talking. And the tab line?"
>
> " 'God's in His heaven, all's right with the world.' "
>
> "That's it in a nutshell. I couldn't have put it better myself."
>
> —P.G. Wodehouse, *The Code of the Woosters*

For the rare occasion on which text contains a quote within a quote *within* a quote, the marks reverse again: double to single to double (or vice versa).

> "You boys heard about the widow Schwartz?" Manzelman asked. "She called the *Tribune* to place a death announcement for her late husband. The fella on the *Tribune* tells her that they charge by the word. 'O.K.,' she says, 'make it "Schwartz dead." ' 'No, madam,' the fella from the *Tribune* says, 'there's a fifty-dollar minimum, and for that you get five words.' The widow thinks a minute, then she says, 'O.K., make it "Schwartz dead. Cadillac for sale." ' "
>
> —Joseph Epstein, *Felix Emeritus*

SETTING OFF CITATIONS

When you cite someone else's words verbatim, you must set them off in some way. This applies whether the original words were spoken or appeared in print.

Style guides differ on the precise conventions. In formal writing, citations that run more than a few lines are customarily set off not by quotation marks but by space: blank lines left above and below, sometimes distinctive line spacing, sometimes indented margins on one or both sides, and sometimes reduced type size. If you are writing to the specifications of a particular guide, follow its instructions. Style guides also differ as to whether the text introducing such a quotation should end in a period, a comma, a colon, or no punctuation at all. Sometimes, the context may dictate using one form or the other.

Quotation marks are used to set off shorter citations that lie within the regular text. They are required whether the quoted words constitute an entire statement or just a fragment.

> Humphries (1995) states that the five considerations for writing good academic prose are "fluency, clarity, accuracy, economy, and grace."

> The delegates agreed that proposals unveiled by the government are "incomplete and contain some irritants."

> He would only say that the report had been leaked to him by a "congressional source."

INDICATING SIGNIFICANCE

Quotation marks around a word or phrase serve to call extra attention to it. There are several reasons for enclosing text this way.

Coined or unusual words

If you are introducing a word, term, or phrase that is recently coined, or that most people would consider specialized or obscure, enclosing it in quotation marks sends a reassuring signal to your readers that they aren't expected to have prior acquaintance with it. Without this signal, readers might momentarily be nonplussed; some might even glance back a paragraph or two to see if they had missed something. Quotation marks make it immediately clear that a word is appropriate, if unusual. If an explanation of the term is required, it should, of course, immediately follow. Do not use quotation marks on subsequent appearances of the word.

> It was not until the advent of von Krankmann, one of Fruitlooper's more brilliant students, a tireless theoretician and jogger and, later, founder of the "neo-Fruitloopian school" of psychoanalysis, that interest in vegetarianism was renewed.
>
> —Glenn C. Ellenbogen, *Oral Sadism and the Vegetarian Personality*

> Some early writing systems used the "boustrophedon" style of alternating the direction of the lines.

Sometimes the absence of quotation marks can make a sentence outright difficult to follow, as the reader struggles to figure out what part of speech an unfamiliar term represents. For example:

> A transom is a horizontal crossbar in a window; over the transom is a publisher's term for unsolicited manuscripts.

> *Better:* A transom is a horizontal crossbar in a window; "over the transom" is a publisher's term for unsolicited manuscripts.

Quotation marks make it clear that these words make up a phrase.

> In a questionnaire, skip instructions tell the respondent to skip certain questions if they are not relevant.

> *Better:* In a questionnaire, "skip instructions" tell the respondent to skip certain questions if they are not relevant.

Quotation marks make it clear that *skip* is part of a compound noun, not a verb.

> Check any utilities issuing blocking ineligible warnings.

> *Better:* Check any utilities issuing "blocking ineligible" warnings.

Quotation marks make it clear—or at least clearer—that "blocking ineligible" is the type of warning that certain utilities are issuing.

With technical and academic terms, note that esotericism is a relative matter. Words that would be unusual to the layperson may be basic terminology to a specialist, so know your audience. It could verge on patronizing to set off a term your readership considers standard, as it would imply that you thought they wouldn't know it.

Quotation marks may also be appropriate for terms that you want to acknowledge as special or unusual in some way, even if they are familiar enough not to have to be defined. For example, they may serve to set off literary references.

> The language of "Newspeak" is alive and well today.

> On the surface all was friendliness, but the "green-eyed monster" was starting to raise its head.

Note however that it is often acceptable or even more appropriate to not include the marks.

Words used in a nonstandard way

If you are introducing a word or phrase that is not unusual in itself, but which you intend in some specific or nonstandard sense, enclose it in quotation marks to alert readers to this fact.

> As applied to technical communicators, the concept of "early involvement" does not mean being present as observers in the initial stages of product development, but having direct participation.

> The outcome was considered to be "poor" if the patient was unable to function for one or more days in the preceding month.

> Note that the national norms are not necessarily "normal" in the sense of being optimal for good health.

Other candidates for quotation marks are phrases or clichés used in a nonliteral manner:

> Physicians need a reliable mechanism that lets them "take the pulse" of their practices so that they can respond to issues of concern to their patients.

> Manuals dealing with the same product should all have the same "look and feel."

Some phrases benefit from being set off by quotation marks when they are functioning as adjectives, in order to stand out better:

> Her "so what" attitude was beginning to wear on the others.

> The "family values" crowd was gaining control of the agenda.

Words used ironically

Quotation marks around a term make it clear that your use of it is ironical or satirical.

> Four soldiers were killed by "friendly fire."

> The "collateral damage" extended to two schools and a medical clinic.

> She would be seen at nothing but the "best" dinner parties.

Note that quotation marks are only needed for this purpose if omitting them might make it look as if you personally endorsed some absurd term or concept. If the irony of a term is self-evident, leave it alone. For example, it would hardly enhance the following passage to have quotation marks around *honest tradesman*:

While Sydney Carton and the sheep of the prisons were in the adjoining dark room, speaking so low that not a sound was heard, Mr. Lorry looked at Jerry in considerable doubt and mistrust. That honest tradesman's manner of receiving the look did not inspire confidence; he changed the leg on which he rested, as often as if he had fifty of those limbs; he examined his finger-nails with a very questionable closeness of attention; and whenever Mr. Lorry's eye caught his, he was taken with that peculiar kind of short cough requiring the hollow of a hand before it, which is seldom, if ever, known to be an infirmity attendant on perfect openness of character.

—Charles Dickens, *A Tale of Two Cities*

SETTING OFF TITLES

Quotation marks are often used to set off references to short stories, poems, magazine or journal articles, book chapters, and songs.

He walked on, tunelessly whistling "Paperback Writer."
One of the assigned readings was Guy de Maupassant's "The Necklace."

They may also be used to set off the titles of books, newspapers, magazines, journals, plays, films, and radio and television programs, although for these more major works it is more conventional to use italics. Not all titles need be set off; for example, names of political parties, geographical locations, and institutions are not, and newspapers and journals often are not. In short, there are many variations and exceptions. If you are writing to the specifications of a style guide, check its rules.

STYLE CONVENTIONS

In addition to knowing when to apply quotation marks, writers need to be familiar with the mechanics of applying them correctly. Quotation marks vary in both appearance and position.

Shape and number

- The opening and closing quotation marks can both appear as straight lines (" "), or they can curve in opposite directions (" "). Ensure consistency: don't mix and match.

- Quotation marks come in both doubles (" ") and singles (' '). The American standard is to use double marks for all purposes, whether marking off dialogue, citations, terms with special meaning, etc. (The occasional style guide may instruct you to use double marks for some purposes and single marks for others, but most keep things simpler.)

If you have one quotation fall within another, make the inner marks single, to distinguish them.

> "Well?" said Miss Higgins. "Are we about to hear your 'the dog ate my hard drive' excuse again?"

If a double and a single mark abut, it is often preferable to separate them with a non-breaking space.

> The authors argue that alphabetic systems "may be the only systems of writing that take full advantage of the processing functions of the so-called 'language hemisphere' " (1982).

If you ever need to set off a quote within a quote within a quote, go from double to single to double. See example on page 184.

British style is traditionally—though not invariably—the reverse: that is, start with single marks, then use double marks for quotes within quotes (and single marks again for quotes within quotes within quotes). Canadians can go either way, but are likelier to start with double marks.

A caution about using single quotation marks: the closing one is indistinguishable from an apostrophe, so if used to enclose a phrase that includes an actual apostrophe, this could lead to momentary confusion. For example, putting the expression *'ladies' man'* within single quotation marks could make it look as though the word *ladies* is set off in quotes. If such a situation arises, it is probably better to recast the sentence.

Position

When text within quotations is immediately followed by some other punctuation, the placement of that other mark relative to the closing quotation mark depends on several factors.

- When the quote marks set off dialogue, the closing punctuation for the dialogue always goes inside the quotations.

> She declared, "I won't go."   [period]
>
> "I won't go," she declared.   [comma]
>
> "I won't go!" she declared.   [exclamation point]

"Will you go?" he asked.   [question mark]

"No, I always—" she began.   [dash]

- With text other than dialogue, the rules vary for the different punctuation marks.

  ○ For **commas** and **periods**, there are two styles: one American and one British. (Canadians may go either way.) In the United States, the convention is to place the comma or period *inside* the quotation marks; in Britain, it is more conventional to place them *outside*.

    US: A questionnaire may include options such as "Don't know," "No opinion," or "Undecided."

    UK: A questionnaire may include options such as "Don't know", "No opinion", or "Undecided".

  ○ **Semicolons** and **colons** always go outside the quotation.

    A questionnaire may include the option of "No opinion"; however, in some cases it may be preferable to force the respondent to make a choice.

    How should I handle things if too many respondents answer "No opinion": should I revise the question?

  ○ For **question marks** and **exclamation points**, the positioning depends on context. These marks go outside the quotation if they apply to the entire sentence, and inside if they apply to just the quoted part.

    Perhaps it would be better in this case to just "live and let live"?
    [entire sentence is a query]

    Small wonder audiences are calling her "the human pretzel"!
    [entire sentence is exclamatory]

    I really have problems with his attitude of "what's in it for me?"
    [only text within quotes is a query]

    Several of the members cried, "Hear, hear!"
    [only text within quotes is exclamatory]

In the last two examples, note that although these sentences would be pronounced as though they ended in a period, they do not take one, since a sentence never takes more than one terminal punctuation mark. The reader will understand that it is only the last segment, not the entire sentence, that is a query or an exclamation.

Ellipsis (…)

THE ELLIPSIS (from the Greek "to leave out" or "fall short"; plural *ellipses*) has three distinct functions:

- Indicating omissions in quoted material
- Indicating hesitation or trailing off in spoken words
- Imparting extra significance

INDICATING OMISSIONS

If you include a quotation from another author in your writing, you may abridge it, but presenting the abridged version as the original would constitute misquoting. If you drop anything, you must put an ellipsis in its place to let readers know that something is missing. (If you are altering or adding anything, use square brackets instead, as described on page 175.)

Ellipses are needed only when you drop something from *within* a quoted passage, or if you need to clarify that a quotation is beginning or ending in midsentence. They are not required if you are presenting selected excerpts or obvious sentence fragments.

There is no limit to how many words you may take out of a quotation, but be sure that the fragments you leave hold together grammatically. More importantly, **be certain that you are not distorting or misrepresenting the meaning of the original**. It is fine to drop words that are irrelevant for your purposes, but the message and the spirit of the source must be retained.

The following shows how an original passage may be abbreviated using ellipses.

Original quotation:

Dear Theo,

Toulouse-Lautrec is the saddest man in the world. He longs more than anything to be a great dentist, and he has real talent, but he's too short to reach his patients' mouths and too proud to stand on anything. Arms over his head, he gropes around their lips blindly, and yesterday, instead of putting caps on Mrs. Fitelson's teeth, he capped her chin. Meanwhile, my old friend Monet refuses to work on anything but very, very large mouths and Seurat, who is quite moody, has developed a method of cleaning one tooth at a time until he builds up what he calls "a full, fresh mouth." It has an architectural solidity to it, but is it dental work?

Vincent

—Woody Allen, *If the Impressionists Had Been Dentists*

Revised quotation:

Toulouse-Lautrec . . . longs more than anything to be a great dentist, and he has real talent, but he's too short to reach his patients' mouths and too proud to stand on anything. . . . he gropes around their lips blindly. . . . Meanwhile, . . . Monet refuses to work on anything but very, very large mouths and Seurat . . . has developed a method of cleaning one tooth at a time until he builds up what he calls "a full, fresh mouth." It has an architectural solidity to it, but is it dental work?

Ellipses can also be used to indicate the omissions in a one-sided dialogue, typically a phone conversation where only one character's words are provided.

I was going to ask to see the rubies when the phone rang, and Gatsby took up the receiver.

"Yes. . . . Well, I can't talk now. . . . I can't talk now, old sport. . . . I said a small town. . . . He must know what a small town is. . . . Well, he's of no use to us if Detroit is his idea of a small town. . . ."

He rang off.

—F. Scott Fitzgerald, *The Great Gatsby*

INDICATING HESITANT OR TRAILING SPEECH

In dialogue, ellipses can be used to indicate speech that pauses or trails off (in contrast to the dash, which is used to indicate speech that is abruptly broken off because of an interruption or sudden change of mind).

The effect of ellipses can be to make speech appear indecisive or nervous,

"Could we go there and take a look at it?"

Sherman's mouth had gone dry. He could feel his lips contracting.

"The car?"

"Yes."

"When?"

"Soon's we leave here's good a time as any, for us."

"You mean now? Well, I don't know . . ." Sherman felt as if the muscles of his lips were being constricted by a purse string.

"There's certain things that's consistent with an incident like this. If a car don't have those things, then we keep on going down the list. At this point we're looking for a car. We don't have a description of a driver. So—that okay with you?"

"Well . . . I don't know . . ." No! Let them look at it! There's nothing for them to find! Or is there?

—Tom Wolfe, *The Bonfire of the Vanities*

laid-back or musing,

They said when Healey arrived he had got the highest ever marks in a scholarship entrance. Once, in his first term, Cartwright had been bold enough to ask him why he was so clever, what exercises he did to keep his brain fit. Healey had laughed.

"It's memory, Cartwright, old dear. Memory, the mother of the Muses . . . at least that's what thingummy said."

"Who?"

"You know, what's his name, Greek poet chap. Wrote the Theogony . . . what *was* he called? Begins with an 'H'."

"Homer?"

"No, dear. Not Homer, the other one. No, it's gone. Anyway. Memory, that's the key."

—Stephen Fry, *The Liar*

or mysterious or dreamy.

"Little man," I said, "I want to hear you laugh again."

But he said to me:

"Tonight it will be a year . . . My star, then, can be found right above the place where I came to the Earth, a year ago . . ."

"Little man," I said, "tell me that it is only a bad dream—this affair of the snake, and the meeting-place, and the star . . ."

But he did not answer my plea. He said to me, instead:

"The thing that is important is the thing that is not seen . . ."

"Yes, I know . . ."

—Antoine de Saint-Exupéry, *The Little Prince*
(translated by Katherine Woods)

Ellipses can also be used to indicate multiple speakers completing a single sentence. (Em dashes could serve this purpose as well, but would convey an impression of a series of forcible interruptions rather than of one speaker pausing to let the next one begin.)

> Ten minutes. I strap on my right pad. Preoccupied with time and equipment and not yet the game, the room is quieter, if no more serious. Too quiet. Uneasy, thinking of Cournoyer, the team's captain, at home, his distinguished career probably over, Lapointe says, "Hey, let's win this one for Yvan," and instantly the room picks up. "Poor little guy," he continues, "his back all busted up, probably just lyin' at home . . ." and as he pauses as if to let his words sink in, Shutt and Houle jump in before anyone else can.
>
> ". . . havin' a little wine. . ."
>
> ". . . a little Caesar salad . . ."
>
> ". . . poor little bastard," Lapointe muses sadly, and we all laugh.
>
> —Ken Dryden, *The Game*

IMPARTING SIGNIFICANCE

Ending a sentence in an ellipsis rather than a period adds a certain ineffable weight. The effect can be to underscore a point that need not be stated explicitly,

> "I don't care what you do with your whiskers; I don't care what *anybody* does with his whiskers," said the King, still soothing his own tenderly; "I want the King of Euralia's blood." He looked round the Court. "To anyone who will bring me the head of the King, I will give the hand of my daughter in marriage."
>
> There was a profound silence . . .
>
> "Which daughter?" said a cautious voice at last.
>
> "The eldest," said the King.
>
> There was another profound silence . . .
>
> —A.A. Milne, *Once on a Time*

to impart a haunting, surreal or dreamy aspect,

> The sea is high again today, with a thrilling flush of wind. In the midst of winter you can feel the inventions of spring. A sky of hot nude pearl until midday, crickets in sheltered places, and now the wind unpacking the great planes, ransacking the great planes . . .
>
> I have escaped to this island with a few books and the child—Melissa's child. I do not know why I use the word "escape." The villagers say jokingly that only a sick man would choose such a remote place to rebuild. Well, then, I have come here to heal myself, if you like to put it that way . . .
>
> —Lawrence Durrell, *The Alexandria Quartet*

or to create a sense of suspense.

> It was a fine night and he walked home to Bertram's Hotel after first getting into a bus which took him in the opposite direction. It was midnight when he got in and Bertram's Hotel at midnight usually preserved a decorous appearance of everyone having gone to bed. The lift was on a higher floor so the Canon walked up the stairs. He came to his room, inserted the key in the lock, threw the door open and entered!
> *Good gracious, was he seeing things?* But who—how—he saw the upraised arm too late . . . Stars exploded in a kind of Guy Fawkes' display within his head . . .

—Agatha Christie, At Bertram's Hotel

STYLE CONVENTIONS

- Leave spaces between the points that make up an ellipsis. That is, type it as (. . .), not as (...).

- An ellipsis always consists of three points, although it sometimes appears to have four. Use three points in the following situations:

  - In quotations, if you are omitting text in the middle of a sentence or at the beginning of the first sentence.

  - In dialogue, to indicate a pause in the middle of a sentence or when a sentence trails off unfinished.

- A four-point ellipsis is actually a three-point ellipsis plus a period. (The marks, of course, are indistinguishable.) Use four points in the following situations:

  - In quotations, if you are omitting either the last part of a sentence, the beginning of a sentence other than the opening one (here, the first point is the period of the previous sentence), or an entire sentence or more. If the sentence whose last part is being omitted (or the sentence that precedes the one whose first part is being omitted) ends in a question mark or an exclamation point rather than a period, then instead of four points, use that mark plus three points.

  - In a one-sided telephone conversation (here, the first point is the period ending the speaker's words).

  - In dialogue, to indicate a pause that follows a complete sentence (here, the first point is the period ending that sentence). When using an ellipsis at the end of a sentence to impart significance or suspense, some writers put down three points and some four.

- With three points, leave a space on either side of the ellipsis. With four points, place the first one immediately next to the text that precedes it, to show that it is a period.

- In quotations, if you drop the first part of a sentence, you may either capitalize the word that now begins that sentence or keep it lowercase (which is truer to the original). A third option is to capitalize it and enclose the first letter in square brackets to indicate your change. For an illustration of this, see Use brackets to shorten a quoted sentence on page 177.

- In quotations, you may choose to either drop or retain any punctuation that immediately precedes an ellipsis, depending on whether or not it helps readability. You may, for example, find it desirable to keep a semicolon or colon that comes before the text you dropped. Put a space between that punctuation mark and the ellipsis.

Apostrophe (')

THE APOSTROPHE OFTEN is'nt used correctly: peoples' misunderstandings about it's function range from omitting it when its required, to putting it in the wrong place, to adding bevy's of apostrophe's where they dont' belong. Not too many sentences contain as many apostrophe errors as the above (seven), but misuses show up remarkably often. The confusion over this much-abused mark probably arises out of the fact that it has three completely independent uses, each of which applies under some circumstances but not others. These functions are the following:

- Indicating omissions in contracted words
- Indicating possessives
- Indicating plurals

INDICATING OMISSIONS

The apostrophe is used as a stand-in for missing letters in a contraction, signaling that something has been taken out. Contractions may be applied to two words that are combined into one, to single words, or to numerical dates.

Two-word contractions

When two words are run together and one or more letters get dropped in the process, the apostrophe takes the place of the missing letters.

She couldn't make it.	[could not]
You're looking great.	[you are]
We've no time to lose.	[we have]

They'd rather not do it.	[they would]
They'd finished the job.	[they had]
Let's go.	[let us]
Who's on first?	[who is]
Who's got the time?	[who has]
'Tis a pity.	[it is]
It's a pity.	[it is]
It's already been done.	[it has]

These types of contractions are not appropriate for all genres of writing; for example, they are often viewed as too informal for academic journals (which isn't to say they may never be used there, just that they must be used with discretion). On the other hand, they are fine for informal writing and virtually mandatory for dialogue, as speech would sound ridiculously stilted and unnatural without them. In fact, in dialogue you can even get away with double contractions such as "You shouldn't've said that" or "I'd've known him anywhere."

Different words may sometimes form the same contraction. This doesn't usually create a problem, since the context should make your intentions clear, but occasionally you might need to spell things out to avoid ambiguity. For example, *I'd let* could mean either "I would let" or "I had let."

Single-word contractions

Single words are sometimes shortened to make them less formal. Letters may be dropped anywhere in a word: from the beginning, the end, the middle, or both ends.

For some such contractions, an apostrophe is mandatory. Since the contraction is not a "real" word, the apostrophe is needed as a signal that something is intentionally missing. If you omitted it, it might look as though you were simply ignorant of how the word should properly appear.

So, how's life in the 'burbs?

How are you doin'?

Please hurry, 'cause we're late.

C'mon, I want to get out of here.

In other cases, the contraction may be considered a legitimate variant, so the apostrophe is optional. That is, it's not incorrect to include it, but the shortened form of the word may stand alone as well.

'Copter Pilot Safe After Crash   [could be *copter*]

If I had my 'druthers, we'd be elsewhere.   [could be *druthers*]

We've been working 'round the clock.   [could be *round*]

In other cases (usually involving phrases), the contracted form has become the standard spelling, and is what appears in the dictionary entry.

Their son turned out to be a ne'er-do-well.

His girlfriend sings in a rock 'n' roll band.

She's always pursuing will-o'-the-wisp dreams.

A caution: in the case of contractions where the apostrophe is placed at the start of the word, it is a common error to use an opening quotation mark (') in place of ('), such as *rock 'n' roll, 'round the clock,* and *if you can't beat 'em, join 'em.* The contracted words must appear as *'n', 'round,* and *'em.*

In yet other cases, the shortened form has come to replace the original word, or has at least become the more common version. Here, including the apostrophe would look pedantic or old-fashioned rather than correct. After all, language continuously evolves, and today's slang may be tomorrow's standard usage. Few modern writers would think to put apostrophes in *bus* (from *omnibus*), *flu* (from *influenza*), or *cello* (from *violoncello*).

It may be debatable as to whether a given contraction has become "standard" enough to lose its apostrophe, so judgment is needed in some cases. Go by your own comfort level and the tone of your writing. More formal, keep the apostrophe; less formal, drop the apostrophe.

Date contractions

If the century of a date is obvious, it is often permissible to drop the first two digits. (This may not be allowed in more formal styles of writing.) In such a case, some writers will replace the missing century with an apostrophe.

She graduated in '06.

Remember the summer of '68?

He was born in the '30s.

If there could be any question as to what the missing numbers are, do not omit them. Most dates will of course refer to the current or the immediate past century, so dropping the first two digits shouldn't leave any ambiguity; similarly, if your text is dealing exclusively with some other era, the context should make any abbreviated dates there sufficiently clear. (Everyone knows in which century Clementine's father, the forty-niner, was around.) Just be certain there's no possible doubt.

If a shortened date contains an apostrophe for some other purpose, it is better to not use an apostrophe to indicate the contraction, as it would look awkward to have more than one.

> The 80's excesses gave way to the frugality of the 90s.

INDICATING POSSESSIVES

This section first presents the basic rules about possessives and then details the exceptions and problem areas. There are admittedly quite a few aspects to this topic, but fortunately the basic rules cover the vast majority of situations.

For singular nouns, add an apostrophe plus *s*

> the planet's orbit
> that student's schedule
> Mr. Smith's apartment

For plural nouns that end in *s*, add just an apostrophe

> the planets' orbits
> those students' schedules
> the Smiths' apartment

For plural nouns that don't end in *s*, add an apostrophe plus *s*

> children's books   [not *childrens'*]
> men's shoes   [not *mens'*]
> the people's choice   [not *peoples'*]
> the alumni's lounge   [not *alumnis'*]

Note that this rule means that words where the plural is the same as the singular will have the same possessive form in both cases: For example, *the sheep's wool* could refer to the wool of one sheep or of multiple sheep. If you are ever faced with this sort of construction, ensure that the context makes your meaning unambiguous.

For personal pronouns, add just *s*, no apostrophe

This one is yours.	[not *your's*]
That one is hers.	[not *her's*]
The house on the left is ours.	[not *our's*]
I'll do my share if they do theirs.	[not *their's*]
Put everything in its place.	[not *it's*]

A particularly common error is confusion of the possessive *its* with the contraction *it's*, which means either "it is" or "it has." (Consider the difference in meaning between *A wise dog knows its master* and *A wise dog knows it's master*!) Those who insist that the possessive *its* take an apostrophe because a possessive "always" takes one should take note of the fact that *yours, hers, ours,* and *theirs* do not take one either. For more on this, see the discussion on page 273.

Other possessive pronouns do take an apostrophe:

It is everybody's responsibility to help clean up.

No one is admitting ownership, but this has to be *somebody's*.

After giving one's best years to the company, isn't it reasonable to expect something more?

For joint possession, make only the last noun possessive; for separate possession, make each noun possessive

my mother and father's house	[not *my mother's and father's*]
Neil and Nancy's sons	[not *Neil's and Nancy's*]
Robert and Martha's partnership	[not *Robert's and Martha's*]
New York's and Washington's subway systems	[not *New York and Washington's*]
my brother's and sister's weddings	[not my *brother and sister's*]
the Browns and the Murphys' vacation plans	[if these families travel together]
the Browns' and the Murphys' vacation plans	[if these families have separate plans]

Even armed with the above rules, writers often feel they are on shaky ground in certain circumstances. In some cases there are genuine exceptions to the rules; in others, writers mistakenly think that something is an exception, and so fail to follow a rule when it should apply. These problem areas are described below.

Sibilants

Writers are often unsure how to deal with the possessives of nouns ending in *s* or another sibilant sound (*ce, x, z*), or in a silent *s*. The answer is, in most cases treat such words exactly as you would any other. Thus, to form the possessive of the singular, add apostrophe plus *s*; to form the possessive of the plural, add *es* to the singular to make it a plural, and then add an apostrophe.

Ms. Jones's property	the Joneses' property
Mr. Harris's store	the Harrises' store
the actress's contract	the actresses' contracts
the box's contents	the boxes' contents
the quiz's answers	the quizzes' answers

However, if it would sound awkward to have two *s*'s next to each other (one belonging to the word itself and another added to make the word possessive), you may consider dropping the second one. A sensible way of deciding which way to go is to say the word aloud, spontaneously. If it feels natural to pronounce the second *s*, include it; otherwise, drop it. Many authorities would consider either of the following acceptable:

Dickens's novels	Dickens' novels
Jeff Bridges's films	Jeff Bridges' films
Mr. Williams's dog	Mr. Williams' dog
the Riverses' car	the Rivers' car

If you're not sure which way to go, it's usually best to include the extra *s*, since technically it is correct. There is really no excuse for creating constructions such as *Charles' wife* or *the Ferris' house*.

In a few cases (very few, mind you), convention dictates that the possessive *s* must be dropped.

Achilles' heel
Euripides' plays

Graves' disease
Brahms' lullaby
Mr. Rogers' Neighborhood®
for goodness' sake
for appearance' sake

Some such phrases have their own dictionary listing, so often you can turn to the dictionary to confirm if a possessive *s* is needed.

Compound nouns

With compound nouns, whether closed, open, or hyphenated, put the possessive apostrophe at the end of the compound rather than on the principal word. The possessive appears the same way for the singular and the plural.

a passerby's umbrella	the passersby's umbrellas
her brother-in-law's business	her brothers-in-law's business
the postmaster general's duties	the postmasters general's duties

These constructions are undeniably awkward for plural possessives. It may be preferable to recast them as, for example, *the duties of the postmasters general.*

Words with *y* singulars

There is frequent confusion over words whose singular ends in *y* and plural ends in *ies*. Yet such words simply follow the standard rules: apostrophe plus *s* for the singular possessive; apostrophe alone for the plural possessive.

the baby's crib	the babies' cribs
the lady's purse	the ladies' purses
the daisy's petals	the daisies' petals

Inanimate possession

Some authorities hold that it is not good idiom to create possessives for inanimate things, since they are not capable of ownership. For instance, with reference to some earlier examples, rather than *the quiz's answers* and *the 80's excesses*, one should write *the answers to the quiz* and *the excesses of the 80s.* Other authorities argue that this restriction can lead to unnecessarily stilted constructions and should be disregarded.

The possessive form is used in references to time and to money: *a week's vacation, a minute's reflection, a year's worth of trouble, my two cents' worth, ten dollars' worth of candy.*

INDICATING PLURALS

It's far more often the case that apostrophes are mistakenly added to plural words than they are mistakenly omitted. The only time such an apostrophe is appropriate is when a word might be hard to interpret without it.

Pluralizing numerals or letters

Most authorities agree that the plural of a numeral or a single letter should take an apostrophe if it is likely to be misread without one.

One such scenario is when the combination of the letter or numeral and the pluralizing *s* may coincidentally look like another word.

> The binary system uses 0's and 1's.   [otherwise could look like "Os" and "Is"]
>
> The game tonight is against the Oakland A's.   [otherwise could look like "As"]
>
> To put the program in "Insert" mode, type two i's.   [otherwise could look like "is"]

Another scenario is when the pluralizing *s* could not otherwise be distinguished from the root word because they are both of the same case. For example, say you are writing a technical manual and need a heading for a section that describes how to create an entity referred to by its abbreviation of DBC. The title of this section, then, is *Creating DBCs*. With a lowercase *s*, this works fine without an apostrophe. If, however, your style requires that headings be set in uppercase, the title becomes *CREATING DBCS*—and it now looks as though the *S* is part of the term itself. Writing it as *CREATING DBC'S* would avoid this problem.

In cases of numbers and letters where no ambiguity is likely, some authorities say to include an apostrophe; others say not to. The trend today is toward the latter, but this is certainly not universal. Whichever approach you take, be consistent.

> His best work was done in the 1990s.   [or 1990's]
>
> The airline will be purchasing four more 787s.   [or 787's]
>
> She belongs to two YWCAs.   [or YWCA's]
>
> The hospital is anticipating a shortage of RNs.   [or RN's]

Pluralizing non-noun words

When a word that is not a noun is used as one, and appears in plural form, an apostrophe often helps make it clearer just how that word is intended. Without the apostrophe, readers might have to pause or backtrack to pick up on the meaning.

Copy editors must know their *which's* from their *that's*.

I'm not taking any more "sorry's."

Her speech was riddled with "you know's" and "um's."

The response from the class was a chorus of no's.

Using apostrophes in this case can be a matter of judgment. Some writers would exclude them in such familiar expressions as "no ifs, ands, or buts"; others would include them. Make your decisions about such plurals on a case-by-case basis.

When not to use a pluralizing apostrophe

It is a common error to include apostrophes when pluralizing words that end in a vowel, words that end in *y*, and names. Consider the following:

Apostrophe's can be tricky.

The quota's will be set next month.

The tomato's are three for a dollar.

All the puppy's were barking at once.

Jamaican patty's sold here.

Both their sons are jockey's.

The Smith's were invited to dinner.

The Schultz's can't make it.

Be sure to send a card to the Jenkins'.

In the first set, the nouns should appear simply as *apostrophes*, *quotas*, and *tomatoes* (note the added *e*). Just because a word ends in a vowel doesn't mean it should be treated any differently from one that ends in a consonant. For nouns whose singular ends in *y*, the majority form the plural as *ies*: thus, *puppies* and *patties*. Those that end in *ey*, such as *jockeys*, stay the same and add an *s*. In neither case is an apostrophe needed. And treat names exactly as you would any other noun: thus, the *Smiths*, *Schultzes*, and *Jenkinses* (note the *es* ending for names ending in sibilants).

For more, see Plural Formations on page 40.

Part 3

Structure and Syntax

> [Laura] felt quite at home with Mr. Williams while she diagrammed sentences on her slate and rapidly parsed them.
>
> *Scaling yonder peak, I saw an eagle*
> *Wheeling near its brow.*
>
> " 'I' is the personal pronoun, first person singular, here used as the subject of the verb 'saw', past tense of the transitive verb 'to see'. 'Saw' takes as its object the common generic noun, 'eagle,' modified by the singular article 'an.'
>
> " 'Scaling yonder peak' is a participial phrase, adjunct of the pronoun 'I,' hence adjectival. 'Wheeling' is the present participle of the intransitive verb, 'to wheel,' here used as adjunct to the noun, 'eagle,' hence adjectival. 'Near its brow' is a prepositional phrase, adjunct of the present participle of the verb 'to wheel,' hence adverbial."
>
> After only a few such sentences, Mr. Williams was satisfied.
>
> —Laura Ingalls Wilder, *Little Town on the Prairie*

While all parts of this book are concerned with aspects of grammar, the topics addressed in this chapter are ones that are often viewed as its essence: structure and syntax, meaning the forms that words can take and the ways in which the elements of a sentence can be put together. The very word "grammar" makes some people quail, evoking an image of unfathomable, rigid, and often arbitrary rules buttressed by a mountain of terrifying terminology. In fact, for the most part grammar consists of sensible conventions designed to support unambiguous and meaningful expression, and it's often the case that if a rule isn't followed, some uncertainty or misinterpretation could result.

Achieving clear expression shouldn't be a writer's only motivation for observing the rules. Unconventional grammar may be seen as an indication of carelessness or ignorance, with the result that readers may take the content itself less seriously. Thus, even though some conventions may be based more on tradition than on logic, the mere fact of their existence means that it is important to abide by them.

Since many aspects of structure and syntax are intuitively understood, the focus here is on just a few topics that present frequent stumbling blocks. They are **agreement between subject and verb** (ensuring that these words match each other in form), **parallel structure** (ensuring grammatical equivalence between elements that play similar roles), **positioning of modifiers** (ensuring that a description acts on the right target), **tense** and **mood** (using the verb form that indicates the time of an action and its reality), **pronouns** (using the right word to represent a noun), and **active and passive voice** (putting the focus on either the performer or the recipient of an action). A final section addresses a few miscellaneous grammar topics, including some supposed rules that may in fact often be safely disregarded.

Agreement Between Subject and Verb

THIS CHEESE SMELLS MOLDY / These cheeses smell moldy. He isn't in a rush / They aren't in a rush. My class has already started / My classes have already started. English speakers instinctively realize that when a noun or pronoun is singular, the verb that applies to it takes a singular form, and when the noun or pronoun is plural, the verb takes a plural form. This is known as **agreement between subject and verb**.

When sentences are straightforward, errors in agreement are rare. Few would say *These cheeses smells moldy, He aren't in a rush,* or *My classes has already started.* When the structure becomes more complex, however, mistakes become more likely. The causes fall into two general categories: uncertainty as to which words in a sentence represent the subject, and so matching the verb to the wrong noun; and uncertainty as to whether a given subject is in fact singular or plural.

Difficulties in the first category, discussed under the heading The Subject, the Whole Subject, and Nothing But the Subject on page 209, may arise when sentences contain any of the following:

- Compound subjects
- Distracting parenthetical, modifying, or predicate nouns
- Inverted subject-verb order

Difficulties in the second category, discussed under the heading Forest or Trees? on page 215, may arise when sentences contain any of the following:

- Collective nouns
- Terms of quantity
- Indefinite pronouns
- Numerical phrases
- Nonstandard plurals or singulars

THE SUBJECT, THE WHOLE SUBJECT, AND NOTHING BUT THE SUBJECT

The **subject** of a sentence can be any sort of entity: a person, a place, an object either concrete or abstract—in short, a noun. It can also be a pronoun that refers to an entity identified elsewhere, or a verb form (a gerund or an infinitive) functioning as a noun. The subject is the focus of the sentence; the actor or the center of interest. It either does something, has something done to it, or is described in some way. Thus, it is always tied to an accompanying verb. For more, see Basic Sentence Structure on page 72.

This section describes scenarios where writers may fail to recognize precisely which words in a sentence represent the subject, and consequently use a plural verb where a singular should go or vice versa. In the illustrative sentences that follow, the subjects are shown in **bold** and the verbs with an <u>underline</u>.

Compound subject linked by *and*

A sentence may contain a **compound subject**: two or more nouns, pronouns, gerunds, or infinitives that share the same verb and are linked by the conjunction *and*. With a few exceptions, the verb for a compound subject is plural. This applies whether each part of the compound is itself singular or plural.

Your **enthusiasm** and **participation** <u>are</u> much appreciated.	[both parts singular]
The **books** and **papers** <u>go</u> in the study.	[both parts plural]
Frank's **résumé** and **writing samples** <u>are</u> ready to be sent, now that the **typos** and **grammatical mistake** <u>have</u> been fixed.	[one part singular, one part plural, either order]

When the element closest to the verb is singular, writers sometimes mistakenly make the verb agree with just that part. The following examples are *in*correct:

Her **understanding** and **attention span** <u>has</u> improved greatly.	[should be *have*]
Whether a relationship between these events actually exists and if so **whether it is causal** <u>remains</u> to be shown.	[should be *remain*]

It is particularly easy to miss the fact that there is more than one subject if the elements are long, complex, or abstract.

Exceptions:

- If two elements make up a single entity, they take a singular verb:

    Gin and tonic <u>was</u> his preferred drink.

    Drinking and driving <u>is</u> a crime.

Gin and *tonic* combine to form one beverage; *drinking* and *driving* are not crimes in isolation, only in combination.

Sometimes the status may be a matter of interpretation:

    Plucking and **cleaning** a chicken <u>was</u> an unpleasant task for many of our grandmothers.

    Calculating and **plotting** the points on the graph <u>is</u> the most time-consuming part of the exercise.

Closely related actions may be considered to function as a single activity. It would be grammatical to use plural verbs and change the descriptions above to *tasks* and *parts*, but doing so would slightly alter the implied relationships.

- If a subject is preceded by *each* or *every*, the verb associated with the subject is always singular, even if the subject would otherwise be treated as a plural. Thus, while a sentence such as "The **invoice** and **purchase order** have to be approved by the manager" takes a plural verb, all the following sentences take a singular one:

    Each invoice and purchase order <u>has</u> to be approved.

    Every invoice and purchase order <u>has</u> to be approved.

    Each of the invoices and purchase orders <u>has</u> to be approved.

    Every one of the invoices and purchase orders <u>has</u> to be approved.

    Each and every invoice and purchase order <u>has</u> to be approved.

If *each* comes after a compound subject rather than before it, the verb is plural. (No one ever said English was logical.)

    The **invoices** and **purchase orders** each <u>have</u> to be approved.

Compound subject linked by *or*

When two subjects that share a verb are linked by the conjunction *or*, *nor*, or *but*, the verb agrees with whichever part is closest to it.

Either the **bookcases** or the **filing**   [both parts plural, so verb is plural]
cabinets <u>need</u> to go somewhere else.

Either the **bookcase** or the **filing**   [both parts singular, so verb is singular]
cabinet <u>needs</u> to. . . .

Either the bookcase or the **filing**   [noun closest to the verb is plural, so verb
cabinets <u>need</u> to. . . .   is plural]

Either the bookcases or the **filing**   [noun closest to the verb is singular, so
cabinet <u>needs</u> to. . . .   verb is singular]

Similarly,

One or the other of you <u>has</u> to compromise.

Not only the students but also the teacher <u>has</u> signed the petition.

Whether the workers or the supervisor <u>was</u> responsible was a matter of debate.

Whether the tablecloth or the placemats <u>go</u> on the table is up to you.

Note that constructions that include a plural subject but use a singular verb may sound awkward. If possible, consider switching the components around (*Not only the teacher but also the students have signed the petition*); if not, it may be best to recast the sentence entirely.

Distracting parenthetical nouns

When a subject is followed by a mention of another entity, there is a risk of mistaking this other entity for the second part of a compound subject. Consider the following:

Both the **principal** and the **vice principal** <u>are</u> away at a conference.

The **principal**, as well as the vice principal, <u>is</u> away at a conference.

The first sentence contains a compound subject, *the principal and the vice principal*, and hence takes a plural verb. The second one contains a singular subject, *The principal*, followed by a parenthetical element (see page 86) that names the vice principal but is not part of the subject. Thus, *The principal, as well as the vice principal, <u>are</u> away at a conference* would be incorrect. If a parenthetical phrase is removed, the sentence should still read grammatically. It is obvious that you would not say *The principal are away at a conference*.

Similarly,

His chronic **tardiness**, as well as his negative attitude, <u>disrupts</u> the class.

The **professor**, accompanied by some graduate students, <u>was</u> just entering the building.

A **parcel**, along with a multitude of letters, <u>was</u> delivered the next day.

Anxiety about her health, in addition to her financial woes, <u>has</u> led her to seek counseling.

His **perseverance**, no less than his pleasant manner, <u>makes</u> him a credible candidate for the job.

The entire **room**, except for the two side doors, <u>is</u> to be painted.

Of course, if the subject preceding the parenthetical phrase is plural, the verb will be plural (*The guidance counselors, as well as the secretaries, are away at a conference*).

Note that the parenthetical elements in the above examples are enclosed in commas. While technically these are required, they may sometimes be dropped for reasons of style. If you omit them, this does not affect the rule described above: you would still disregard the parenthetical text as far as the verb is concerned.

The **library** as well as the chapel <u>stands</u> on a rolling green hill.

The new **workload** on top of my other duties <u>is</u> unreasonable.

A final word on this type of construction: it is correct but may sometimes look awkward. If there is no need to put more weight on one element than another, it may be preferable to join them with *and* instead.

The professor and some graduate students were just entering the building.

A parcel and a multitude of letters were delivered the next day.

Distracting modifying nouns

When a subject is followed by an element that further defines it, there is a risk of mistaking the noun contained in this element for the subject itself. Consider the following:

This **set** <u>is</u> not complete.

These **instructions** <u>are</u> not complete.

This **set** of instructions <u>is</u> not complete.

In the last sentence, it would be an error to say *This set of instructions are not complete*. The subject is the singular *set;* the plural word *instructions* is merely modifying the subject.

Similarly,

An extensive **collection** of medieval   [subject is *collection*, not *manuscripts*]
manuscripts is maintained in the library.

Engaging in contact sports is not for   [subject is *engaging*, not *sports*]
the faint of heart.

An **assortment** of ribbons and bows   [subject is *assortment*, not *ribbons and bows*]
was lying in the drawer.

The **inclusion** of intervening words   [subject is *inclusion*, not *words*]
between subject and verb often causes
confusion.

The **use** of correction fluid or other   [subject is *use*, not *methods*]
methods that mask the original data is
not permitted.

Errors attributable to this type of sentence structure seem limited to when the subject is singular and the phrase contains a plural noun. When it's the other way around, the effect of the intervening words is less distracting. Few people would make errors such as *The pupils in her class is extraordinarily well behaved* (subject is clearly the plural *pupils*, not the singular *class*) or *The inscriptions on the tombstone was almost worn away* (subject is clearly the plural *inscriptions*, not the singular *tombstone*).

Distracting predicate nouns

While the subject is the center of interest in a sentence, the **predicate** is what provides information about the subject, either describing it or identifying an action that it performs or that is performed upon it. See Basic Sentence Structure on page 72.

If the predicate happens to include a noun, there is a risk of mistaking this noun for the subject itself. This will cause errors in agreement if the subject is singular and the predicate noun plural, or vice versa. Consider the following:

Her never-ending **rants** are the biggest irritant.

The biggest **irritant** is her never-ending rants.

In the first sentence, the subject is the plural noun *rants*: don't be decoyed by the singular *irritant*. In the second, the wording is turned around so that the subject is *irritant*.

Similarly,

The only deductible **item** on my tax return <u>is</u> my charitable expenses.

My charitable **expenses** <u>are</u> the only deductible item on my tax return.

Her best **feature** <u>is</u> her eyes.

Her **eyes** <u>are</u> her best feature.

The ongoing **crises and tantrums** in the office <u>were</u> a nightmare.

The main **thing** needed <u>is</u> cooler heads.

The most annoying **problem** with the house <u>was</u> its creaky floors.

The error of focusing on the wrong noun is likelier to happen if other words intervene between the subject and the verb. Remember, it is not proximity to the verb that determines which word acts as the subject.

Inverted subject-verb order

In English, the subject usually precedes the verb: **Seth** <u>has</u> a good memory; the quick brown **fox** <u>jumps</u> over the lazy dog; his **idea** <u>was</u> pooh-poohed. However, this order is reversed in sentences that are constructed as questions, or that open with phrasings such as *there were* or *it is*, or that say *what* was done before saying *who* did it. In these situations, writers are more apt to make errors in agreement, either because they are focusing only on whatever immediately follows the verb and neglect to look further, or because they get distracted by a noun that precedes the verb. However, the same rules described above apply here as well.

Into each project <u>go</u> **hours** of hard work.	[subject is *hours*, not *project* or *work*; verb is plural]
Included in the total <u>are</u> the five spare **components**.	[subject is *components*, not *total*; verb is plural]
Among the guests coming tonight <u>is</u> my cousin's new **fiancé**.	[subject is *fiancé*, not *guests*; verb is singular]

If you're ever uncertain about how to deal with an inverted sentence, try mentally turning it around or dropping any distracting elements:

the **components** <u>are</u> included

my cousin's **fiancé** <u>is</u> coming

With compound subjects linked by *and*, the subject is always plural and therefore the verb is always plural, just as in the case where the subject comes first (see page 209).

<u>Have</u> the **plates** and **glasses** been put away?	[both subjects plural; verb is plural]
<u>Do</u> your **brother** and **his friend** need a place to stay tonight?	[both subjects singular; verb is plural]
Walking purposefully up to the house <u>were</u> the **trainer** and **his assistants**.	[one subject singular, the other plural; verb is plural]
There <u>are</u> only **five textbook**s and **one computer** available for the entire class.	[one subject plural, the other singular; verb is plural]

With compound subjects linked by *or* or *nor*, the noun closest to the verb determines its form, just as in the case where the subject comes first (see page 210).

<u>There's</u> no **paper** or pencils to be found anywhere.	[subject closest to the verb is singular; verb is singular]
<u>There is</u> neither **prestige** nor profits to be gained.	[subject closest to the verb is singular; verb is singular]
There <u>are</u> no **pencils** or paper to be found anywhere.	[subject closest to the verb is plural; verb is plural]
<u>Are</u> neither my **rights** nor my reputation to be considered?	[subject closest to the verb is plural; verb is plural]

Be particularly careful when using contractions for *there is, what is,* and the like, since contractions tend to obscure the verb. It is common to see faulty constructions such as *What's the main issues at stake here?* or *Where's my shoes?* or *There's still tons of debris to be cleared.* Such constructions are frequent (and forgivable) in speech, but the standard must be higher in writing.

FOREST OR TREES?

The second category of problems when it comes to agreement between subject and verb involves scenarios where a singular subject may be mistaken for a plural or vice versa, and hence matched with the wrong verb.

Collective nouns

A **collective noun** refers to an entity made up of more than one thing or person: *crowd, government, flock.* Whether such a word functions as a singular or a plural depends on several factors.

Some are always singular or always plural

The **mob** <u>was</u> turning ugly.

A mob is treated as a unit, since by definition the people who make it up could not individually exhibit mob traits.

Where <u>are</u> the **binoculars**?

Items that are made up of two connected parts often take a plural construction—*scissors, glasses, pants, pliers, tweezers*. They are only properly treated as singular if preceded by the phrase *a pair of*.

Some are singular when used in one sense, and plural in another

The new **headquarters** <u>are</u> in Paris.	[the physical entity]
Headquarters <u>is</u> waiting for an answer.	[the corporate entity]
Statistics <u>is</u> the most difficult course in the program.	[the field of knowledge]
The **statistics** <u>show</u> that highway accidents are decreasing.	[the individual items of information]

Some can go either way

Some collective nouns may be treated as either plurals or singulars depending on whether the focus is on the unit or on the members it comprises.

The **staff** <u>seems</u> very competent / The **staff** <u>seem</u> very competent.

The **couple** <u>has</u> two young daughters / The **couple** <u>have</u> two young daughters.

His **family** constantly <u>interferes</u> in his life / His **family** constantly <u>interfere</u> in his life.

Some are determined by context

For those collective nouns that can normally go either way, the context sometimes dictates whether one form or the other is appropriate.

The **staff** <u>have</u> many specialized skills.	[reference is to the individual staff members; verb is plural]
The **couple** <u>get</u> along very well together.	[reference is to the two individuals who make up the couple; verb is plural]
His **family** <u>is</u> very close-knit.	[reference is to the unit; verb is singular]

Be consistent with collective nouns

With a collective noun that can go either way, be careful that you do not start referring to it as singular and then switch to plural, or vice versa. This can entail using either the wrong verb form or the wrong pronoun. The following examples are *in*correct:

> The couple <u>lives</u> in New York but <u>go</u> to Florida for the winter.

> The committee <u>is</u> adamant that <u>their</u> recommendations be adopted.

> My company <u>has</u> an employment policy that <u>they've</u> adhered to for years.

> After <u>their</u> big win, the team <u>feels</u> more relaxed.

> The group of ticketholders <u>was</u> furiously demanding refunds of <u>their</u> money.

If you have created such a construction, think about whether the focus should be on the whole or on the individuals it comprises—and whichever way you go, be consistent.

> The couple <u>live</u> in New York but <u>go</u> to Florida for the winter.

> The committee <u>is</u> adamant that <u>its</u> recommendations be adopted.

Terms of quantity

Although most plural subjects take plural verbs, plural nouns that refer to measurements of money, time, or distance are treated as singulars. That is, the sum is viewed as a unit.

> **Two hours** <u>is</u> plenty of time.

> **Twelve yards** of material <u>seems</u> like more than enough for a doll's dress.

> Lying there in plain view <u>was</u> the missing **four hundred thousand dollars**.

> **Eleven cents** <u>is</u> hardly going to cover lunch.

Of course, if the emphasis is intended to be on the individual items, use a plural.

> The **forty minutes** of the class <u>were</u> dragging by with agonizing slowness.

> The **thirteen dollars** <u>were</u> laid on the table one by one.

Other terms of quantity may sometimes be treated as singulars as well.

<u>Is</u> **three pinches** of salt too much?   [focus is on the total quantity, not the
                                                 individual pinches]

A generation ago, no one in the world of   [focus is on the achievement of this
figure skating would have believed that **four** feat, not the individual revolutions]
revolutions in the air <u>was</u> possible.

Indefinite pronouns

Pronouns that refer to a specific person, place, or thing don't cause difficulty when
it comes to agreeing with a verb (*it is, they are,* and so on). Somewhat trickier are
indefinite pronouns, which are not tied to something specific. The ones that tend
to be misused are those that refer to multitudes but are singular in construction,
and those that go both ways.

Pronouns in the first category include *each, every, either, neither, anyone, anybody,
someone, somebody, nobody, everything, everyone,* and *everybody.* They always take a singular verb.

Either candidate <u>seems</u> credible.

Either of the candidates <u>seems</u> credible.

Neither of us <u>wants</u> to go.

Neither of the options <u>is</u> acceptable.

Everything in the boxes <u>goes</u> into the large filing cabinet.

Where <u>has</u> **everybody** gone?

They are even singular when used in combination.

Anything and everything <u>goes</u>.

Anybody and everybody <u>is</u> welcome.

Each and every dish <u>was</u> chipped.

As with nouns, don't be distracted by parenthetical or modifying phrases intervening between subject and verb.

Everything about her presentation—the talk, the overheads, and the handouts—<u>was</u>
rated highly.

Pronouns in the second category include *all, more, most, some, any,* and *none.* These pronouns take a plural verb when associated with a multitude (indicating how many) and a singular verb when associated with a unit (indicating how much).

All the chores <u>have</u> been completed.	[how many; verb is plural]
All the snow <u>was</u> melted.	[how much; verb is singular]
<u>Is</u> there **any** pepper in that shaker?	[how much; verb is singular]
<u>Are</u> there **any** questions?	[how many; verb is plural]

The pronoun *none* is somewhat controversial. Some authorities insist it must always be treated as a contraction for *not one,* which makes it singular. However, constructions such as *None of the residents is wealthy* or *None of the customers seems satisfied* can sound a bit pedantic, and there are many literary precedents to support using this word to mean *not any* as well. The decision as to how to treat it depends partly on whether a singular or a plural notion predominates, and partly on how formal a tone you wish to achieve.

The candidates seem interchangeable; none <u>stands</u> out as the best.	[*not one*; verb is singular]
None but the foolhardy <u>eat</u> at this place.	[*not any*; verb is plural]
None of these options <u>is</u> satisfactory / None of these options <u>are</u> satisfactory.	[either is acceptable; the first is more formal]

Numerical phrases

When it comes to subject-verb agreement, phrases having to do with notions of singularity or plurality cause more than their share of confusion.

TEST YOUR KNOWLEDGE

In the following, which of the verbs in parentheses is correct?

1. My roommate is one of those people who (is, are) late for everything.

2. I believe Zoë is the only one of the guests who (needs, need) a lift.

3. As the witnesses filed out, more than one (was, were) overcome by emotion.

4. Included with each set (is, are) one or more evaluation forms.

5. It is estimated that one in four adults (has, have) difficulty reading.

6. A number of students (has, have) already registered.

7. The number of cars on the city's roads are increasing by five percent every year.

8. All but one candidate (was, were) male.

9. All but one of the candidates (was, were) male.

10. All but one (was, were) male.

ANSWERS

1. *one of those people who are late for everything.* The key to understanding this construction is recognizing that the sentence is saying two things: there are some people (plural) who are late for everything, and the roommate (singular) is one of them.

2. *the only one of the guests who needs a lift.* This sentence is saying that there is one guest (singular) who needs a lift. It is not saying that there are guests (plural) who need lifts.

3. *more than one was overcome by emotion.* Logically, "more than one" implies a plural, but by convention this construction is treated as singular. (Note that you would say *more than one witness*, not *more than one witnesses*.)

4. *Included with each set are one or more evaluation forms.* This might seem to be a case of subjects linked by *or* where the part closest to the verb is singular and hence the verb should be singular. However, by convention, the phrase "one or more" is taken to be plural.

5. *one in four adults has difficulty.* Although this obviously refers to a plurality, grammatically the subject is *one*, so the verb is singular. However, many people feel, with some reasonableness, that the plural form should be considered acceptable as well; certainly, it is common idiom. Which way you choose to go may depend on the formality of your writing.

6. *A number of students have.* The phrase "a number of" is always treated as plural, even though it looks like a singular entity.

7. *The number of cars on the city's roads is increasing.* The phrase "the number of" is always treated as singular.

> 8. . . . and 9, and 10: *All but one candidate <u>was</u> male. All but one of the candidates <u>were</u> male. All but one <u>were</u> male.* In all three cases, of course, the reference is to a plurality; however, the quirks of the language dictate that if the phrase *all but one* is immediately followed by a noun, the verb is singular.

Nonstandard plurals or singulars

As discussed under Plural Formations on page 40, not all nouns in English form their plurals by adding *s*. The majority of nonstandard plurals do not cause confusion, but a few are regularly misused as singulars; conversely, some singular nouns are taken to be plurals. Misunderstandings of either type lead to errors in subject-verb agreement; sometimes because the subject is wrong, sometimes because the verb is wrong.

TEST YOUR KNOWLEDGE

Correct the following sentences by changing either the subject or the verb:

1. A virus needs a host cell in order to reproduce; a bacteria does not.
2. The most important criteria for admission to the program is good leadership abilities.
3. The media of television is the focus of the first half of the course.
4. Rickets are prevented by adequate vitamin D and exposure to sunlight.
5. The study may be stopped at any time if new clinical data becomes available.
6. The phenomena of road rage has attracted the attention of social psychologists.
7. Where's the other dice?
8. Dominoes are an easy game to learn.
9. Customs are responsible for levying the following taxes:
10. The mathematics of the problem haven't been worked out yet.

ANSWERS

1. *a <u>bacterium</u> does not.* One virus, multiple viruses; one bacterium, multiple bacteria.
2. *the most important <u>criterion</u> for admission is.* One criterion, multiple criteria.

3. *the _medium_ of television is.* One medium; multiple media. The plural form is properly used when referring to some combination of television, radio, newspapers, magazines, etc., or to the people who work for such entities, as in *The media were swarming around the hotel.* (Note though that *multimedia* would be treated as singular, because it refers to a field. See the example for *mathematics*, below.)

4. *Rickets _is_ prevented.* Despite its *s* ending, rickets is simply the name of a disorder, and hence is singular. The same holds for some other diseases: for example, shingles, measles, mumps.

5. *if new clinical data _become_ available.* Data is the plural of the rarely (if ever) used *datum*, a single piece of factual information, and means the total body of facts accumulated. As a plural noun, it properly takes a plural verb. However, it is increasingly being treated as a singular, so which way you handle it may depend on your audience. In scientific and academic writing, plural usage is required; in business and informal writing, singular usage is accepted and may even be mandatory. (Words do of course change over time. For example, the uncontroversial singular *agenda*, a list of individual to-do items, originated as a plural of *agendum*.)

6. *The _phenomenon_ of road rage has.* Like *criteria*, *phenomena* is plural. One phenomenon *is*; multiple phenomena *are*.

7. *Where's the other _die_.* One die; two dice. If referring to a pair, this would be *Where _are_ the other dice.*

8. *Dominoes _is_ an easy game.* The individual pieces used in the game are plural (one domino, multiple dominoes), but when referring to the game, this word is simply a singular noun that ends in *s*. The same holds for other games that are described as plurals: for example, checkers or draughts, horseshoes or quoits, ninepins or tenpins, tiddlywinks.

9. *Customs _is_ responsible.* Used in the sense of traditions or habits, *customs* is of course plural (one custom, multiple customs), but the agency responsible for border control is singular.

10. *The mathematics _hasn't_.* Despite the *s* ending, *mathematics* is always singular in construction. The same applies to many other academic or professional fields: for example, physics, linguistics, genetics.

Parallel Structure

THE VERSATILITY OF THE ENGLISH LANGUAGE enables its users to express the same concept in many ways. The problem is, this freedom makes it all too easy to start composing a thought one way and then switch tactics midstream. The result may be a passage guilty of **faulty parallelism**—a clumsy construction in which the elements fail to mesh. Each may be perfectly grammatical in itself, but it doesn't fit with the others.

Ensuring parallelism in a piece of writing does *not* mean that every sentence and passage should be structured the same way, which would quickly become tedious. What it does mean is that within a sentence, a list, or a passage that contains elements related in purpose or structure, these elements should be presented in a consistent manner. For example, you must not go arbitrarily from the active voice to the passive, from the second person to the third, from the present tense to the past, or from a series of adjectives to a noun. You must also be consistent in your handling of words such as prepositions, articles, and conjunctions.

The effects of faulty parallelism range from barely noticeable to jarring. As with many other grammar rules, you may at times decide to bend this one if you feel that doing so would make a sentence more vibrant or capture your intended meaning more precisely. That is, don't avoid a catchy phrasing out of an over-devotion to technicalities. Be certain, however, that you have a valid reason for rejecting the more correct alternatives.

TEST YOUR KNOWLEDGE

Each of the following sentences contains a problem with parallel structure. What is it, and how would you correct it?

1. The lecture was long, a bore, and uninspiring.

2. Planning a surprise party calls for organizing, scheduling, and cunning.

3. He had always preferred talking to listening, and to give rather than to take direction.

4. Her main responsibilities were the management of the PR department and to attend trade shows.

5. A computerized database index needs to be reorganized when it has become fragmented, or to correct the skewing of values.

6. The consultant objected to the proposal, saying that the costs would be exorbitant and because the training facilities were insufficient.

7. It may be necessary to either add or subtract items from this list.

8. Courses are offered in spring, summer, and in fall.

9. The revised plan called for reduced salaries, operating budgets, and longer hours.

10. Writers who work on a freelance basis don't get steady paychecks, but one has the advantage of extra tax breaks.

11. Participants should sign in by noon and pick up your registration materials at the front desk.

12. Go to the Options menu to change the display colors, fonts, type size, set predefined breaks in your program, or open the dictionary.

13. Customers may either pick up the merchandise themselves, or the company will deliver it for a small fee.

14. In just twenty minutes, he not only shoveled the entire driveway but also the stairs and balcony.

15. If some text that appears on the screen does not show on the printout, it is marked as hidden. To remove this marking, do the following:

    i. The text must be selected

    ii. On the **Font** tab, the user clicks on the icon to open the dialog box

    iii. Deselect the **Hidden** checkbox

SUGGESTED REVISIONS:

Note that this heading is not titled "Answers," since there is more than one right way to reword these sentences. What is important is to be able to recognize the problem in each case.

1. . . . *long, a bore, and uninspiring.* The words *long* and *uninspiring* are adjectives, while *a bore* is a noun. **Better:** long, boring, and uninspiring.

2. . . . *organizing, scheduling, and cunning.* Despite the common endings of these words, they are not grammatically equivalent. *Organizing* and *scheduling* are gerunds, words that function as nouns by adding *ing* to verbs, while *cunning* is a straightforward noun that just happens to end in *ing*. (There is no verb "to cun.") The series should contain all gerunds or all nouns. *Organize* can be made to fit either form, but the other two must be altered. **Better:** *organizing, scheduling, and scheming* (all gerunds) **or** *organization, cunning, and scheduling skills* (all nouns).

3. . . . *preferred talking to listening, and to give rather than to take direction. Talking* and *listening* are gerunds, while *to give* and *to take* are infinitives. **Better:** *He had always preferred talking to listening, and giving over taking direction.*

4. . . . *the management of the PR department and to attend trade shows.* The first element contains a noun, the second an infinitive. **Better:** *Her responsibilities were to manage the PR department and to attend trade shows* **or** *Her responsibilities were management of the PR department and attendance at trade shows.*

5. . . . *when it has become fragmented, or to correct the skewing of values.* The focus switches here from what is happening to the database index (passive voice) to what the person using this index should do (active voice). Since the subject of this sentence is the index, not the user, the passive voice is more appropriate. **Better:** *when it has become fragmented or when its values have become skewed.*

6. . . . *saying that the costs would be exorbitant and because the training facilities were insufficient.* There is no reason to switch from *that* to *because.* In addition to the faulty parallelism, note that this slightly changes the meaning, turning the consultant's second objection from a matter of opinion into

a statement of fact. **Better:** *The consultant objected to the proposal, saying that the costs would be exorbitant and that the training facilities were insufficient.*

7. *. . . either add or subtract items from this list.* If words in a sentence take different prepositions, each preposition must be included. Writers sometimes include only the last preposition, without checking to see if it's appropriate for all. In this example, it's not: you can't add something *from* something. **Better:** *It may be necessary to either add items to or subtract them from this list.*

8. *. . . in spring, summer, and in fall.* When the same preposition applies to a series, it may be either repeated for each item or used just once—but you must be consistent. Don't include it for some items and drop it for others. **Better:** *Courses are offered in spring, in summer, and in fall* **or** *in spring, summer, and fall.* (The more concise version would usually be preferred, but you may sometimes for reasons of style decide to repeat the preposition.)

9. *. . . reduced salaries, operating budgets, and longer hours.* The adjective *reduced* is intended to apply to the first two items, but fails to connect with the second one because the third one (hours) takes a different adjective. This leaves "operating budgets" standing alone, without a modifier. **Better:** *The revised plan called for reduced salaries, reduced operating budgets, and longer hours* **or** *reduced salaries and operating budgets, as well as longer hours.*

10. *Writers who work on a freelance basis don't get steady paychecks, but one has . . .* The subject switches from the plural noun *writers* to the singular pronoun *one.* **Better:** *Writers who work on a freelance basis don't get steady paychecks, but they have the advantage of extra tax breaks* **or** *As a freelance writer, one doesn't get a steady paycheck, but one has the advantage of extra tax breaks.*

11. *Participants must sign in by noon and pick up your materials.* The sentence switches from the third person to the second. **Better:** *Participants should sign in by noon and pick up their registration materials* **or** *Sign in by noon and pick up your registration materials.*

12. *Go to the Options menu to change the display colors, fonts, type size, set predefined breaks in your program, or open the dictionary.* The verb *change* is intended to apply to only the first three items, but then keeps going,

latching on to the next item as well. Grammatically, this sentence is saying that you can change the display colors, change fonts, change type size, and "change set predefined breaks in your program"—the last, of course, making no sense. **Better:** *Go to the Options menu to change the display colors, fonts, and type size; to set predefined breaks in your program; or to open the dictionary.*

13. *Customers may either pick up the merchandise themselves, or the company will deliver it.* Opening with the words *Customers may either* sets up an expectation that customers will be able to do one of two things—but then the focus switches to a different actor, the company. In any "either/or" sentence, the two options must be parallel. A reliable way to check for parallelism is to see if the syntax still stands up if you put the second option in place of the first. *Customers may either the company will deliver it for a small fee* clearly doesn't work. **Better:** *Customers may either pick up the merchandise themselves or have it delivered for a small fee* **or** *Either customers may pick up the merchandise themselves, or the company will deliver it for a small fee.*

14. *. . . he not only shoveled the entire driveway, but also the stairs and balcony.* In any "not only/but also" sentence, *not only* must be placed immediately before the first of the two elements being contrasted. If two actions are being contrasted, *not only* goes before the first action; if one action is affecting two objects, it goes before the first object. Putting it before the action "shoveled" would be appropriate if a second action followed: for example, *he not only shoveled the entire driveway but also salted the icy patches.* In this case, however, it must go before the first object (driveway). **Better:** *In just twenty minutes, he shoveled not only the driveway but also the stairs and balcony.*

15. *If some text that appears on the screen,* etc. This final example is not a single sentence but a list, and items in a list should all be presented the same way. Here, the first item uses the passive voice (*the text must be selected*), the second uses the third person (*the user clicks on the icon*), and the third uses the imperative, addressing the user directly (*deselect the checkbox*). As this is instructional text, the imperative should be used for all. **Better:**

---

i. *Select the text*

ii. *On the Font tab, click on the icon to open the dialog box*

iii. *Deselect the Hidden checkbox*

Another issue with list items is that you must not phrase some as complete grammatical sentences and others as single words or sentence fragments. Both styles are fine, but not in combination. If you are creating a list where certain items must be phrased as complete sentences, rework the others so that they become complete sentences as well.

---

* * *

Apart from the grammatical requirement of maintaining a consistent structure, parallelism can be employed as a literary device to achieve an appealing cadence or to lend emphasis. Note how it is used in the following extracts:

> He was a good mixer, and in three days knew everyone on board. He ran everything. He managed the sweeps, conducted the auctions, collected money for prizes at the sports, got up quoit and golf matches, organized the concert, and arranged the fancy-dress ball. He was everywhere and always. He was certainly the best-hated man in the ship.
>
> —W. Somerset Maugham, *Mr Know-All*

> The external world could take care of itself. In the meantime it was folly to grieve, or to think. The prince had provided all the appliances of pleasure. There were buffoons, there were improvisatori, there were ballet-dancers, there were musicians, there were cards, there was Beauty, there was wine. All these and security were within. Without was the "Red Death."
>
> —Edgar Allan Poe, *The Masque of the Red Death*

In poetry, of course, the device of parallelism is common.

> "One kiss, my bonny sweetheart, I'm after a prize tonight,
> But I shall be back with the yellow gold before the morning light;
> Yet, if they press me sharply, and harry me through the day,
> Then look for me by moonlight,
> Watch for me by moonlight
> I'll come to thee by moonlight, though hell should bar the way."
>
> —Alfred Noyes, *The Highwayman*

Should you ask me,
whence these stories?
Whence these legends and traditions,
With the odors of the forest
With the dew and damp of meadows,
With the curling smoke of wigwams,
With the rushing of great rivers,
With their frequent repetitions,
And their wild reverberations
As of thunder in the mountains?

—Henry Wadsworth Longfellow, *The Song of Hiawatha*

"Forward, the Light Brigade!"
Was there a man dismay'd?
Not tho' the soldier knew
Someone had blunder'd:
Theirs not to make reply,
Theirs not to reason why,
Theirs but to do and die:
Into the valley of Death
Rode the six hundred.

—Alfred, Lord Tennyson, *The Charge of the Light Brigade*

Positioning of Modifiers

A **MODIFIER** IS AN ELEMENT of a sentence that describes or qualifies some other element. Adjectives and adverbs are the most common modifiers (*gorgeously plumaged* parrots squawked *raucously* atop the *soaringly tall* trees), but a phrase or dependent clause can act as one too.

All elements in a sentence must be positioned so that any modifier is acting upon what it is supposed to. Failure to do so may lead to some disconcerting results. There are three types of problems to look out for:

- Dangling modifiers
- Misplaced modifiers
- Squinting modifiers

These are described in turn below, followed by an exercise that presents examples of all three.

DANGLING MODIFIERS

If a sentence is carelessly constructed so that the entity to be modified is implied rather than explicitly stated, the modifier is left "dangling"—left at loose ends as it were—and in the absence of the intended "modify-ee", ends up latching onto whatever happens to come next, resulting in a nonsense sentence. For example:

Just two years after finishing graduate school, Adelaide's career took off.

Presumably it was Adelaide who finished grad school, but she makes no direct appearance in the sentence; only her career does. Grammatically, what is being said here is that Adelaide's career finished grad school and then took off (what did it do—leave her for another woman?). The problem can be remedied by rewording either the phrase or the clause.

> Just two years after Adelaide finished graduate school, her career took off.

> *or:* Just two years after finishing graduate school, Adelaide saw her career take off.

The absurdities that result from dangling modifiers can range from the obvious to the subtle. Fortunately, even when syntax is garbled, readers are usually able to process a sentence in the way the writer intended it.

MISPLACED MODIFIERS

Like a dangling modifier, a misplaced modifier acts on something other than what the writer intended. In this case, the problem is not that the intended subject isn't clearly identified in the sentence but that the modifier is in the wrong position relative to what it should be affecting. (Whenever possible, the two elements should lie right next to each other.) For example:

> We put out an appeal for more volunteers to help with the fall program at last week's meeting.

Presumably what happened at last week's meeting was an appeal for help with the fall program, but the positioning of the modifier makes it sound as if the fall program itself was held at last week's meeting. The problem can be remedied by moving the modifying phrase.

> At last week's meeting, we put out an appeal for more volunteers to help with the fall program.

SQUINTING MODIFIERS

In some cases, the placement of a modifier is not so much wrong as ambiguous, in that it could apply to either the element that precedes it or the one that follows. Such constructions are called "squinting modifiers" or "two-way modifiers", as they seem to be looking in both directions. For example:

> The coach said on Thursday we'd have to start working harder.

Was this said on Thursday, or would the hard work begin on Thursday? This sentence should read as one of the following:

On Thursday, the coach said we'd have to start working harder.

or: The coach said we'd have to start working harder on Thursday.

A squinting modifier can be particularly difficult to notice, since if you read the sentence the right way it doesn't appear to contain a problem. It's a good example of why it is always advisable to have someone else look over your work: this is the sort of error a fresh eye is likelier to spot.

More examples of problems with modifiers follow. Note how you may have to read such sentences a couple of times before you pick up on the fact that there is something wrong with them.

TEST YOUR KNOWLEDGE

Correct the following sentences:

1. Upon opening the pantry door, a stack of cans flew out at her.

2. Unlike dashes, a writer may use parentheses to enclose an entire sentence, not just part of a sentence.

3. Awaiting the starter's gun, Pierre's heart began to thump rapidly.

4. After ransacking the house, Ben's wallet finally turned up under the dog's water bowl.

5. Thumbing through the newspaper, my eye was suddenly caught by a small item.

6. Leaning over the hospital bed, she looked into the vacant man's eyes but could see no spark of recognition.

7. At its next meeting, the Board of Education will debate whether teachers should be allowed to administer adrenaline to students who experience severe allergic reactions without written permission.

8. The formerly glamorous countess is now continually mocked in the tabloids for her taste in clothing, weight, and overspending.

9. The suspect's condition was upgraded from serious to fair after he fell from a third-story balcony while trying to evade arrest.

10. The gallery that was featured in the evening news recently had another major exhibit.

11. The tramp being asked to leave rudely replied that no one could tell him what to do.

12. Climbing stairs very rapidly gets you into good condition.

SUGGESTED REVISIONS

Sentences 1 to 5 contain dangling modifiers. Note that it is not enough to simply have the intended target of the modifier mentioned in the sentence, if it's not acting as the subject.

1. *Upon opening the pantry door, a stack of cans flew out at her.* How did the stack of cans manage to open the pantry door? **Better:** *When she opened the pantry door, a stack of cans flew out at her.*

2. *Unlike dashes, a writer may use parentheses to enclose an entire sentence, not just part of a sentence.* This seems unfair: if writers may use parentheses this way, why shouldn't dashes be permitted to do so as well? **Better:** *Unlike dashes, parentheses may be used to enclose an entire sentence, not just part of a sentence.*

3. *Awaiting the starter's gun, Pierre's heart began to thump rapidly.* Pierre's heart must have good ears. **Better:** *Awaiting the starter's gun, Pierre felt his heart begin to thump rapidly.*

4. *After ransacking the house, Ben's wallet finally turned up under the dog's water bowl.* That is one active wallet. **Better:** *After ransacking the house, Ben finally found his wallet under the dog's water bowl.*

5. *Thumbing through the newspaper, my eye was suddenly caught by a small item.* Unusual ocular anatomy. **Better:** *As I thumbed through the newspaper, my eye was suddenly caught by a small item.*

Sentences 6 to 9 contain misplaced modifiers:

6. *Leaning over the hospital bed, she looked into the vacant man's eyes but could see no spark of recognition.* The man himself is vacant? **Better:** *Leaning over the hospital bed, she looked into the man's vacant eyes but could see no spark of recognition.*

7. *At its next meeting, the Board of Education will debate whether teachers should be allowed to administer adrenaline to students who experience severe allergic reactions without written permission.* One has to admire the discipline of those

students who *do* first obtain permission. **Better:** *At its next meeting, the Board of Education will debate whether teachers should require written permission to administer adrenaline to students who experience severe allergic reactions.*

8. *The formerly glamorous countess is now continually mocked in the tabloids for her taste in clothing, weight, and overspending.* What's wrong with the countess's taste in weight or her taste in overspending? **Better:** *The formerly glamorous countess is now continually mocked in the tabloids for her taste in clothing, her weight, and her overspending* **or** *for her weight, overspending, and taste in clothing.*

9. *The suspect's condition was upgraded from serious to fair after he fell from a third-story balcony while trying to evade arrest.* Who knew that falling off a balcony could have health benefits? **Better:** *The suspect, who fell from a third-story balcony while trying to evade arrest, has had his condition upgraded from serious to fair.*

Sentences 10 to 12 contain squinting (two-way) modifiers, so which correction is applied depends on the intended meaning:

10. *The gallery that was featured in the evening news recently had another major exhibit.* The gallery was recently featured, or it recently had an exhibit? **Better:** *The gallery that was recently featured in the evening news had another major exhibit* **or** *The gallery that was featured in the evening news had another major exhibit recently.*

11. *The tramp being asked to leave rudely replied that no one could tell him what to do.* Who was speaking rudely: the tramp or the person asking him to leave? **Better:** *Upon being rudely asked to leave, the tramp replied that no one could tell him what to do* **or** *The tramp being asked to leave replied rudely that no one could tell him what to do.*

12. *Climbing stairs very rapidly gets you into good condition.* Does this mean that racing up the stairs will eventually get you into good condition—or that trudging up them at any pace is a quick way of getting into shape? **Better:** *Climbing stairs very rapidly is a way of getting into good condition* **or** *Climbing stairs gets you into good condition very rapidly.*

Tense and Mood

The major problem [with time travel] is quite simply one of grammar, and the main work to consult in this matter is Dr. Dan Streetmentioner's Time Traveler's Handbook of 1001 Tense Formations. It will tell you, for instance, how to describe something that was about to happen to you in the past before you avoided it by time-jumping forward two days in order to avoid it. The event will be described differently according to whether you are talking about it from the standpoint of your own natural time, from a time in the further future, or a time in the further past and is further complicated by the possibility of conducting conversations while you are actually traveling from one time to another with the intention of becoming your own mother or father.

Most readers get as far as the Future Semiconditionally Modified Subinserted Plagal Past Subjunctive Intentional before giving up; and in fact in later editions of the book all the pages beyond this point have been left blank to save on printing costs.

—Douglas Adams, *The Restaurant at the End of the Universe*

A **tense** is the form that a verb takes to indicate the time of its action. How many tenses are there? A glib answer would be three: present, past, future. Not so fast. . . .

Tenses are one of the banes of people learning English as a second language, and they can be complex enough that even native speakers who use them correctly are often doing so intuitively, without an underlying understanding. This section describes many—by no means all—of the tenses in English, explaining the subtleties involved in deciding when to use each one and cross-referencing others where applicable. To begin, here is an overview of some terms and concepts that are vital to understanding this topic.

1. The present, past, and future tenses each have the following four variants:

- **Simple** tenses are the most straightforward—at least grammatically. In terms of usage, there is sometimes more to them than meets the eye.

- **Progressive** tenses are used to describe an action or state that is *in progress* at the present time, or that was or will be in progress at the time being discussed. Progressive tenses are also called **continuous**.

- **Perfect** tenses, disappointingly, refer merely to an action or state that has been completed (perfected) at the present time, or that was or will be completed at the time being discussed.

- **Perfect progressive** tenses combine the concepts of progressive and perfect, referring to an action or event that is/was/will be in progress at a particular time *and* that is/was/will be completed at a particular time. These tenses are also called **perfect continuous.**

A few other variants that have less broad application (that is, they do not apply to each of the present, past, and future) are discussed here as well. These are **present emphatic** and **past emphatic**, to accentuate statements in the simple present and simple past, respectively; **habitual past**, to describe something that used to occur on a regular basis; and **future in the past**, to express the idea that at an earlier time point, there had been an expectation that something would later happen.

2. Every verb can be formed in four ways, with different forms used in different tenses:

- The **base form** is the root word (*work, scrape, binge, shop, stand, write, eat, choose*). If you were looking up a verb in the dictionary, its base form is what would appear as the main entry.

- The **past form** is formed for regular verbs by adding *ed* to the base form (*worked*), or just *d* if the base form ends in *e* (*scraped, binged*), and sometimes doubling the last consonant (*shopped*). For irregular verbs, don't look for rhyme or reason (*stood, wrote, ate, chose*).

- The **present participle** is formed by adding *ing* to the base form (*working, standing, eating*). If there is an *e* at the end of the base form, it is usually dropped (*scraping, writing, choosing*) but is sometimes kept (*bingeing*); and in some cases, the last consonant of the base word is doubled (*shopping*).

- The **past participle** is the same as the past form for regular verbs (*worked, scraped, binged, shopped*). For irregular verbs, it is sometimes the same (*stood*) but more often differs, usually ending in *en* (*written, eaten, chosen*).

3. The nature of a verb restricts which tenses it can take on. One of the ways in which verbs can be categorized is as either **dynamic** or **stative**:

- **Dynamic** verbs, also called **normal**, involve actions or processes: for example, *jump, write, whisper, cough, melt, memorize*. These actions or processes do not have to be observable, but they all involve something happening or being done, with a start and a finish.

- **Stative** verbs, also called **non-continuous**, involve perceptions, emotions, or the relationship between things: for example, *want, like, need, believe, prefer, contain, resemble*. They describe a state of being, as opposed to a start-and-finish action. Verbs classified as stative cannot be used with progressive (continuous) tenses.

- To further complicate things, a verb with multiple meanings may be either dynamic or stative, depending on which of its meanings is intended. For example, *think* can be either an action of sorts ("Your money or your life!" "I'm thinking, I'm thinking!"), which makes it a dynamic verb, or the expression of an opinion ("I think all politicians are dirty rascals"), which makes it stative.

4. In addition to the main verb that describes a state or action, almost all tenses include **auxiliary verbs** that play a supporting role. (A slightly infantilizing term that some grammar books use for these parts of speech is "helping verbs".) Only two tenses—the simple present, which consists of just the base form of the verb, and the simple past, which consists of just the past form—do *not* include auxiliary verbs.

- Common auxiliary verbs are *have, be, will, can,* and *would*.

- In speech and in informal writing, auxiliary verbs are often contracted. Thus, *I am* becomes *I'm; we had* becomes *we'd;* etc. In most of the examples below, the auxiliary verbs are presented as contractions.

5. Most of the discussion below is concerned with the active voice (X does something), but examples are included to show how the verb form changes if the passive voice is used (something is done to X). See page 289 for a discussion of the use of voice. Passive

voice constructions always include a form of the auxiliary verb *to be* followed by the past participle of the action verb, regardless of tense. Some passive constructions are very awkward-sounding and are included here only for completeness.

6. The **mood** of a verb deals with the concept of whether a statement is expressing a fact (indicative mood), a possibility or likelihood (conditional mood), or a command or instruction (imperative mood). A sentence is characterized by both its tense and its mood. The discussion of mood is presented following that of tenses.

Two summary tables are presented on pages 265-266. Table 1 shows the conjugation of a verb in all the tenses discussed here, in the active voice, while Table 2 compares the forms of a verb in the active and passive voices. These summaries should be helpful as a quick reference.

PRESENT TENSES

Simple present
Formed by using just the **base form** of the action verb, with *s* added for the third-person singular (*he*, *she*, or *it*). This tense has a surprising number of applications, and it can be used in some contexts to refer to the past or future as well as the present.

- Use it to describe a habitual action, circumstance, or state of affairs: a trait, a routine, a custom. It works for this purpose with both dynamic verbs:

  I **go** for an ear candling therapy session every Wednesday.

  My aunt **plays** the kettle drums.

  and stative verbs:

  He **knows** his way around a pool hall too well.

  The queen **likes** corgis.

- Use it with stative verbs to describe something happening right now, at (forgive the cliché) this point in time:

  What do you think of this sculpture? I **hate** it.

  Which flavor ice cream does your son want? He **wants** banana bubblegum chocolate chip, please.

For dynamic verbs, use the present progressive tense instead for this purpose (page 241).

- Use it in statements referring to the future that include any expression having to do with time (*when, once, if, unless, after,* etc.), even though the event has not yet happened:

    I'll pay you as soon as he **pays** me. [not: as soon as he *will pay* me]

    When the timer **goes** off, please turn the heat down under the haggis. [not: when the timer *will go* off]

- In dialogue (not in formal writing), optionally use it with dynamic verbs to describe something scheduled to happen in the near future:

    My flight **leaves** in two hours—gotta go.

    I **see** my hairdresser next Thursday, so I'll get the dirt then.

Saying *my flight will leave* (simple future, page 252), while accurate, would sound a bit stilted; the simple present is more natural in speech. In the second example, note that the simple present is an appropriate choice for the verb *see*, which is referring here to something scheduled and therefore definite, but not for *get*, which is describing something that is an assumption rather than a certainty and therefore more properly takes the future tense.

- In dialogue, optionally use it to indicate something that happened in the recent past:

    Your mother **tells** me you're engaged. [the telling is not happening at this very moment]

    I **hear** that he's thinking of writing The Great American Novel. [ditto for the hearing]

This is slightly more casual than using the simple past (page 247): *your mother told me, I heard.*

- It is sometimes employed as a literary device, and can be used deliberately throughout a narrative in place of the past tense. This usage of simple present tense is referred to variously as the **vivid present**, the **dramatic present**, or the **historical present**. It can have the effect of imparting a sense of immediacy,

    Woods has the puck in the corner; Robinson winds around him, but the puck dribbles out in front. I bob and weave, searching for the player I can't see but

I know is there. *Whaack.* A shot speeds for the net. My eyes hack at legs and torsos in front of me, but it's no use. I see nothing. Unaware, my arm moves, my legs split to either side, my fingers pull away, then snap back tightly closed. From a crush of noise, there's a profound silence, then suddenly a roar. I look in my glove – a good save, maybe better.

—Ken Dryden, *The Game*

or a certain intimacy, as if the reader is experiencing the events along with the characters:

"Well, at the very least you need a hat," she tells him. "I know a place nearby. Do you need to be back at work right away?"

She leads him to a little boutique on Madison. The window is crowded with women's hats perched on gray, featureless heads, with sloping necks nearly a foot long.

"They have men's stuff in the back," she says. The shop is crowded with women. The back is relatively tranquil, stacks of fedoras and berets arrayed on curved wooden shelves. He picks up a fur hat, a top hat, trying them on as a joke. The glass of wine has made him tipsy. Moushumi begins rummaging through a basket.

"This will be warm," she says, placing her fingers inside a thick navy cap with yellow stripes on the brim. She stretches the hat with her fingers. "What do you think?" She puts it on his head, touching his hair, his scalp. She smiles, pointing to the mirror. She watches as he studies himself.

—Jhumpa Lahiri, *The Namesake*

- *Negative formation*: For most tenses, all that's needed to turn a positive statement negative is to add the word **not**, but the simple present additionally requires the auxiliary verb **do** (*I/you/we/they do not; he/she/it does not*). In speech, these are usually run together as *don't* and *doesn't*. Another difference from the positive form is that for the third-person singular (*he/she/it*), the action verb drops the *s* at the end.

  I **like** porcupines / I **don't like** porcupines.

  She **takes** an hour to get ready / She **doesn't take** an hour to get ready.

  Sending the cat outside to get the mail **sounds** like a good idea / Sending the cat outside to get the mail **doesn't sound** like a good idea.

- *Passive formation:* Use the **simple present** of the auxiliary verb **be** (*am*, *are*, or *is*) followed by the past participle of the action verb.

    His magnificence overwhelms her / She **is overwhelmed** by his magnificence.

    My parents always give me socks for my birthday / I **am** always **given** socks for my birthday.

Present progressive

Also called the present continuous. Formed by combining the **simple present** of the auxiliary verb **be** (*I am, you are*, etc.) with the **present participle** of the action verb. This tense can be used only with dynamic verbs.

- Use it to refer to an action or event that is occurring right now and has not yet finished:

    Sorry, she can't come to the phone right now—she's **playing** her kettle drums.

    He's **finishing** his coffee—he'll be with you in a sec.

    Have you decided yet what you'll order? No, I'm still **thinking**.

This tense does not work with stative verbs. The following examples are *in*correct:

    What do you think of this sculpture? I am hating it.

    Which flavor ice cream does your son want? He is wanting the banana bubble-gum chocolate chip, please.

Use the simple present (*I hate, he wants*), as discussed on page 238.

- Like the simple present, the present progressive can be used to refer to a scheduled future event.

    He's **starting** university in the fall.

    Their train **is leaving** in an hour.

    It's not on my calendar, but I'm positive we **are having** tea with the duchess next Saturday.

The above examples could be phrased in the simple future (page 252) as *I'll start, their train will leave*, etc. In some cases, however, there can be a shade of difference in meaning between the two phrasings. Consider the following scenario: Person A asks Person B out to dinner, which B declines on the basis of unavailability. Grammatically (if not quite graciously), B could respond with either of the following:

> Present progressive: I can't, **I'm seeing** another friend that evening.

> Simple future: I can't, **I'll see** another friend that evening.

Both these wordings describe the same circumstance (seeing a friend) that will happen at the same time (the evening in question), but the former indicates that the competing activity was already in place before the invitation, whereas the latter carries just a suggestion that plans will be hastily made in order to have a reason to decline.

If a future event is *not* something planned and definite, it cannot be described with either the simple present or the present progressive. The following example is *in*correct:

> His race is next—I'm positive he is beating them all.

Such a statement can only be phrased in the simple future (page 252): *he will beat* or *he's going to beat*.

- *Passive formation:* Use the **present progressive** of **be** (*am being, are being,* or *is being*) followed by the past participle of the action verb.

  > I think she's manipulating him / I think he**'s being manipulated** by her.

  > The maitre d' is totally ignoring us / We**'re being** totally **ignored** by the maitre d'.

Present perfect

Formed by combining the **simple present** of the auxiliary verb **have** (*I have, he has,* etc.) with the **past participle** of the action verb.

Confusingly, this tense refers to something that has *already* happened (or hasn't happened, in a negative sentence). In that case, why call it "present," and why not use the simple past tense (page 247) instead? Because the simple past merely reports that something occurred or was done at some prior time, without connecting that event or act to the present. The present perfect captures the idea that there is some *current relevance* to the past action, or that as of this time, one *has had the experience* of doing something. (Recall that "perfect" refers to some action or event that is completed; i.e., perfected.) For example, "I saw *Travesties* last Sunday" describes a specific act that you did on that particular day, whereas "Yes, I**'ve seen** *Travesties*" states that at the present time, your experience includes having seen this particular play; *when* you did so is not relevant. Sometimes the distinction is negligible, other times not.

- Use the present perfect to describe something that has only just completed and has immediate relevance for the present,

> OK, I**'ve finished** building the Great Pyramid: what next? [focus is not on the completed task but on the builder's current availability]

> Oh no—the dog**'s eaten** the pastries I put out for the guests! [focus is not on the completed action of canine digestion but on the current absence of dessert]

> Is Iris still here? No, she**'s gone** home. [focus is not on Iris's completed journey, but on the current fact of her absence]

or to describe events at any time in the past, provided there is current relevance:

> She**'s raised** six kids, so she should know what she's talking about.

> We**'ve blown** too many chances: we've got to get it right this time.

- Use it with the time indicators *since* or *for* to refer to an event or state of affairs that started earlier and is *still in effect* at the present time. This tense works with both dynamic verbs,

> He**'s lived** in a tree house for the last two years.

> She**'s raised** iguanas since 2007.

and stative verbs:

> I**'ve known** him since kindergarten.

> He**'s owned** that car for twelve years.

Do not use it to refer to an event that took place at a specified time in the past. The following examples are *in*correct:

> He's written six letters to the editor last week.

> They've gone to their country house on Sunday.

Use the simple past (*he wrote, they went*) in these cases, as discussed on page 247.

- *Passive formation:* Use the **present perfect** of **be** (*have been* or *has been*) followed by the past participle of the action verb.

They've given him a huge grant to study the preservation of the broom crowberry / He's **been given** a huge grant to study the preservation of the broom crowberry.

I trusted them, but I think they've taken me for a ride / I trusted them, but I think I've **been taken** for a ride.

For some irregular verbs, it is a common error to use the past form instead of the past participle in a passive construction. (Recall that the past form and the past participle are always the same for regular verbs, but often differ for irregular ones.) The following examples are *in*correct:

He's worked with lab rats for years, but he's never been bit. [should be *bitten*]

Our team's only been beat once in the last eight games. [should be *beaten*]

There are no injuries, but she's been shook up a bit. [Elvis notwithstanding, should be *shaken*]

Present perfect progressive

Also called the present perfect continuous. Formed by combining the **simple present** of the auxiliary verb **have** (*I have, he has,* etc.), the auxiliary verb **been**, and the **present participle** of the action verb. (Note that *been* in this case is used differently from the *been* used to designate the passive voice for the perfect present.) This tense works only with dynamic verbs. It is used to indicate that an action or event that started earlier is still happening or still holds true.

- Use it to indicate ongoing action. (While the present perfect can also be used for this purpose, it requires a time indicator such as *since* or *for*. In contrast, the present perfect progressive *always* means that the action is still ongoing, whether or not a time indicator is included.)

    You're right: I've **been watching** that pot, and it hasn't boiled yet.

    You've **been spying** on me, haven't you?

    My husband **has been following** the Extreme Ironing competition all week.

The distinction between the present perfect and the present perfect progressive can be subtle. Always use the former when the action referred to has ended, and (except for sentences with time indicators, where you have a choice of which tense to use), always use the latter when the action is still ongoing:

I've **racked** my brains to try to come up with a good example. [I'm giving up]

I've **been racking** my brains to try to come up with a good example. [I'm still working on it]

You've **done** only one chore in all this time? [at least you got *one* completed]

You've **been doing** only one chore in all this time? [and you're *still* at it?]

Consistent with this distinction of completed versus ongoing, use the present perfect when referring to *the number of times* something has occurred, and the present perfect progressive when referring to *a period of time*:

I've **tried** his number ten times, but no answer. [not: *I've been trying* his number ten times]

I've **been trying** his number for the last hour, but no answer. [not: *I've tried* his number for the last hour]

She's **written** six books about her grievances already. [not: *She's been writing* six books]

She's **been writing** about her grievances for years. [not: *she's written* for years]

- Use it with the time indicators *since* or *for* to convey essentially the same meaning as the present perfect. Compare the following with the examples shown on page 242:

  He's been living in a tree house for the last two years. [same meaning as *he's lived*]

  She's been raising iguanas since 2007. [same meaning as *she's raised*]

In this situation, the present perfect progressive arguably puts slightly more emphasis on the present, the present perfect slightly more emphasis on the past. The distinction is trifling, however, and either tense could be used in these sentences with no essential difference in meaning.

This tense does not work with stative verbs, either with or without time indicators. The following examples are *in*correct:

I've been knowing him since kindergarten.

He's been owning that car for twelve years.

Use the present perfect (*I've known, he's owned*), as discussed on page 243.

- *Passive formation:* The passive voice does not lend itself well to any of the perfect progressive tenses, and is usually better avoided. Here, it takes the **present**

perfect continuous of **be** (*have been being* or *has been being*) followed by the past participle of the action verb. The result does not exactly trip off the tongue.

> They've been renovating their house for months / Their house **has been being renovated** for months.

> She's been stringing him along for too long / He**'s been being strung** along by her for too long.

Present emphatic

Formed by combining the **simple present** of the auxiliary verb **do** (*I/you/we/they do, he/she/it does*) with the **base form** of the action verb. This tense indicates the same time of action as the simple present but, as its name makes obvious, underscores a point more strongly. It is not used frequently.

Use it when the intention is to stress a point; typically when either contradicting a preceding statement,

> Why did you bother buying that exercise bike, when you never use it? I **do use** it. [more emphatic than *I use*]

> I'm afraid she doesn't like me. Nonsense, she **does like** you. [more emphatic than *she likes*]

or strongly agreeing with it:

> I like her voice. Yes, she **does sing** beautifully. [more emphatic than *Yes, she sings beautifully*]

> I think these plaid pants and paisley shirt are a good combination, don't you? Yes, they **do go** well together. [more emphatic than *Yes, they go well together*]

Note that negative statements in the simple present also take **do** (see page 240), but the inclusion of this word in that circumstance does not carry a suggestion of emphasis. If emphasis is wanted for a negative statement, it is necessary to use italics (see page 60) or some other strategy.

PAST TENSES

Next, the past. The past tense has a certain capacity that the present tense does not. Whereas the present tense by definition is concerned with only one point in time (you can't have two simultaneous "now's"), the past has a continuum to work with. That is, while making reference to some event that happened prior to now, you can also specify whether that event took place before *another* past event.

Simple past

Formed by using just the **past form** of the action verb. No surprises here: it always refers to an event that took place prior to the present time.

- Use it when referring to a past event, whether the time is specified,

    I **graduated** ten years ago.

    She **left** the company a year ago.

  or not:

    I **graduated** with honors.

    She **left** her executive position to become a personal shopper.

- *Negative formation:* For a negative statement, add the past form of **do** (*did*) plus the word **not**, and put the action verb in the base form rather than the past tense form.

    She saw him / She **didn't see** him.

    They handled that well / They **didn't handle** that well.

- *Passive formation:* Use the **past form** of **be** (*was* or *were*) followed by the past participle of the action verb.

    They downed their food in about two minutes / Their food **was downed** in about two minutes.

    The mosquitoes dive-bombed us / We **were dive-bombed** by mosquitoes.

The simple past is of course the standard tense used in narrative, in both fiction writing and non-fiction.

Past progressive

Also called the past continuous. Formed by combining the **past form** of the auxiliary verb **be** (*I was, you were,* etc.) with the **present participle** of the action verb. It can be used only with dynamic verbs. There are two main applications for this tense:

- Use it to convey the idea of one activity or state of affairs being in progress when another event happened:

    She **was minding** her own business when this blackbird came along and pecked off her nose.

    The tub **was overflowing** by the time he figured out how to turn the tap off.

- Use it to describe ongoing activities that were taking place in parallel:

> Mr. Phillips **was** back in the corner **explaining** a problem in algebra to Prissy
> Andrews and the rest of the scholars **were doing** pretty much as they pleased,
> **eating** green apples, **whispering**, **drawing** pictures on their slates, and **driving**
> crickets, harnessed to strings, up and down the aisle.
>
> —L.M. Montgomery, *Anne of Green Gables*

Do not use the past progressive to refer to an event that took place at a specified time in the past. The following examples are *in*correct:

> I was graduating ten years ago.
>
> She was leaving an hour ago.
>
> We were going to Helsinki last year.

Use the simple past (*I graduated, she left, we went*) in these cases, as discussed on
page 247.

- *Passive formation:* Use the **past progressive** of **be** (*was being* or *were being*)
  followed by the past participle of the action verb.

  > She was treating him rudely / He **was being treated** rudely.
  >
  > Ten men were pulling on the ropes / The ropes **were being pulled** on by ten men.

Past perfect

Formed by combining the **past form** of the auxiliary verb **have** (*had* in all cases, frequently contracted to *'d*) with the **past participle** of the action verb. Use this tense to
indicate that an action or event in the past happened earlier than some other action
or event in the past, or that it happened earlier than some specified time in the past.

- When referring to two or more past actions or events, use the past perfect to
  indicate that event A was completed before event B occurred:

  > It was only when the hostess introduced them that she remembered she **had**
  > **met** him once before. [*met* happened prior to *introduced* or *remembered*]
  >
  > The road suddenly ended at the top of a cliff, at which point we realized we **had**
  > **missed** the turn-off. [*missed* happened prior to *ended* or *realized*]

With stative verbs, use it to indicate that action A was in effect at the point at
which action B occurred:

I'**d known** that she was rich, but I was still taken by surprise when she presented me with a yacht for my birthday.

He'**d liked** her a lot until he found out about the bodies buried in her cellar.

With dynamic verbs, use the past perfect progressive (see below) for this purpose instead.

- When a sentence refers to a single action or event, this tense indicates that the action or event took place or was in effect at some time prior to the time under discussion:

    We'**d heard** all his stories a million times already.

    I'**d** never **seen** such a mess.

    We were told that the cup **had belonged** to the Borgia family.

- *Passive formation:* Use the past perfect of **be** (*had been*) followed by the past participle of the action verb.

    We had given him enough chances / He **had been given** enough chances.

    He'd driven her to appointments countless times / She'**d been driven** to appointments by him countless times.

Past perfect progressive

Also called the past perfect continuous. Formed by combining the **past form** of the auxiliary verb **have** (*had* in all cases, frequently contracted to '*d*), the auxiliary verb **been**, and the **present participle** of the action verb. This tense can be used only with dynamic verbs.

- Use it to indicate that some action or event A that began in the past was still ongoing when some later action or event B occurred:

    We **had been stirring** the potion for just a few minutes when it began to spew green smoke. [the stirring was still in progress when the spewing began]

    He'**d been waiting** on tables for years before he finally got his big break. [the server job was still in progress at the point that the studio came calling]

This tense does not work with stative verbs. The following examples are *incorrect*:

I'd been knowing that she was rich, but . . .

He'd been liking her a lot until . . .

Use the past perfect (*I'd known, he'd liked*), as discussed on page 248.

- Use it to indicate that a single action or event took place over some period of time:

    I couldn't report on what had been said at the teleconference because I**'d been playing** online solitaire the whole time.

    They**'d been living** in a commune before they started their family.

- *Passive formation:* As with the present perfect continuous, the passive voice becomes very clumsy in this tense and is not recommended. It consists of the **past perfect progressive** of **be** (*had been being*) followed by the past participle of the action verb. The result is not pretty.

    Women had been chasing him for years / He **had been being chased** by women for years.

    Beavers had apparently been chomping on the tree trunks / The tree trunks **had** apparently **been being chomped** on by beavers.

Past emphatic

Formed by combining the **simple past** of the auxiliary verb **do** (*did* in all cases) with the **base form** of the action verb. As with the present emphatic, it refers to the same time of action as the simple past but carries more weight. Use it to stress a point, particularly in contradiction to a previous statement.

Why didn't you return my call? I **did return** it, you weren't home. [more emphatic than *I returned*]

I don't think she knew about the concert. She **did know**—she told me she was planning to go. [more emphatic than *she knew*]

Note that the negative of a statement in the simple past also takes this form, but in this case there is no implication of emphasis.

They finished on time / They **didn't finish** on time.

We gave it our best shot / We **didn't give** it our best shot.

Habitual past

Formed by combining the auxiliary verb **would** with the **base form** of the action verb. Use it to describe something that occurred in the past on a regular or at least occasional basis.

> In my university days, I **would sleep** till noon.

> She **would** always **bring** a bottle of wine when she came for dinner.

> On summer nights at the lake, we **would lie** on the dock and gaze at the stars.

An important note here: *would* is a multi-purpose verb that plays several roles, and in this context is acting as the past tense of *will*. The same combination of *would* plus the base form of the action verb is also used in both the conditional simple (page 260) and the future in the past (page 256), which have very different meanings. The context, however, differentiates these three uses. The above examples make it clear that the scenarios are ones that occurred repeatedly in the past, whereas a conditional sentence would contain a word such as *if* to indicate the future (*If I didn't have to go to work tomorrow, I would sleep till noon*), and future in the past would include a reference to both past and future (*She told me this morning that she would bring a bottle of wine tonight*).

In the following, note two different strategies for describing the habitual past:

> A magician's house is expected to have certain peculiarities, but the most peculiar feature of Mr Norrell's house was, without a doubt, Childermass. In no other household in London was there any servant like him. One day he **might be observed** removing a dirty cup and wiping crumbs from a table like a common footman. The next day he **would interrupt** a room full of admirals, generals and noblemen to tell them in what particulars he considered them mistaken. Mr Norrell had once publicly reprimanded the Duke of Devonshire for speaking at the same time as Childermass.
>
> —Susanna Clarke, *Jonathan Strange & Mr Norrell*

The passive construction of "he might be observed" is capturing the same notion of habitual action in the past as the active construction "he would interrupt".

FUTURE TENSES

On to the future. Unlike some other languages, English does not have a dedicated verb form for the future tense, equivalent to the *ed* ending for the past. Therefore, for even the simple future, auxiliary verbs are needed. (Some grammar references insist that, technically, English does not have a future tense. This is strictly true, but obviously does not prevent us from describing it.)

Like the past tense, the future can deal with a continuum, specifying not only that an event has not yet taken place but also whether it will take place after another as-yet-uncompleted event.

Simple future

Formed by combining the auxiliary verb **will** (frequently contracted to *'ll*) with the **base form** of the action verb. But just to complicate things—yes it's called "simple", what's your point—the simple future can also be formed with **be going to**. Both forms describe something that has not yet happened but is expected to happen at some later time. They are often interchangeable and a matter of choice, but in some cases carry subtly different meanings.

It is preferable to use **will** under the following circumstances:

- When there is an likelihood but not a certainty of something happening, and no prior plan or schedule:

  Just throw those crusts in the yard; the birds **will eat** them.

  There's no need for medication, as the symptoms **will resolve** on their own.

- When a statement about a future action is arising out of what is happening now:

  I'**ll be** right with you—hang on.

  Well, I'**ll see** what I can do.

  Don't yell, we'**ll clean up** when we're done.

- When making an offer to do something, without an earlier understanding:

  Anybody here able to host the next meeting? Sure, I **will**. [*I'm going to* would imply that the arrangement was already in place.]

  "Dear Pig, are you willing to sell for one shilling
  Your ring?" Said the piggy, "**I will**".

  —Edward Lear, *The Owl and the Pussycat*

- When there is outright uncertainty about the outcome:

    Maybe she**'ll change** her mind. [one can always hope]

    Perhaps the neighbors **will relent** and return our baseball. [should we offer to pay for the broken window?]

The use of *going to* would imply a likelihood that cannot under the circumstances be assumed.

- When writing in a formal style:

    The study **will enroll** 300 patients. [not *is going to* enroll]

    The investigator **will be responsible** for obtaining informed consent from the subjects. [not *is going to be responsible for*]

- When emphasizing an action. The future cannot employ *do* to achieve emphasis as in the present emphatic (page 246) and past emphatic (page 250). But in speech at least, where *will* is almost always contracted to *'ll*, an emphatic effect can be achieved by using the full word:

    If you don't hurry, you won't make that deadline. I **will make** it. [more emphatic than *I'll make it*]

    It looks like Eden won't be showing up. She **will show up**. [more emphatic than *she'll show up*]

It is preferable to use **be going to** under the following circumstances:

- When the future act or event is something planned or intended, or can be predicted with certainty:

    I**'m going to pass by** the market this afternoon: can I pick anything up for you?

    We're **going to catch** a movie tonight: care to join us?

    I heard it**'s going to rain** tomorrow. [assuming that the forecast can be trusted]

    My nephew insists he**'s going to be** a fireman when he grows up.

(In the last example, note the use of the simple present in *grows* following the time expression *when*. See page 239.)

- When expressing a stronger intention than the use of **will** indicates. Compare the following two statements:

    I**'ll call** tonight to see how you're doing. [I assume you're okay with that]

    I**'m going to call** tonight to see how you're doing. [whether you like it or not]

Yet a third way of forming the simple future is with the verb **shall**. Its use is less common, and is usually reserved for the following:

- When extra emphasis is wanted:

    I **shall do** as I please.

    You most certainly **shall not**.

- In legal terminology, such as that used in contracts, where the intention is to clarify that something is not optional:

    The Author **shall deliver** to the Publisher one copy of the complete manuscript for the Work, in content and form satisfactory to the Publisher. The Publisher **shall**, within eighteen months after accepting the Author's satisfactory complete and final manuscript, publish the Work at its own expense . . .

- *Passive formation:* Use the **simple future** of **be** (*will be* or *going to be*), followed by the past participle of the action verb.

    The dog will eat anything that falls on the floor / Anything that falls on the floor **will be eaten** by the dog.

    Alfie is going to organize the next safari / The next safari **is going to be organized** by Alfie.

As discussed above, the simple present (page 239) and present progressive (page 241) can be used under some circumstances in place of the simple future.

Future progressive

Also called the future continuous. Formed by combining the auxiliary verbs **will be** or **be going to be** with the **present participle** of the action verb.

- Use this tense to indicate that an action or event that will begin in the future will still be in progress at some later time, or will be continuing for some time. It can be used only with dynamic verbs.

    He'**ll be working** late tonight, so you probably won't see him.

    We'**ll be following** your career as an alligator wrestler with great interest.

- **Be going to be** is more appropriate than **will be** if there is a wish to emphasize that something is planned.

I'**m going to be** outside shoveling—just holler if you need me.

My kids will be running in the marathon, but I'**m going to be walking**.

- *Passive formation:* The passive voice again fares very poorly here, consisting of the **future progressive** of **be** (*will be being*) followed by the past participle of the action verb. It is not recommended.

We'll be watching them carefully / They'll **be being watched** carefully.

Future perfect
Formed by combining the auxiliary verbs **will have** with the **past participle** of the action verb.

- Use this tense to indicate that an event or action A that has not yet happened will have been completed before another more distant event or action B occurs, or that an event will occur before some specified time in the future. This is the same concept as the past perfect but goes in the opposite direction, time-wise; and in this case involves references to both the future and the past in one breath.

She'**ll have gone** by the time you get here.

Everyone **will have eaten** by eight o'clock.

Hell **will have frozen over** before those idiots figure out what to do.

As with the simple future, **be going to have** can be used instead, although this is less common. Its meaning is the same as **will** but carries a slight implication of greater certainty.

I'**m going to have finished** my entire book before this stupid flight even takes off!

You'**re going to have tidied** your room by the time I get back, or else.

- *Passive formation:* Use the **future perfect** of **be** (*will have been*) followed by the past participle of the action verb.

I am confident that the butler will have polished the silver to perfection / I am confident that the silver **will have been polished** to perfection.

She will have written over a thousand pages of drivel on that subject / Over a thousand pages of drivel on that subject **will have been written** by her.

Future perfect progressive

Also called the future perfect continuous. Formed by combining the auxiliary verbs **will have been** (or **be going to have been**) with the **present participle** of the action verb.

This is about as complex as a tense can get, but there is a clear logic to it. As with the future perfect, this tense combines concepts of both the future and the past. Imagine that some scenario is happening right now, at the present time, and will continue to happen for some time into the future. Or, the scenario has not yet begun, but it will, and once it does, it will continue for some time. Hold that thought. Now, imagine jumping into the future while this scenario is still in progress, looking back on it, and observing how long it has been in progress *at that point*. That is the future perfect progressive.

- Use it to indicate that an action or event will be either ongoing or completed at some later time.

    In another few months, I'**ll have been living** in this city for more than half my life.

    Expect him to arrive grumpy: he'**ll have been travelling** for thirty-six hours.

    This is ridiculous: we'**re** soon **going to have been waiting** over forty minutes for this bus.

- *Passive formation:* Again, the passive voice works very poorly here. It consists of the **future perfect progressive** of **be** (*will have been being*) followed by the past participle of the action verb.

    They'll have been showing all their artwork to the guests / All their artwork **will have been being shown** to the guests.

Use this one at your peril.

Future in the past

Formed by combining the auxiliary verb **would** with the **base form** of the action verb. It is the equivalent of the simple future, which puts *will* before the base form. Here, *would* is acting as the past tense of *will*.

- This tense expresses the idea that at some earlier point, reference was made to an intended action or expected event that *at that time* was still in the future.

Sentences that use future in the past include actions such as thinking, knowing, informing, planning, predicting, or promising.

I knew he **would cough up** what he owed eventually.

He had been so convinced that he **would win** the lottery, he quit his job.

Note that the same combination of *would* plus the base form of the action verb is used for both the habitual past (page 251) and the conditional simple (page 260). The presence in the sentence of another verb in the past form (*knew, was*) provides the necessary context to differentiate this tense from those others.

• Like the simple future, the future in the past can use **be going to** instead of **would**; in this case, in the past form.

She was afraid he **was going to ramble on** forever.

They told me they **were going to make** the first payment last week.

CONDITIONALS

If not language itself, perhaps the Great Leap Forward [the appearance in the archaeological record about 40,000 years ago of artwork, musical instruments, and other artifacts of culture] coincided with the sudden discovery of what we might call a new software technique: maybe a new trick of grammar, such as the conditional clause, which at a stroke, would have enabled 'what if' imagination to flower. Or maybe early language, before the leap, could be used to talk only about things that were there, on the scene. Perhaps some forgotten genius realised the possibility of using words referentially as tokens of things that were not immediately present. It is the difference between 'That waterhole which we can both see' and 'Suppose there was a waterhole on the other side of the hill.'

—Richard Dawkins, *The Ancestor's Tale: A Pilgrimage to the Dawn of Life*

The remainder of this section deals with the construct of **mood**. The mood of a verb conveys the overall purpose for which it is being used.

The **imperative mood** expresses a command, request, or instruction (*go away; pass the salt please; press any key to continue*), with the subject of the sentence always understood to be *you*. This mood presents no grammatical challenges—it always uses the base form of the verb—and needs no further discussion.

Most sentences are crafted in the **indicative mood**, which presents a statement as fact (whether or not it is true is irrelevant). In the discussion of tenses above, all the examples use the indicative mood, since the assumption—grammatically, at least—is that the scenario described in each one did in fact happen or is happening or will happen. Tenses don't pass judgment on likelihood; they are concerned only with the timing.

In contrast, the **conditional** or **subjunctive mood** is used to convey ideas of likelihood and necessity. It deals with uncertain events that are dependent on something else, and is used to express the speaker's or writer's attitude about the reality or desirability of a statement—the "woulda coulda shoulda" experiences of life. Confusingly, some grammar references use these terms interchangeably, while others make a distinction, with "conditional" being used to describe possible, realistic scenarios, and "subjunctive" reserved for those that are hypothetical, impossible, or contrary to fact. Resolving the terminology dissonance is beyond the scope of this book. The main thing is to understand how to apply these grammatical formations correctly, whatever you choose to call them.

A conditional sentence contains two clauses. One of these, the condition clause, presents a condition, and the other, the result clause, presents a result that is dependent on that condition. (See the definition of clauses on page 74.) The condition clause includes a word such as *if*, *when*, or *unless*. (*When* carries a suggestion of something happening with more frequency or likelihood than *if* does.) Usually the clause that describes the condition comes first and the result clause comes second, but either order is possible.

A **real conditional** describes a situation that really does exist or did exist under certain circumstances, or that is likely to or expected to exist. Real conditionals differ from indicative sentences only in that they contain a conditional word such as *if*.

Real conditional in the present

Describes routine or habitual acts. The verbs in both clauses take the **simple present** tense (base form), consistent with the first application of this tense described on page 238.

> If I **see** a spider in the house, I **squash** it.
>
> When he **falls** off his bike, he **climbs** right back on it.
>
> She always **throws** a tantrum unless she **gets** her way.

Real conditional in the past

Describes something that once was routinely or repeatedly done, but carries an implication that it is no longer done. Again, the condition clause contains a word such as *if* or *when*, and the result clause contains a qualifying adverb such as *always*, *often*, or *usually*. The verbs in both clauses take the **simple past** tense (past form).

If I **went** into town, I always **gave** my neighbor a lift.

When he **called** the dogs, they usually **came** running.

Real conditional in the future

Describes something that can realistically happen in the future. Both clauses in this case describe specific acts that have not yet happened, but only the verb that states the result or outcome uses the **simple future** tense (*will* plus base form.) The verb that states the condition, despite the fact that it too is describing a future event, uses the **simple present** tense (base form). Recall that one of the applications of the simple present (page 239) is to indicate the future when the sentence includes an expression of time. In this case, the word *if* carries such an implication.

If you **fall**, I'**ll catch** you.

Unless you **object**, I'**ll invite** my parents to move in with us.

He'**ll call** you back if he **can**.

On to the unreal scenario. An **unreal conditional** (or subjunctive) describes a hypothetical situation that does not now exist, never existed, or is unlikely to ever exist. Unreal conditionals can be set in the present (if a certain hypothetical condition existed at this time, then a hypothetical result would also now exist), in the past (if a certain hypothetical condition *had* existed, then a hypothetical result would also have existed), or in the future (if a certain hypothetical condition comes true at some later time, then a hypothetical result will come true as well).

Unreal conditionals employ the auxiliary verbs *would*, *could*, *should*, and *might*, among others. Such verbs are called **modals**, meaning that they modify the *mood* of the action verb. Just like verbs in the indicative mood, they can take the simple form (*I would do*), progressive form (*I would be doing*), perfect form (*I would have done*), or perfect progressive form (*I would have been doing*).

Unreal conditional in the present

Describes a scenario whereby *if* hypothetical event A (the condition) existed at this time, then hypothetical event B (the result) would follow.

Consider the following sentence:

> If I **lived** downtown, I **would bike** to work.

Note the apparent use of the past tense in *I lived*. However, the statement is not making reference to having lived downtown at some earlier time. So what is happening here? The verb is indeed in the **past form** (see page 246), which is most commonly used for the simple past. In this case, however, it is being used to indicate not the past tense but the **subjunctive mood**. The subjunctive describes hypothetical situations, ones that are contrary to fact. In this example, it is describing a circumstance that does not in fact exist for our SUV-driving suburbanite. The scenario of living downtown might theoretically come true for this person in the future, but it is not true at the present time.

The verb that describes the result (*would bike*) is in the **conditional simple**, which consists of the modal auxiliary verb **would** (often contracted to *'d*) plus the **base form** of the action verb. The conditional simple describes something that *might* happen in the future but is not happening now.[1]

Similarly,

> If I **knew** what was wrong, I **would fix** it. [but I don't know]

> If she **had** any brains, she**'d see** what he was up to. [too bad she doesn't]

> If I **had** a hammer, I**'d hammer** in the morning. [but I don't have one, so world peace will have to wait]

A number of other constructions for unreal present conditional sentences are presented below.

- *Conditional sentences with no explicit "if" clause.* A conditional sentence does not have to contain an explicit *if* clause; the *if* can be implied. Consider the following:

---

[1] Note that the habitual past, described on page 251, takes exactly the same form for a completely different purpose. If this sentence read as <u>*When*</u> *I lived downtown, I would bike to work*, then "I lived" would be the simple past tense and "I would bike" would be in the habitual past. It is the *if* that changes everything.

> A law that **required** recently licensed drivers to have no more than one passenger under the age of nineteen **would reduce** the number of vehicle accidents involving teenagers.

As with *lived* in the earlier example, *required* is not in the past tense, it's in the subjunctive mood. Use of the subjunctive in the above sentence indicates that this particular law did not and does not now exist, but the writer believes there would be good consequences *if* it existed. (Aside: a proposed law in Ontario on this topic was axed after howls of outrage from the recently licensed.)

- *Conditional sentences with progressive verbs.* Conditional sentences can contain verbs in the progressive form, to indicate a hypothetical event that, if true, would be ongoing at this time. A progressive verb in the *if* clause takes the **past progressive**, while the verb in the result clause takes the **conditional simple**, formed by **would** plus the base form of the action verb:

> If they **were living** together, they **would save** a lot of money. [too bad they can't stand each other]

> If you **were behaving**, I **would buy** you a treat. [as it is, forget it]

If the progressive verb is in the result clause, it takes the **conditional progressive**, formed by **would be** plus the **present participle** of the action verb. The verb in the *if* clause takes the **simple past**:

> If he **understood** the urgency, I'm sure he **would be helping** you. [but he doesn't, so you're on your own]

> If I **had** the energy, I**'d be tidying** the house right now. [maybe next week]

- *Use of "was" versus "were" in the subjunctive.* For the *if* clause, a grammatical quirk associated with the subjunctive is that when it is applied to the verb *to be*, the past form for the first and third person (*I was, he was, she was, it was*) changes to *were*:

> Perhaps this software would work if the moon **were** in the right phase.

> If he **were** younger, it would be a different story.

> He treats his girlfriend as if she **were** a child.

> If I **were** you, I would . . . [insert helpful advice of choice here].

It is a common error to use *was* in such sentences (if he was younger, if I was you).

Less commonly, in what can be termed "hypercorrection," writers sometimes use the subjunctive when it is inappropriate: that is, when a sentence is describing a real rather than an unreal scenario. The following examples are *in*correct:

> At the end of the afternoon, we put everything that remained unsold out at the curb, and if anyone were interested, it was free for the taking.

> He looked as if he were expecting to be praised for his misbehavior.

Despite the "if's," these sentences are stating factual scenarios, not ones that are wishful thinking or contrary to fact or possibilities that may never come to be. Accordingly, the appropriate form of the verb is *was* (if anyone was interested; he looked as if he was expecting).

Unreal conditional in the past

Describes some hypothetical event that did not in fact ever happen, but *if* it had happened, then a hypothetical result would have followed. Unlike the unreal conditional in the present, which allows for the possibility that the hypothetical event might later come true, in this case it is too late and fulfillment is impossible.

Conditional sentences in the past are the hypothetical equivalent of the past perfect tense (page 248), which states that actual event A occurred before actual event B occurred. In this case, the message is that if hypothetical event A had occurred at a certain time, then hypothetical event B would have resulted. The verb in the *if* clause takes the **past perfect tense** (**had** plus past participle), and the verb in the result clause takes the **conditional perfect** (**would have** plus past participle).

> If I**'d known** you were coming, I **would have baked** a cake.

> If he **had listened** to his mother, he **would have applied** to medical school.

> If she **had realized** that the tiara that had been left to her was set with genuine diamonds, she **would** not **have sold** it for two dollars at the garage sale.

In the last example, if hypothetical event A had occurred, then actual event B would *not* have occurred.

A number of other constructions for unreal past conditional sentences are presented below.

- *Conditional sentences with no explicit "if" clause.* A conditional sentence does not have to have an explicit *if* clause:

> In hindsight, he realized it **would have been** a good idea to drill drainage holes in the planters before mounting them on the balcony railing.

Implication: *If* such holes had been created, a somewhat foreseeable consequence would have been averted.

- *Conditional sentences with progressive verbs.* As with the conditional in the present, these sentences can contain verbs in the progressive form, to indicate something ongoing. A progressive verb in the *if* clause takes **the past perfect progressive**, while that in the result clause takes the **conditional perfect**, formed by the auxiliary verbs **would have** plus the past participle of the action verb:

> If I **had been paying** more attention, I **would have stopped** the hairdresser before he applied the airplane glue.

> If they **had been sleeping** at the time, they **would** never **have heard** the bear going through the garbage.

If the progressive verb is in the result clause, it takes the **conditional perfect progressive**, formed by the auxiliary verbs **would have been** plus the **present participle** of the action verb. The verb in the *if* clause takes the **past perfect**:

> If she **had married** her elderly admirer, she **would have been living** in the lap of luxury. [big mistake that she went instead for the handsome young artist]

> You **wouldn't have been laughing** if it **had happened** to you. [a little empathy would be nice]

> If we**'d missed** that bus, we **would have been waiting** for the next one for an hour. [good thing I made us run for it]

- *Use of the correct participle with irregular verbs.* A common error in this construction is to use the past form of the verb instead of the past participle. (This is only an issue with irregular verbs, since for regular verbs the past form and past participle are always the same.) The following examples are *in*correct:

> I would have went if you'd asked me to. [should be *I would have gone*]

> If I hadn't stopped her, she would have drank the whole thing. [should be *she would have drunk*]

> You couldn't possibly have wrote that yourself. [should be *you couldn't possibly have written*]

Unreal conditional in the future

Describes a hypothetical event in the future where the intention is to emphasize that fulfillment of the event is uncertain, unlikely, or impossible. The verb in the *if* clause takes the **subjunctive** (past form of the action verb), while that in the result clause takes the **conditional simple** (**would** plus **base form** of the action verb).

> I may have to make a business trip to Tokyo. Wow, that sounds exciting—if you **went**, when **would** you **go**?

If the trip were a given, this would be worded as *When **will** you go?*

> If I **had** time next week, I **would clean** the garage. [implication: I won't have time, so this won't get done]

Contrast this with the real conditional in the future, *If I **have** time, I **will** clean the garage*, which lets the garage hold out a little more hope.

One or both clauses can take the progressive form instead of the simple form:

> If I **were going** your way, I **would give** you a lift.

> If he **were graduating** in time, he'**d be joining** you at the firm this year.

> If I **weren't playing** darts tonight, I **would** gladly **join** you in a game of chess.

* * * * *

The following tables summarize the verb forms described above. Table 1 conjugates an irregular verb in the active voice, while Table 2 contrasts the different verb forms used in the active and passive voice.

TABLE 1: CONJUGATION OF THE VERB *TO WRITE*

	Simple	Progressive	Perfect	Perfect Progressive	Emphatic	Habitual Past	Future in the Past
Present	I write	I am writing	I have written	I have been writing	I do write	--	--
Past	I wrote	I was writing	I had written	I had been writing	I did write	I would write *	
Future with *will*	I will write	I will be writing	I will have written	I will have been writing	--	--	I would write *
Future with *be going to*	I am going to write	I am going to be writing	I am going to have written	I am going to have been writing	--	--	--
Conditional	I would write *	I would be writing	I would have written	I would have been writing	--	--	--

More context is needed to differentiate the three starred tenses:

* Conditional simple: If I had the time, I **would write** him a letter. (But I don't have the time, so I won't.)

* Habitual past: Whenever I had the time, I **would write** him a letter. (I did this on a number of occasions.)

* Future in the past: I promised that I **would write** him a letter. (And at some later point I did so.)

TABLE 2: ACTIVE AND PASSIVE VERB FORMS OF THE VERB *TO GIVE*

	Simple	Progressive	Perfect	Perfect Progressive
Present, Active	she gives	she is giving	she has given	she has been giving
Present, Passive	she is given	she is being given	she has been given	she has been being given *
Past, Active	she gave	she was giving	she had given	she had been giving
Past, Passive	she was given	she was being given	she had been given	she had been being given *
Future, Active	she will give	she will be giving	she will have given	she will have been giving *
Future, Passive	she will be given	she will be being given *	she will have been given	she will have been being given *

* The starred tenses are awkward and should usually be avoided.

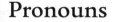

Pronouns

WITHOUT PRONOUNS to act as stand-ins for nouns, language would be very cumbersome. Imagine if every sentence had to be along the lines of *Betty Lou does whatever Betty Lou pleases and usually gets Betty Lou's own way* instead of *Betty Lou does whatever she pleases and usually gets her own way*. Pronouns improve flow, enabling the avoidance of repetitiveness at no cost of clarity. Most pronouns are easily and intuitively understood: everyone knows that a bull is *he*, a toaster is *it*, and something that belongs to the Joneses is *theirs*. Some constructions, however, are dicier. This section looks at a few issues that are frequent stumbling blocks:

- Determining the right pronoun
- Referring to the right antecedent
- Ensuring that a pronoun agrees with its antecedent

In addition, some considerations around choosing between first, second, and third person are reviewed at the end of the section.

DETERMINING THE RIGHT PRONOUN

For many weeks he pressed in vain
His nose against the window-pane,
And envied those who walked about
Reducing their unwanted stout.
None of the people he could see
"Is quite" (he said) "as fat as me!"
Then, with a still more moving sigh,
"I mean" (he said) "as fat as I!"

—A.A. Milne, *When We Were Very Young*

Unlike nouns, pronouns change form depending on what role they play in a sentence. You would say *Leora called Jonah* and *Jonah called Leora*, but if the names were replaced by pronouns, these sentences become <u>she</u> *called* <u>him</u> and <u>he</u> *called* <u>her</u>. The different forms that a pronoun can take on are called **cases**.

There are three cases: subjective, objective, and possessive. The **subjective case** is used when a pronoun represents the subject, or actor: <u>I</u> *will be late*. The **objective case** is used for a pronoun that represents the object, the entity affected by the action of the subject: *Don't wait for* <u>me</u>. The **possessive case** is used to indicate ownership, and differs depending on whether the pronoun precedes or follows the possessed object: *That's* <u>my</u> *soup / That soup is* <u>mine</u>. No one would say *Me will be late, don't wait for I*, but in some situations the correct pronoun is not so obvious.

A word on this topic before beginning. There is often disparity between what the rule books say and how people actually use the language; and educated speakers who wouldn't dream of saying *I seen him yesterday* or *she don't sing so good* will readily use pronouns in ways that contravene grammar rules, possibly because they feel that the correct word would sound pedantic. Most modern guides to English usage recognize the reality of common idiom, and stop short of dictating that every pronoun rule be followed under every circumstance. This book is no exception. It is important, however, that you be familiar with the rules so that if you choose to bend them you do so consciously. Experienced writers can distinguish between those situations where disregarding a rule is reasonable and those where disregarding it would seem just plain ignorant. In situations where you don't feel comfortable using either a stilted-sounding correct pronoun or a more natural-sounding but technically incorrect one, it may be best to recast the sentence.

Personal pronouns

Personal pronouns are used as stand-ins for the names of specific people or things. The **subjective personal pronouns** are *I, you, he, she, it, we,* and *they,* and are used when the pronoun represents the subject of the sentence—the actor or the focus of interest. The **objective personal pronouns** are *me, you, him, her, it, us,* and *them,* and are used when the pronoun represents the object of the sentence—something that is acted on or affected by the subject. (Note that *you* and *it* are the same in both cases; the others change.) A third category, **possessive personal pronouns**, is discussed on page 272.

Confusion between the subjective and objective cases is most likely to occur in the following situations:

When the sentence has more than one subject

The correct pronoun is obvious in a simple construction such as *I bought some shoes today*, but a remarkable number of speakers would say *Sarah and me bought some shoes today*, or *me and Sarah bought*, or *her and me bought*, instead of the subjective *Sarah and I*. If you are ever uncertain, mentally drop any distracting elements. It should be apparent that it is incorrect to say *me bought some shoes*; the addition of another subject does not change this.

When the sentence has more than one object

Possibly because of an awareness that *me* is often used incorrectly, many people use constructions such as *If you have any questions, please let Shayne or I know*, likely believing that *I* sounds more genteel. (Some grammarians are kind enough to call this type of usage "hypercorrectness." A better term for it is "wrong.") Again, mentally drop any distracting elements. It should be apparent that it is incorrect to say *let I know*.

This type of error is particularly likely to occur when the pronoun is the object of a preposition rather than the object of a verb. The objective case is always required when a pronoun follows a preposition: *give that to me; she went to the appointment with him*. If another object intervenes between the preposition and the pronoun, the subjective case may be mistakenly used: *The news came as a shock to Sam and I* instead of *to Sam and me*. If you mentally drop the intervening object, it becomes clear that it would be incorrect to say *The news came as a shock to I*.

When the pronoun is immediately followed by the noun it represents

The noun in such a case is called an **appositive**, a word that renames an adjacent word. The presence of an appositive can be distracting, but it doesn't alter the subject/object distinction. In this situation, simply treat the pronoun as you would if the appositive weren't there: that is, use the subjective case if the pronoun is the actor, and the objective case if it is the target of an action. It is common to see sentence formations such as *Us drudges would like to have the day off* or *Just give that job to we drudges*. Take away the noun, and it should be clear that it would be incorrect to say *Us would like to have the day off* and *Just give that job to we*. Therefore, these sentences must appear as *We drudges would like* and *give that job to us drudges*. If you are ever uncertain, mentally drop the noun to determine whether the pronoun is acting as a subject or an object.

When the sentence has an elliptical construction

This refers to wording in which some element that can be inferred from the context is dropped. Since a subject is usually followed by a verb (an action or a description) whereas an object is not, it is an understandable error to assume that an objective pronoun should be used whenever no verb follows. Many people would believe it correct to say *Louie can yell louder than him* and *She thinks she's better than me*. In fact, these are elliptical constructions for *Louie can yell louder than he can yell* and *She thinks she's better than I am*, and therefore should properly appear as *Louie can yell louder than he* and *She thinks she's better than I*. A sentence such as *The explosion startled Oscar as much as they* is also incorrect, because here the meaning is *The explosion startled Oscar as much as it startled them*. If you are uncertain, mentally fill in the missing words to determine whether the pronoun is acting as a subject or an object.

If you feel that the subjective case sounds too pedantic in these situations—which it can—then avoid the elliptical construction and spell out all the words. In speech or informal writing, the objective case is often perfectly acceptable. Determine your own comfort level.

When the pronoun follows any form of the verb **to be**

This includes all tense formations: *am, are, is, was, were, will be, being, been, had been, have been,* etc. In such constructions, the pronoun always takes the subjective case. Thus, *Old King Cole was a merry old soul, and a merry old soul was he,* or *The only attendees still awake at the lecture were Michelle and I*. If you switch the wording around, it becomes clear that the pronoun is acting as the subject: *he* (not *him*) *was a merry old soul;* and *I* (not *me*) *was still awake*. If you don't feel comfortable with this, recast the sentence: *Michelle and I were the only attendees still awake*.

TEST YOUR KNOWLEDGE

Which pronoun is correct?

1. Felicia and (I/me) polished off the roast ox.

2. Both Aunt Minnie and (I/me) were hauled off for interrogation.

3. My brother can crochet better than (I/me).

4. The guys at the office gave Alice and (I/me) matching garden gnomes.

5. Thank you for inviting Roland and (I/me), but we both have to wash our hair that night.

6. Just between you and (I/me), I think he's lying through his teeth.

7. Sidney wanted the job more than (I/me).

8. Sally's not nearly as persnickety as (she/her).

9. The space shuttle landing in the backyard excited Abe more than (they/them).

10. I felt that the last person I could trust with the chocolate truffles was (he/him).

11. A fine pair of fashion plates are (we/us)!

12. The dean told (we/us) jocks that we'd better shape up academically.

13. The dean said that (we/us) jocks had better shape up academically.

14. For (we/us) baby boomers, the economic future is looking less rosy than the past.

15. There wasn't much attention left over for the second-place finisher (I/me).

ANSWERS

1. *Felicia and I polished off the roast ox.* Don't be distracted by the two subjects. You wouldn't say *me polished off the roast ox.*

2. *Both Aunt Minnie and I were hauled off.* Again two subjects, here the recipients of an action rather than the performers. Don't be distracted by either the other subject or the passive construction. You wouldn't say *me was hauled off for interrogation.*

3. *My brother can crochet better than I.* An elliptical construction that effectively is saying *My brother can crochet better than I can crochet.*

4. *The guys at the office gave Alice and me.* Don't be distracted by the two objects. The pronoun is one of the objects of the verb *gave.*

5. *Thank you for inviting Roland and me.* Again, two objects. The pronoun is one of the objects of the verb *inviting.*

6. *Just between you and me.* The pronoun is one of the objects of the preposition *between.* ("Between you and I" is a *very* common error.)

7. *Sidney wanted the job more than . . . ?* The choice of pronoun here depends on the meaning. It is *I* if what's meant is *Sidney wanted the job more than I wanted the job* (an elliptical construction where the pronoun is a subject), and *me* if what's meant is *Sidney wanted the job more than he wanted me* (an elliptical construction where the pronoun is an object). Since the distinction is subtle, it would probably be better to fill in the implied words.

8. *Sally's not nearly as persnickety as she.* An elliptical construction meaning *as persnickety as she is.*

9. *[It] excited Abe more than them.* An elliptical construction meaning *more than it excited them.*

10. *. . . the last person I could trust was he.* The pronoun follows a form of the verb *to be* (*was*), and is therefore subjective.

11. *A fine pair of fashion plates are we!* Again, a subjective pronoun following a form of *to be* (*are*).

12. *The dean told us jocks that we'd better shape up.* Don't be distracted by the appositive *jocks.* Both the pronoun and the noun are objects of the verb *told.*

13. *The dean said that we jocks had better shape up.* Again, don't be distracted by the appositive. Here, both the pronoun and the noun are subjects.

14. *For us baby boomers.* Here, both the pronoun and its appositive are the objects of the preposition *for*, and the pronoun therefore takes the objective case.

15. *There wasn't much for the second-place finisher, me.* The pronoun is an appositive to *second-place finisher.* Both are the objects of the preposition *for*, and the pronoun therefore takes the objective case.

Possessive pronouns

The **possessive personal pronouns** are used to define who owns something. They are *mine, yours, hers, his, its, ours,* and *theirs.* Such a pronoun either comes after the noun being possessed *(The house on the left is ours; Are these enchanting children yours?)* or is independent of it *(My bathrobe is green. His is pink; Whose crib notes are these? Mine.)*

Possession is also expressed using *my, your, her, his, its, our,* and *their* (note that *his* and *its* are the same in both cases). These words always come before the noun being possessed (*That's <u>our</u> house; Are these <u>your</u> children?*), and cannot stand alone. Since they act to modify the noun that follows, they are labeled by some grammarians as possessive adjectives rather than pronouns. Regardless of what they are called, their role is that of a pronoun.

Possessive pronouns are mostly handled without difficulty, but there are two problem areas: the inclusion of needless apostrophes, and confusion of certain pronouns with words that are homonyms.

- **Apostrophe or not?** Likely because the possessive form of names and nouns takes an apostrophe plus *s* (*Joe's place; the cat's meow*), some people assume that possessive pronouns ending in *s* must take an apostrophe as well, and write them as *your's, her's, our's,* and *their's*. No such words exist.

- ***Its* or *it's*?** A strong contender for the most frequent error in the English language. As described above, some people just can't shake the conviction that every possessive must take an apostrophe; the difference in this case is that adding an apostrophe does create a real word, albeit with a different meaning. *Its* is the possessive of *it* (*has your car had its oil checked lately; every dog has its day*). *It's* is a contraction for either *it is* (*it's not fair; do you think it's going to snow*) or *it has* (*it's barely begun; it's been a long day*).

- ***Your* or *you're*?** *Your* is the possessive of *you* (*here's your coat; how's your dad doing*). *You're* is a contraction for *you are* (*you're very welcome; you're not so easy to please*). Errors such as "Your welcome" or "Your kidding" are very common.

- ***Their* or *they're*?** *Their* is the possessive of *they* (*is that their house; I just met their daughter*). *They're* is a contraction for *they are* (*I heard they're not coming; She told me they're moving to Italy*).

For more, see the discussion of the possessive apostrophe on page 200.

Interrogative pronouns

Costello: I'm asking YOU who's on first.

Abbott: That's the man's name.

Costello: That's whose name?

Abbott: Yes.

> **Costello:** Well go ahead and tell me.
> **Abbott:** That's it.
> **Costello:** That's who?
> **Abbott:** Yes.

—Abbott and Costello, *Who's on First*

Interrogative pronouns are used to open questions that require an informative answer, more than just a yes or no. They are *who, whom, whose, which,* and *what.*

The first three are used to refer only to people, and, like personal pronouns, differ in case: *who* for a subject, *whom* for an object, and *whose* to determine possession. *Who left these muddy footprints on the carpet? Whom will you be taking to the ball? Whose Fabergé egg is this?*

What is used to refer only to things, and does not change case. Subject: *What's the problem here?* Object: *What will you be bringing to the potluck?*

Which is less open-ended than the others, being used to specify one or more possibilities out of a restricted group. It can be used to refer to either people or things and, like *what,* does not change case. Subject: *Which is your teacher? Which is the best route?* Object: *Which do you prefer?*

Two common errors made with interrogative pronouns are confusion between *who* and *whom* and between *whose* and its homonym *who's.*

- **Who or whom?** Use the subjective *who* when the pronoun is associated with an action or a description: *Who wants a cupcake?* Use the objective *whom* when the pronoun is the target of someone else's action: *Whom are you trying to fool?*

  A helpful mnemonic is to determine whether the answer to the question would take *him* or *he,* which are more intuitively understood. If it would take *him,* go with *whom,* both of which end in the letter *m;* if it would take *he,* go with *who,* neither of which ends in *m.* Thus: *Who wants a cupcake? He wants a cupcake. Whom are you trying to fool? I'm trying to fool him.* (This trick also works with *them* and *they,* but not with *her* and *she,* since neither of those words ends in *m.*)

  In speech, it usually feels more natural to use *who* in both cases. In writing, decide which to use based on the formality of your work.

- **Whose or who's?** This error exists only in writing, not in speech, since these words sound the same. *Whose* is possessive: *Whose car is blocking the driveway? Who's* is a contraction for either *who is* or *who has: Who's driving my way? Who's eaten all the cherries?* If unsure about which one to use, mentally substitute *who is* or *who has* for the word and see if it makes sense. If yes, go with *who's;* if no, go with *whose*. It becomes readily apparent that you could say <u>*Who is*</u> *driving my way* but not <u>*Who is*</u> *car is blocking the driveway*.

Relative pronouns

Relative pronouns are used to open a particular type of dependent clause (see page 74) called a **relative clause**. Such a clause provides information about a noun mentioned earlier in the sentence. Relative pronouns include *who, whom, whose,* and *which* (which also function as interrogative pronouns), as well as *that, where,* and *when,* plus the derivatives *whoever, whomever,* and *whichever*. For example, *The jelly-beans* <u>*that the kids left in the car*</u> *are now stuck to the seat,* or *Students* <u>*who hand assignments in late*</u> *will have marks deducted.*

The following words are commonly confused:

- ***Who* or *whom*?** Just as when these words are used as interrogative pronouns, the distinction between them has to do with their use as subject and object. It can be helpful to mentally recast a sentence so that it would take a personal pronoun, and then determine whether this pronoun would be subjective or objective. As with the "who/whom" distinction described for interrogative pronouns, a good mnemonic is to think of the pronouns *he/him* or *they/them,* because of the "m" versus "no m" ending. Thus,

She was the one <u>whom</u> we wanted to support.	[we wanted to support <u>him</u> (i.e., *her*)]
I was hoping to meet this mystery man, <u>who</u> she said is her masseur.	[<u>he</u> is her masseur]
We asked only those employees <u>who</u> we figured would be interested.	[we figured <u>they</u> would be interested]
We assigned only those employees <u>whom</u> we figured the customers would trust.	[the customers would trust <u>them</u>]

- ***Whoever* or *whomever*?** The same strategy as before.

  Subject:

Would <u>whoever</u> borrowed the karaoke machine please keep it.	[<u>he</u> borrowed it]
<u>Whoever</u> is responsible for this mess should clean it up.	[<u>he</u> is responsible]

Object:

Please return that hideous lampshade to <u>whomever</u> you got it from.   [I got it from <u>him</u>]

Feel free to go sky-surfing with <u>whomever</u> you want.   [I'll go with <u>him</u>]

In everyday speech, most people would say *whoever you got it from* or *whoever you want*. How you handle the subjective/objective distinction should depend on the formality of your writing.

- ***Whose* or *who's*?** Just as when these pronouns are interrogative, *whose* is possessive, *who's* is a contraction. Possessive: *It was an idea <u>whose</u> time had come; I don't care <u>whose</u> fault it is.* Contraction: *We need to find out <u>who's</u> responsible; anyone <u>who's</u> finished may leave now.* Again, mentally substitute "who is" or "who has" for the word and see if the sentence still makes sense. If yes, go with *who's;* if no, go with *whose*. Note that as a relative pronoun (but not as an interrogative pronoun), *whose* can apply to objects as well as people.

- ***Which* or *that*?** The distinction here is not one of subject versus object, but of how the information that follows the pronoun relates to the subject of the sentence. Briefly, use *that* when the dependent clause is providing identifying information about the subject. For example, *Spiders <u>that</u> live underground do not spin webs.* The subject of the sentence is spiders—but not all spiders. The dependent clause *that live underground* applies to only some species of spider, and hence is acting to further identify the subject. Use *which* when the clause is simply providing additional information about a subject that is already fully identified. For example, *Spiders, <u>which</u> have four pairs of legs, are classified as arachnids, not insects.* Again, the subject is spiders, and in this case we mean all spiders. The relative clause *which have four pairs of legs* applies to every species of spider; hence, it is not serving to further identify the subject.

  A fuller discussion of the which/that distinction is provided in the section on restrictive versus nonrestrictive elements, on page 89.

- ***That* or *who*?** The issue here is whether or not the subject is a human being. It is usual to use *who* when referring to people (*The Man Who Fell to Earth; The Boy Who Cried Wolf*) and *that* when referring to animals or objects (*The Mouse That Roared; The House That Jack Built*). This distinction, however, is not universally followed. Some writers use *who* for animals, at least for individual animals that are viewed (or should that be "who are viewed"?) as having human-like personalities (*The Dog Who Wouldn't Be*). Occasionally, *who* is used to refer to corporate entities (*We went with the management company who offered the lowest bid*). Some authorities accept *that* for people when the reference is general rather than specific (*I can't stand people that never listen; She always seems to end up with men that only want her for her brains*). It is usually considered preferable, though, to go with *who* for people and *that* for everything else.

Reflexive pronouns

Reflexive pronouns are pronouns that end in *-self*. The most common error involving these pronouns is to use them when they are completely uncalled for. Many people seem to think it sounds more genteel to say *myself* when plain *I* or *me* would do. Negative. If the pronoun is acting as a subject, use *I*; if it is acting as an object, use *me*. The only circumstances in which the *-self* form of a pronoun is appropriate are the following:

When the subject and object are the same entity (that is, when they reflect each other):

You take <u>yourself</u> too seriously.

She looked at <u>herself</u> critically.

The machine turned <u>itself</u> off automatically.

The little piggy took <u>himself</u> off to the market.

When you need to clarify that the subject has performed some action alone or unassisted:

I couldn't possibly go by <u>myself</u>.

Shoshanna did all the cooking <u>herself</u>.

Did you finish that entire sugar pie <u>yourself</u>?

They cleaned up all by <u>themselves</u>.

When the pronoun acts to emphasize another word (in this role, it is called an **intensive pronoun**):

I <u>myself</u> would never sink that low.

Morris <u>himself</u> has no idea how the sour cream got into the DVD player.

We <u>ourselves</u> expected the worst.

My reputation <u>itself</u> was at risk.

I insist on having an appointment with Monsieur André <u>himself</u>.

TEST YOUR KNOWLEDGE

Which pronoun is correct?

1. Elmer and (I/myself) were jointly responsible for the riot.

2. Imelda gave the report directly to Hubert and (me/myself).

3. The director and (I/myself) had a long discussion about the recipe for blintzes.

4. Why does this sort of thing always happen to (me/myself)?

ANSWERS

In none of the above cases is the reflexive pronoun correct. The answers are *I* for items 1 and 3 and *me* for items 2 and 4.

REFERRING TO THE RIGHT ANTECEDENT

"Ugh!" said the Lory, with a shiver.

"I beg your pardon!" said the Mouse, frowning, but very politely. "Did you speak?"

"Not I!" said the Lory, hastily.

"I thought you did," said the Mouse. "I proceed. 'Edwin and Morcar, the earls of Mercia and Northumbria, declared for him; and even Stigand, the patriotic archbishop of Canterbury, found it advisable—' "

"Found *what?*" said the Duck.

"Found *it*," the Mouse replied rather crossly: "of course you know what 'it' means."

"I know what 'it' means well enough, when I find a thing," said the Duck: "it's generally a frog or a worm. The question is, what did the arch-bishop find?"

> The Mouse did not notice this question, but hurriedly went on, " '—found it advisable to go with Edgar Atheling to meet William and offer him the crown. . . .' "
>
> —Lewis Carroll, *Alice's Adventures in Wonderland*

The **antecedent** of a pronoun is the noun to which it refers. For example, in the preceding sentence, the word *pronoun* is the antecedent of the pronoun *it*. The antecedent may exist in the same sentence as the pronoun or in an earlier sentence; or, less commonly, it may come after. Interrogative pronouns logically do not have antecedents: for example, *Who was at the door?* And certain pronouns are themselves antecedents for other pronouns; more on this below.

The relationship between a pronoun and its antecedent must be crystal clear. Watch for errors such as the following:

Missing antecedents

Sometimes a writer fails to notice that the entity a pronoun is intended to refer to hasn't in fact been explicitly named. For example:

> Research has shown that men are generally more satisfied than women with marriage, and that they seek divorce less often. It also has shown that they live longer than bachelors.

Men live longer than bachelors? The writer obviously means *married* men, but the preceding sentence doesn't actually contain that term, so *they* ends up latching onto the wrong entity.

> *Better:* Research has shown that men are generally more satisfied than women with marriage, and that they seek divorce less often. It also has shown that married men live longer than bachelors.

Similarly,

> The use of free-format tables for writing software specifications may seem counter to the general trend; however, they give the developer certain advantages.

Here, *they* is intended to refer to *free-format tables*, but note that the subject of the sentence is actually *the use of*. Although the term *free-format tables* does appear in the sentence, it is not in a position to act as the antecedent.

> *Better:* The use of free-format tables for writing software specifications may seem counter to the general trend; however, such tables give the developer certain advantages.

Intervening antecedents

If a noun that could act as an antecedent—from a grammatical standpoint if not a logical one—comes between the pronoun and the "real" antecedent, the pronoun will latch onto this interloper instead. Thus, you must ensure that no interfering noun comes between a pronoun and its intended antecedent.

> Keep the drug stored at room temperature. A special insulating container is provided. If it is exposed to extremes of heat or cold, its properties may degenerate.

Presumably the writer didn't intend to say that the insulating container may degenerate, but since this noun lies closer to the pronoun *it* than does the noun *drug, container* grabs the role of antecedent. There are three possible solutions: repeat the intended noun instead of replacing it with a pronoun; move the intervening noun to a position where it won't cause a problem; or enclose the reference to the intervening noun in parentheses, which effectively removes it from the picture. (See Parentheses on page 154.)

> *Better:* Keep the drug stored at room temperature. A special insulating container is provided. If the drug is exposed to extremes of heat or cold, its properties may degenerate.
>
> *or:* Keep the drug stored at room temperature. If it is exposed to extremes of heat or cold, its properties may degenerate. A special insulating container is provided.
>
> *or:* Keep the drug stored at room temperature. (A special insulating container is provided.) If it is exposed to extremes of heat or cold, its properties may degenerate.

Do not have a pronoun and its antecedent lie too far away from each other, even if no interfering noun lies between them. Readers should not have to puzzle over a *they* or an *it* popping up unexpectedly and be faced with backtracking to find its origin.

Ambiguous antecedents

Watch out for constructions where a pronoun could refer to more than one antecedent. If this is the case, you will have to rephrase the sentence. For example:

> As the dog pounced on the cat, it let out a snarl.

Which one let out the snarl—the dog or the cat? Either of the following might be correct:

> The dog pounced on the cat, snarling as it did so.
>
> The dog pounced on the cat, which let out a snarl.

Note that the ambiguity exists only because both possible antecedents take the same singular pronoun. If there were two or more dogs and just one cat, or vice versa, there wouldn't be a problem.

> As the dogs pounced on the cat, it let out a snarl.
> [*it* refers unambiguously to the cat]

> As the dog pounced on the cats, it let out a snarl.
> [*it* refers unambiguously to the dog]

Similarly,

> Marvin's uncle told him he would have to leave.

Which one would have to leave: Marvin or his uncle? Either of the following might be correct:

> Marvin's uncle told him to leave.

> Marvin's uncle told him, "I have to leave."

If Marvin's *aunt* were involved instead, the male pronoun would not be ambiguous.

AGREEMENT BETWEEN PRONOUN AND ANTECEDENT

The rules of English grammar state that within a sentence, certain types of words must "agree" with other types—that is, be grammatically consistent with them. For example, a singular noun takes a singular verb and a plural noun takes a plural verb: one snowflake *falls*, multiple snowflakes *fall*. See Agreement Between Subject and Verb on page 208.

In the case of pronouns, a pronoun must agree with its antecedent (and with any other pronouns referring to the same antecedent) in three ways: **gender**, **number**, and **person**.

Agreement in gender

Agreement in gender is straightforward: male entities take *he, him, his*; female entities take *she, her, hers*; gender-neutral entities take *it, its*. Errors in this type of agreement don't arise too often. If writing about an animal, be sure you don't carelessly alternate between *it* and one of the other pronouns: for example, *The cat arched his back and switched its tail*. Also, do not write a sentence such as *Either of his sisters is likely to do well for themselves*: the word *either* requires a singular pronoun and *sisters* makes it clear that this pronoun must be female, so the sentence should read *Either of his sisters is likely to do well for herself*.

If you have chosen to alternate between *he* and *she* when referring to persons of unspecified sex, do not do so with jarring frequency. At a minimum, finish a topic or a paragraph before switching to the other gender. For further discussion, see Avoidance of Bias on page 318.

Agreement in number

No competent English speaker would say *where did I put them* when looking for a single book or *where did I put it* when looking for a stack, or refer to one's best friend as *they* or to a group of girlfriends as *she*. In most cases, singular and plural pronouns are used appropriately. Occasionally, however, problems arise.

Avoidance of male-only pronouns

In an effort to avoid gender bias—that is, the use of *he, him*, and *his* to refer to both sexes—it is common to employ *they, them*, or *their* as singular pronouns when the sex of the person being referred to is unknown or irrelevant. For example, *If a student wants to drop a class without penalty, they must do so in the first month*. In speech, this is completely acceptable, but in formal writing it sometimes draws censure. The problem is, in standard English, *they* is a plural pronoun, and using it in combination with a singular antecedent (student) constitutes an error in agreement. There are many historical and literary precedents for using plural pronouns to denote a single person, and there are strong arguments for legitimizing this use; in fact, some dictionaries already do. For a discussion of this issue, see Avoidance of Bias on page 316.

Singular indefinite pronouns

The indefinite pronouns *each, every, either, neither, everybody, everyone, somebody, someone, nobody, no one, anybody*, and *anyone* are all technically singulars, despite some of them being plural in meaning. (See Indefinite pronouns on page 218.) The following examples are *in*correct:

> Each poem and essay in her scrapbook had their own page.

> After the storm, every tree and bush looked as if they had been coated with glass.

These should read as *its own page* and *it had been coated*.

When gender enters into this, the solution is less clear-cut. Many would see the following as perfectly acceptable:

> Each participant was asked if they could bring a snack.
>
> Everyone should stay for the presentation, unless they have an urgent deadline.
>
> No one in their right mind would buy this house.
>
> Someone has lost their wallet.

Strictly speaking, these should appear as *he could bring, he has a deadline, no one in his right mind,* and *his wallet,* but many writers prefer to avoid this. Substituting *he or she* and *his or her* often sounds clumsy. Your decision on how to handle these constructions should depend on the formality of your writing and the expectations of your audience.

Collective nouns

These are nouns that may be treated as either singulars or plurals—but you must go one way or the other. If you have decided to treat such a word as singular, you cannot then apply a plural pronoun to it, or vice versa. The following examples are *in*correct:

> The board <u>was</u> unable to get <u>their</u> report out by the deadline.
>
> Her family <u>aren't</u> usually that supportive, but <u>it</u> rallied round her this time.

These should read as *its report* and *they rallied.*

Compound subjects

Writers are sometimes unsure which pronoun to use when there is more than one antecedent (a compound subject). The rule is, use a plural pronoun if the antecedents are joined with *and,* whether they are individually singular or plural. If they are joined with *or* or *nor,* have the pronoun agree with whichever antecedent lies nearest to it.

> Bayview High and Riverdale High will be holding <u>their</u> annual reunions on the same night.
> [Two singular antecedents joined by *and;* pronoun is plural]
>
> The salesclerks and the store manager said that <u>they</u> had had enough.
> [A plural and a singular antecedent joined by *and;* pronoun is plural]

Either Ellis or Herb will bring <u>his</u> camera.

[Two singular antecedents joined by *or;* pronoun is singular]

Neither the tree nor the bushes should have <u>their</u> branches pruned just yet.

[A singular and a plural antecedent joined by *nor;* pronoun is plural]

Something was different: either the paintings or the mirror had been moved from <u>its</u>
position. [A plural and a singular antecedent joined by *or;* pronoun is singular]

Note that constructions such as the last two often look awkward, so you may want
to consider recasting them even though they are grammatically correct.

Agreement in person

Pronouns come in the first person (singular *I;* plural *we*), second person (*you* for both
singular and plural), and third person (singular *she, he, it, one;* plural *they*). You must
match the appropriate pronoun to its antecedent, and be consistent: that is, do not
shift unnecessarily from one person to another. The following examples are *in*correct:

You shouldn't have to live behind triple-locked doors, although one has to use a bit
of caution.

A citizen has rights, but you have responsibilities too.

All kinds of people will be affected by these funding cuts: hospital patients; immigrants
learning English as a second language; people who are struggling to hold onto our
present standard of living.

Her firm belief is that one can lead a completely healthy lifestyle regardless of their size
or physical appearance.

CHOOSING A PRONOUN

'I see no harm in reading in itself, Ma'am.'

   'One is relieved to hear it.'

   'It's when it's carried to extremes. There's the mischief.'

   'Are you suggesting one rations one's reading?'

   'Your Majesty has led such an exemplary life. That it should be reading
   that has taken Your Majesty's fancy is almost by the way. Had you invested
   any pursuit with similar fervor eyebrows must have been raised.'

'They might. But then one has spent one's life not raising eyebrows. One feels sometimes that that is not much of a boast.'

'Ma'am has always liked racing.'

'True. Only one's rather gone off it at the moment.'

—Alan Bennett, *The Uncommon Reader*

The decision of which pronoun to use, in cases where there is a choice, has to do not with correctness but with tone, and can make a significant difference to the tenor of your writing.

Appropriateness of first person

Classes in creative writing teach that one of the first decisions is whether to go with a first-person narrative mode, where the story is told through the perceptions of one individual, or the more common third-person mode. With the former, the reader is privy to the private thoughts of only the "I" character; other characters are known solely as they are perceived by the narrator. Third-person mode provides more flexibility, although it can be restricted to the perceptions of one person as well. An occasional author will use the strategy of shifting between first and third person. Discussion of the many variants in narrative mode is beyond the scope of this book, but it is an issue that any aspirant fiction writer should thoroughly explore.

In formal or academic writing, use of the first-person singular to describe your own actions is not forbidden but is usually avoided. A multi-authored paper can safely use the first person plural, but this sounds a bit pompous if you're the sole contributor (it becomes akin to "the royal we"). The usual strategy is to avoid personal pronouns entirely; for example, instead of writing *I used two semi-structured interviews to assess whether potential subjects met the inclusion criteria*, phrasing the sentence as *Two semi-structured interviews were used to assess*. Use of the passive voice is appropriate if the question of who carried out the action is not relevant. However, in modes of writing where you are voicing opinions or interpretations that should be attributed to yourself, it would be better to go with the first person. For more on this, see Active Versus Passive Voice on page 289.

In writing that addresses the reader directly, such as user manuals and how-to books, it often sounds falsely intimate to use the first person plural, such as *Now that we have defined our terms, let's work through an example*. The focus of "user-friendliness" should be on clear communication and avoidance of bafflegab; not on a pretense that you're holding hands with your readers as they turn the pages.

Appropriateness of second person

Use of the second person ("you") is, of course, standard in any instructional writing. Apart from this, sometimes an interesting strategy is to use it where the first person would normally go. This tends to generalize what the speaker is saying, inviting the reader to relate more personally to the text even if it obviously is describing the experiences of the narrator.

> A little smoke couldn't be noticed now, so we would take some fish off the lines and cook up a hot breakfast. And afterwards we would watch the lonesomeness of the river, and kind of lazy along, and by and by lazy off to sleep. Wake up by and by, and look to see what done it, and maybe see a steamboat coughing along upstream, so far off toward the other side you couldn't tell nothing about her only whether she was a stern-wheel or a side-wheel; then for about an hour there wouldn't be nothing to hear nor nothing to see—just solid lonesomeness. Next you'd see a raft sliding by, away off yonder, and maybe a galoot on it chopping, because they're most always doing it on a raft; you'd see the ax flash and come down—you don't hear nothing; you see that ax go up again, and by the time it's above the man's head then you hear the *k'chunk!*—it had took all that time to come over the water. Once there was a thick fog, and the rafts and things that went by was beating tin pans so the steamboats wouldn't run over them. A scow or a raft went by so close we could hear them talking and cussing and laughing—heard them plain; but we couldn't see no sign of them; it made you feel crawly; it was like spirits carrying on that way in the air. Jim said he believed it was spirits; but I says:
>
> "No; spirits wouldn't say, 'Dern the dern fog.' "
>
> —Mark Twain, *The Adventures of Huckleberry Finn*

More unusual is literal use of the second person in literature, with the narrator addressing a specific other character, not the reader. Done skillfully, this can impart an intimacy that gives the reader the feeling of entry into a private communication from one individual to another.

> In the morning icicles hung from our windows and a foot of snow blanketed the ground. The trifle, which we had been too tired to wait for the night before, emerged for breakfast along with toast and tea. It was not what I'd expected, the hot mixture I'd helped beat on the stove now cold and slippery, but you devoured bowl after

bowl; your mother finally put it away, fearing that you would get a stomachache. After breakfast our fathers took turns with the shovel, clearing the driveway. When the wind had settled I was allowed to go outside. Usually, I made snowmen alone, scrawny and lopsided, my parents complaining, when I asked for a carrot, that it was a waste of food. But this time you joined me, touching the snow with your bare hands, studying it, looking happy for the first time since you arrived. You packed a bit of it into a ball and tossed it in my direction. I ducked out of the way, and then threw one at you, hitting you in the leg, aware of the camera hanging around your neck.

"I surrender," you said, raising your arms. "This is beautiful," you added, looking around at our lawn, which the snow had transformed. I felt flattered, though I had nothing to do with the weather.

—Jhumpa Lahiri, *Unaccustomed Earth*

Appropriateness of "one"

Speakers sometimes employ *one* instead of *I* to refer to themselves, despite *one* actually being in the third person. In dialogue, this strategy can be used to impart certain nuances, such as pomposity, to a character's words. (In the case of the Queen, of course, nothing less would be expected.)

[Bish] picked up the menu again. "I wonder whether I should have something sweet. . . one's Bengali tooth, you know. . . ."

Lata began to wish that he were up-and-going.

Bish had begun to discuss some matter in his department in which he had acquitted himself particularly well.

". . . and of course, not that one wants to take personal credit for it, but the upshot of it all was that one secured the contract, and one has been handling the business ever since. Naturally"—and here he smiled smoothly at Lata—"there was considerable disquiet among one's competitors. They couldn't imagine how one had swung it."

. . . . Bish, perhaps sensing that Lata had not taken to him, made an excuse and disappeared after dinner.

—Vikram Seth, *A Suitable Boy*

It can also be used to achieve a tone of cynicism, detachment, or slight self-mockery.

Ben: Christ, I feel awful. (*Pause.*) Do you know, all the time you were away, I didn't have one telephone call. I consider that very frightening. Not even from Tom.

Joey: Oh. (*Pause.*) I thought you found his company intolerable.

Ben: But one likes, as they say, to be asked. Also one likes people to be consistent, otherwise one will start coming adrift. At least this one will. (*Stands up.*) Also, how does one know whether Tom is still the most boring man in London unless he phones in regularly to confirm it. This is the fourth week running he's kept me in suspense. . . .

—Simon Gray, *Butley*

One can sometimes be used instead of using the second person; that is, it can be worked in as an occasional alternative to *you* in writing that speaks to the reader—although be aware that it becomes tedious if overused. It also may occasionally be an effective substitute for *he* in cases where you wish to describe something without making reference to gender. For a discussion and example, see Avoidance of Bias on page 314.

Active Versus Passive Voice

GRAMMATICALLY SPEAKING, **voice** refers to whether the subject of a sentence is on the giving or receiving end of the action. In sentences written in the active voice, the subject is the doer: *Bob caught the Frisbee in his teeth* (subject is *Bob*). In sentences written in the passive voice, the subject is acted upon: *The Frisbee was caught in Bob's teeth* (subject is *the Frisbee*). In a passive construction, the person or object that is actually performing the action may be named in the sentence, but is not the focus of it.

A passive construction is created by combining the appropriate tense of the auxiliary verb **to be** (*am/are/is, was/were, have been/has been, had been, will be, will have been*) with the past participle of the action verb. See Tense and Mood on page 235 for illustrations. This section is concerned not with the "how" but the "when": that is, under what circumstances each voice should be used. Misuses of voice do not constitute actual errors, but do affect tone and sometimes clarity.

USES OF THE ACTIVE VOICE

Many people recall their English teachers issuing a straight dictum to always use the active voice, never the passive. This overly simplistic advice would be better put as, use the active voice as a general rule, and use the passive voice only if there's a specific reason to do so. The active voice has definite advantages over the passive: it's more concise, it's often more informative, and it can make your writing appear more vigorous and confident. The passive voice may sound awkward, plodding, or overly cautious in contrast. For example, compare the following sets of sentences:

Passive: When the F1 key is pressed, help information is shown.

Active: Press the F1 key to see help information.

Passive: The letter received by Estella stated that legal action would be taken by the company, because her outstanding balance of fourteen cents had still not been paid.

Active: The company sent Estella a letter stating that it was going to take legal action because she had still not paid her outstanding balance of fourteen cents.

If the doer of the action isn't mentioned in the sentence and isn't obvious, the result is not only awkwardness but ambiguity.

The gifts given to Harold were much appreciated, although it was wished they smelled a little less pungent.

Who gave Harold the gifts? Who appreciated them? Who wished that they smelled less pungent? Any of the following might be possible:

Harold was very appreciative of the gifts the herbalist gave him, although he wished they smelled a little less pungent.

Harold's wife was very appreciative of the gifts the zookeeper gave him, although she wished they smelled a little less pungent.

Harold was very appreciative of the gifts the mad chemist upstairs gave him, although the next-door neighbor wished they smelled a little less pungent.

It is good practice to scan your writing for sentences that are unnecessarily or inappropriately worded in the passive, and convert them to the active. Online grammar checkers can be set to flag all occurrences of the passive voice.

USES OF THE PASSIVE VOICE

To say that the passive voice is never appropriate is to misunderstand it: why should it exist at all if its only purpose is to be held up as an example of what not to do? It is preferable to the active voice in a number of circumstances.

When the focus is on what is being done TO something rather than BY something

For example, it would be better to say *The wedding cake had to be carried in by eight strong waiters* rather than *Eight strong waiters had to carry in the wedding cake*, because the cake, not the waiters, is the focus of the sentence.

Often, the decision as to which voice is more appropriate can be made only by considering the larger context. Thus, you would say *Very young babies prefer black-and-white images* if you are writing about how babies of various ages respond to colors; however, if your focus is on the colors themselves, it would be better to word this information as *Black-and-white images are preferred by very young babies*. That is, neither form is inherently better: the purpose and context of your writing should determine which voice is used.

When the doer can be inferred or is not of interest

It would be better to say *The cake wasn't served until two in the morning* rather than *The waiters didn't serve the cake until two in the morning*, if (a) it can be inferred that the waiters did the serving and (b) it doesn't matter anyway, and using the active voice would put an inappropriate emphasis on the wrong part of the sentence. If there were some relevance to who served the cake, that would be different: For example, *The bride herself served the cake, and the groom handed out the forks.*

To avoid using the first-person-singular pronoun

In academic writing, it is conventional to avoid saying *I* when referring to one's own work (although *we* may be acceptable). The usual strategy is to word things in the passive voice. Thus, instead of *I assigned subjects to groups using a pre-generated randomization scheme*, saying *Assignment to groups was determined using a pre-generated randomization scheme*. Here again, the focus of the writing is on what is being done, not on who is doing it.

To avoid using all-male pronouns

Many writers prefer not to refer to a generic individual of unspecified sex exclusively as *he*. The problem is, there is no pronoun in English that can be used to indicate a single person of either sex, so more inventive strategies are needed. One approach is to word sentences in the passive voice to avoid the need for pronouns altogether. For example, instead of saying *The average driver trades in his car every four years*, you might say *The average car is traded in every four years*. For a discussion of other strategies, see Avoidance of Bias on page 314.

To deliberately deflect responsibility or conceal information

In speech, the passive voice is often adopted by individuals wishing to minimize or evade personal responsibility for something. A pulled-over driver might acknowledge, "Well, perhaps the car was being driven a bit fast," or a guilty room-mate confess, "Those cookies your mother sent you all got eaten." Speakers may switch between active and passive voice depending on the desire to take owner-ship of an action ("Honey, I've cleared the dining table, put away the food, and loaded the dishwasher, but one of our good wine glasses got broken"). In fiction writing, the passive voice may be applied to dialogue to impart an evasive tone to a character's words.

The passive voice is also handy if one wants to tell the truth and nothing but the truth, but not necessarily the whole truth. This strategy is commonly employed by writers treading on politically delicate ground, as it allows information to be presented in such a way that it cannot be accused of being inaccurate, although it may be incomplete or intentionally ambiguous. Saying *It has been alleged that Mr. Brandon knew about the takeover months in advance* is not the same as saying *Ms. Reisman has alleged that Mr. Brandon knew about the takeover months in advance.* That is, ambiguity in writing is not always the result of carelessness or inattention; some-times it is quite deliberate.

To vary sentence structure

A final legitimate use of the passive voice is for variety in your writing style: using it simply to avoid monotony. Wording every sentence the same way makes for tedious reading, so if you find that you are phrasing every sentence in the active voice, you might consider switching the occasional one to the passive. Of course, do so only in cases where the passive would not raise problems of awkwardness or ambiguity.

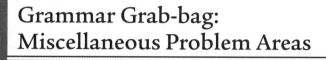

Grammar Grab-bag: Miscellaneous Problem Areas

THE CHALLENGE IN WRITING a book on English usage is not trying to think up topics to include, but deciding where to stop. There are hundreds of candidate subjects, and it seems almost a shame to omit discussion of grammatical constructs with names as alluring as accusative case, copular verb, and free morph. In the interest of keeping this volume under a thousand pages, however, the areas selected for review have been limited to ones that most often pose problems.

This last section addresses a motley group of grammar sticking points that do not individually require a chapter's worth of discussion, but are worth at least a mention.

ADVERB-ADJECTIVE DISTINCTION

Much could be written on adverbs, but the most needful point to make about them is simply, USE THE DAMN THINGS WHEN THEY'RE CALLED FOR! (Note: Primers on e-mail etiquette advise that all-caps text can be interpreted as shouting. Yes, this text is shouting.) Far too many people use an adjective when an adverb is the correct choice.

What is wrong with the following sentences?

I was shaking so bad I could hardly make out what the letter said.

I can't walk as quick as you—please slow down.

It was real nice of you to come.

The roads are slippery, so do drive careful.

The kids are being awful quiet—should we check on them?

Adverbs are not a difficult concept. Like adjectives, they are modifiers, but while adjectives modify nouns, adverbs modify verbs and adjectives. Most (though not all) adverbs are formed by adding *ly* to an adjective. In the sentences above, *shaking, walk,* and *drive* are verbs. *Nice* and *quiet* are adjectives. Accordingly, their modifiers are **NOT** the adjectives *bad, quick, real, careful,* and *awful,* but the adverbs *badly, quickly, really, carefully,* and *awfully.*

INTRANSITIVE AND TRANSITIVE VERBS

Verbs can be categorized in a number of ways: regular versus irregular, dynamic versus stative, main versus auxiliary, and more. (For discussion of these, see Tense and Mood on page 235.) Yet another distinction is **intransitive** versus **transitive**. While both types describe something done by a subject, the meaning of an intransitive verb is complete in itself, while a transitive verb acts directly on an object and its meaning is complete only if the object is named.

Examples of intransitive verbs are *arrive, sneeze, smile,* and *exist.* These all describe actions or states of the subject, but not something that the subject is doing to something else. You could create complete (if brief) sentences such as *they arrived, she sneezed, he's smiling, it exists.* But you can't arrive something, perform a smile on something, do a sneeze with something, exist something.

Examples of transitive verbs are *like, bring, congratulate, avoid.* All of these act on an object. You can't create sentences that contain nothing more than *we like, you bring, I congratulated, he avoids.* (Congratulated whom? Avoids what?) When an object follows, these become grammatically complete: *we like travelling, you bring dessert, I congratulated both of them, he avoids hard work.*

Many verbs can play both roles. You can *walk,* put one foot in front of the other (intransitive), or *walk the dog* (transitive); *grow,* as in get taller (intransitive) or *grow asparagus* (transitive); *move,* as in change homes (intransitive) or *move furniture around* (transitive).

There are a few common errors involving confusion of transitive and intransitive verbs. By far the most frequent is *lay/lie,* discussed in Frequently Misused Words on page 38. Briefly, *lie* is intransitive, describing the action of a subject without reference to an object (*go lie down*), while *lay* is transitive, describing an action done to an object (*would you lay those packages by the door*). Others are *sit/set* and *rise/raise. Sit* is intransitive (*relax, sit for a bit*), *set* is transitive (*next, set the party favors beside the plates*). *Rise* is intransitive (*what time do you usually rise*), *raise* is transitive (*can you raise that up a little*).

SPLITTING INFINITIVES

An **infinitive** is the "to" form of a verb: *to bellow, to whine, to connive, to go.* To split an infinitive means to put some word (usually an adverb) between the *to* and the verb: *to furiously bellow, to peevishly whine, to cleverly connive, to boldly go.*

Just as the spellings and meanings of individual words evolve, so do the rules governing how they should be strung together. When it comes to language, very little is carved in stone: attitudes change, rules become more flexible, authorities eventually bow to common usage and adjust their dictums. There is often not a consensus on the changes, so some writers will choose to bypass conventions they view as cobwebby while others continue to uphold them. Those conventions that are seen as having the least to contribute to clarity are the likeliest to fall by the wayside. For reasons inscrutable to many today, early grammarians decided that some of the rules of English grammar should conform to those of Latin. In Latin, the infinitive is not split; ergo, in English the infinitive should not be split. (The fact that in Latin the infinitive is one word and therefore *can't* be split didn't seem to trouble the rule makers.) The result is a decree that presents the modern writer with a dilemma: should one ignore it, since breaking it usually does no harm, or follow it, since failure to do so may be taken as ignorance?

There is no definitive answer to this, but given the widespread adherence to this convention, it's probably advisable to abide by it within reason. That is, if it's just as easy to word something in a way that avoids splitting an infinitive, do so—if for no better reason than some of your readers will fault you otherwise. For example, rather than saying *Their greatest pleasure was to proudly stroll along the boardwalk with their pet armadillo*, you could put the adverb after the verb: *Their greatest pleasure was to stroll proudly along the boardwalk with their pet armadillo.* Sometimes the adverb must go in front of the *to*: Instead of *I wanted to never see him again*, you could say *I wanted never to see him again.*

In fairness, an infinitive does sometimes function best as a unit, and separating its parts can weaken it by putting undue emphasis on the intervening adverb. And certainly, even if you have no problem with splitting infinitives, don't shatter them. Constructions such as the following seriously interrupt the flow, and make comprehension difficult:

She knew it would be a good idea to before the job interview grow out the green Mohawk.

Better: She knew it would be a good idea to grow out the green Mohawk before the job interview.

He asked me to as soon as I was finished grooming my newts clear off the table.

Better: He asked me to clear off the table as soon as I was finished grooming my newts.

Virtually every modern style guide agrees, however, that it is better to split an infinitive if the alternative would introduce awkwardness or misinterpretation. For example:

It's difficult for us to adequately express our gratitude.

This sentence would sound considerably stiffer as *It's difficult for us adequately to express our gratitude* or as *It's difficult for us to express adequately our gratitude.* Either version would make it look as if you were more concerned with a nitpicky devotion to the rule book than with your reader's ear. A better alternative, if you are determined to avoid the split infinitive, would be to move the interrupter to the end of the sentence: *It's difficult for us to express our gratitude adequately.* In some cases, however, you may feel that it puts too much distance between the verb and its modifier.

Similarly,

We managed to just miss the tree.

Phrasing this as *We managed to miss just the tree* implies that something else was hit. *We managed just to miss the tree,* while better, seems to imply that a failed attempt was made to do something else to the tree. In this case, splitting the infinitive is the most accurate way of expressing what happened.

In sum, use your ear when dealing with this type of construction, and make your decisions on a case-by-case basis. If you feel uncomfortable either splitting an infinitive or putting a modifier in what feels like an unnatural place, recast the sentence.

ENDING WITH A PREPOSITION

Prepositions are the words that define the relationships between other words: *Please put the skeleton <u>in</u> the closet; I'll meet you <u>at</u> the drugstore <u>after</u> the concert; we went <u>across</u> the country; she likes her salad <u>with</u> hot sauce <u>on</u> it.* Many prepositions have to do with time, space, or position.

A persistent myth is that a preposition may never come at the end of a sentence. For example, many students are taught that sentences such as *It's a subject I haven't thought about* and *You have to remember where he's coming from* should be worded as *It's a subject about which I haven't thought* and *You have to remember from where he's coming.* Again, the origins of this custom lie in Latin, in which a preposition cannot come after its target word. In English, however, the effect of ordering words this way is often to turn a phrasing that sounds natural and spontaneous into something tortured.

As with splitting infinitives, you may, as a general rule, prefer to avoid ending sentences in prepositions simply because of your readers' expectations. And indeed, sentences that follow the stricture sometimes do sound more elegant. For example:

> There are a couple of issues I'm willing to be more flexible on.
> *Revised:* There are a couple of issues on which I'm willing to be more flexible.

> It's astonishing that there are people this news comes as a surprise to.
> *Revised:* It's astonishing that there are people to whom this news comes as a surprise.

> There are some questions there are no easy answers for.
> *Revised:* There are some questions for which there are no easy answers.

> This is a matter I'd urge you to make your own decision on.
> *Revised:* This is a matter on which I'd urge you to make your own decision.

If the rewording would sound awkward, however, definitely leave the preposition at the end. Moving it would not "correct" your sentence; it would worsen it.

Part 4

Style

A piece of writing can be entirely free of errors in spelling, grammar, and punctuation—yet still be uncompelling or difficult to follow. The other parts of this book deal with relatively straightforward issues, such as how to spell a word, when to use brackets and when parentheses, or where to position an element in order for it to be unambiguous. Style, in comparison, is a gray area; elusive, subjective, context-dependent.

Obviously there is no one "best" style, since aside from the matter of personal taste, different writing strategies will be appropriate for different genres and audiences. Still, it is undeniable that some writers communicate more clearly and interestingly than others. The following sections review a few aspects of writing having to do with the style aspects of clarity and tone. Some of the topics addressed here are applicable to creative writing, some to informative writing, and some to both. In text whose purpose is to convey facts, clarity must usually be paramount (although other aspects are of course very important as well), while in fiction, this is not necessarily the case.

Note that the topics reviewed here should not be viewed as hard-and-fast rules, merely as factors worth bearing in mind.

Clarity

CLARITY IS ACHIEVED through applying logic and organization at all levels of a piece of writing: sentences, paragraphs, sections or chapters, and the overall work. Only the finer levels are explored here.

SENTENCE BREAKS

How long a sentence should be, before it ends and the next one begins, is determined by both clarity and tone. The aspect of tone is addressed on page 309; in this discussion, the focus is strictly on clear communication. Since a period signals that the end of one unit of information has been reached and a new one is about to begin, words that appear in the same sentence are assumed to be more closely connected to each other than are words that appear in adjoining sentences. Accordingly, putting closely related units of information in separate sentences might make their connection harder to grasp, while merging disparate thoughts into a single sentence might misleadingly imply that they are closely linked. Of course, it can sometimes be a matter of interpretation as to what constitutes "closely related" versus "disparate."

The examples below illustrate this reasoning. The "before" versions are not misleading, but could stand some improvement. The motive behind revising them can be described as follows: readers develop instantaneous, often subconscious expectations about the words they see, and if anything comes along that seems less than completely congruous with these expectations, there may be a need for them to pause momentarily and make a mental adjustment. The writer should anticipate these expectations and ensure that they are met, so that readers will always be on top of the intended meaning.

Example 1:

The disorder occurs in 3% of the general population, and is a chronic and debilitating condition associated with unstable affect and with problems in behavior, cognition, self-image, and interpersonal functioning.

The information presented in the first part of this sentence (percentage of the population affected) is distinct from the remainder (description of the disorder). This distinction would come through more strongly if the two were separated.

Revised: The disorder occurs in 3% of the general population. It is a chronic and debilitating condition associated with unstable affect and with problems in behavior, cognition, self-image, and interpersonal functioning.

Example 2:

It would be expensive and time-consuming to survey the entire population. What you want to do is to select a smaller, representative group (a sample). You use the data derived from this group to make generalizations about the whole.

The third sentence here names the *purpose* of the advice given in the second sentence. This connection would come through more strongly if the two were combined.

Revised: It would be expensive and time-consuming to survey the entire population. What you want to do is to select a smaller, representative group (a sample) and use the data derived from this group to make generalizations about the whole.

Example 3:

If you are hoping to interest a publisher in a book you are writing, the first step is to put together a proposal. The proposal should contain a few paragraphs that outline your goals. A table of contents is helpful. Attach some completed chapters as a sample of your writing. The proposal should include a brief description of yourself, stating your experience and why you are qualified to write this particular book. The publisher may send copies of the proposal to experts in the field for peer review. Thus, it often takes a few months before you can expect to hear whether your proposal has been accepted.

Apart from the choppiness of the short sentences, this paragraph contains a problem in how the information is chunked. There are two subtopics: what a proposal should contain, and what happens after you submit it. However, since each point begins a new sentence, it's not immediately obvious where the first subtopic ends and the next begins. Combining all the information on the first topic into one sentence would make the shift easier to distinguish, as well as allow the passage to flow better.

> *Revised:* If you are hoping to interest a publisher in a book you are writing, the first step is to put together a proposal. The proposal should contain a few paragraphs that outline your goals; a table of contents; some completed chapters as a sample of your writing; and a brief description of yourself, stating your experience and why you are qualified to write this particular book. The publisher may send copies of the proposal to experts in the field for peer review. Thus, it often takes a few months before you can expect to hear whether your proposal has been accepted.

Example 4:

> Our study compared the usefulness of hard copy versus soft copy help information, looking at how subjects employed one or the other of these types of help while performing tasks that included browsing, locating and reading data, and locating and using data to perform calculations.

The above is not strictly speaking a run-on sentence, which is defined as two or more grammatically complete units joined together without any intervening conjunctions or punctuation. However, it's a bit of a strain to follow. There are three distinct, if related, items of information, and these should be broken up. The purpose of the study should appear separately from the methods employed, while the description of the methods should be divided between one sentence that presents high-level information and another that presents the details.

> *Revised:* Our study compared the usefulness of hard copy versus soft copy help information. Subjects were asked to employ one or the other of these types of help while performing various tasks. These tasks included browsing, locating, and reading data, and locating and using data to perform calculations.

SENTENCE ORDER

Sentences may be crafted perfectly on an individual level, but if they are ordered in a way that is confusing or inconsistent, the overall text will not convey its message clearly. The following examples present passages that are muddled and out of sequence. The fact that they aren't impossible to follow is due mostly to the fact that they're short; on a larger scale, poor organization can render writing unintelligible.

Example 1:

When you prepare a research article for publication, set it aside and read it again after a day or two. Does it say what you intended? Try to get a peer review. A fresher or sharper eye may spot areas of weakness, omissions, and other problems in the manuscript that were hidden to you. Does the title accurately describe what the article is about? The discussion should stick to the topic and not ramble. Ensure that you have followed the authors' guidelines provided by the journal. Finally, be sure to run a spell-check before you submit your final copy.

Several problems here. First, the opening two sentences tell the writer what to do personally; the next two deal with getting someone else to give some feedback; then the passage goes back to things that the writer should do. The first category should be completed before the second is begun.

Second, sentence 4 (*a fresher or sharper eye*) is closely related to sentence 3 (*try to get a peer review*), in that it expounds on *why* such a review is important. This relationship would be made more obvious if the two sentences were run together.

Third, two of the aspects that the writer is advised to check for are presented as questions, and two are presented as statements. Apart from the faulty parallelism (information on equivalent matters should be presented in an equivalent way; see Parallel Structure on page 223), this structure almost makes it look as though the text following each question is providing an answer to that question, which is not the case here.

Revised: When you prepare a research article for publication, set it aside and read it again after a day or two. Does it say what you intended? Does its title accurately describe what it is about? Does the discussion stick to the topic and not ramble? Have you followed the authors' guidelines provided by the journal? Try to get a peer review— a fresher or sharper eye may spot areas of weakness, omissions and other problems in the manuscript that were hidden to you. Finally, be sure to run a spell-check before you submit your final copy.

Note that the final sentence has been left where it was, even though it's in the category of things to do oneself. This is because it is stated to be the last step in the process.

Example 2:

The important thing to remember about an oral presentation is that you have only about fifteen minutes to tell the world about your work; hence, preparation is crucial. Design your overheads so that you don't find yourself apologizing for tiny details that aren't showing up clearly. There are no absolutes about how much information should go on a single slide, but use judgment. Don't include anything that you are not planning to talk about.

Begin your talk by explaining the objectives of your study, and then move on to the methods and findings. Leave enough time for a mention of what future directions you hope to take. In your graphics, avoid dark colors, which often do not display well. Don't put too much text in a slide, as it's often better to give details orally. If possible, familiarize yourself beforehand with the LCD projector and room lighting, and ensure that there is a laser pointer available. Keep each slide in mind as you talk so that there is no mismatch between your oral and visual messages. And finally, try to end on a strong note: don't trail off on some feeble line like, "Well, that's all I've got to say."

This text is scattered both time-wise and content-wise, alternating between how to prepare for a presentation and what to do during it. An improved organization would put the information in chronological order.

Revised: The important thing to remember about an oral presentation is that you have only about fifteen minutes to tell the world about your work; hence, preparation is crucial. Design your overheads so that you don't find yourself apologizing for tiny details that aren't showing up clearly, and avoid dark colors, which often do not display well. There are no absolutes about how much information should go on a single slide, but use judgment. Don't put in too much text, as it's often better to give details orally, and don't include anything that you are not planning to talk about.

If possible, familiarize yourself beforehand with the equipment; for example, ensure that there is a laser pointer available and that you know how to handle the LCD projector and the room lighting. Begin your talk by explaining the objectives of your study, and then move on to the methods and findings. Keep each slide in mind as you talk, so that there is no mismatch between your oral and visual messages. Leave enough time for a mention of what future directions you hope to take. And finally, try to end on a strong note: don't trail off on some feeble line like "Well, that's all I've got to say."

CONCISENESS

Too often, writers will make a point, then immediately restate the same information a different way. Sometimes this is done out of sloppiness, but often it is intentional, due to the mistaken belief that repetition will make a point come through more clearly or emphatically. Many people have even specifically been taught in school to do this. The likely effect is actually the opposite: since it is reasonable for readers to

expect that every sentence will have something new to say, they may find it disconcerting or confusing to reencounter the same information, and end up referring back
to earlier sentences to see if there's some subtle distinction they missed. (Of course,
another reason why some writers employ redundancy is to pad out skimpy content, hoping no one will notice that not much is actually being said. It's an old
term-paper trick that didn't fool your profs then, and is unlikely to fool anyone
else now.)

The following passages would benefit from being condensed:

Example 1:

Efficacy has been demonstrated when the duration of the standard Comprehensive Anxiety Management (CAM) protocol is abbreviated from one year to just six
months. Two studies have evaluated the efficacy of six months of CAM. A study by
Masterton and colleagues (3) involved a comparison of six months of CAM with a
treatment-as-usual control in patients diagnosed with anxiety disorders. The findings favored CAM. By the end of the treatment, participants in the CAM group
showed significantly lower occurrences of phobias, panic attacks, and irritability episodes relative to the control group.

In a second study to evaluate a six-month trial of CAM, Lefarge et al. (4) compared CAM to a matched treatment-as-usual control in patients diagnosed with
obsessive compulsive disorder. Results indicated that that there were statistically significant differences favoring CAM in terms of reduced repetitive thoughts and compulsive behaviors.

Sentences in this passage contain needlessly overlapping information. Line 1 says
that six months rather than a year of the CAM treatment has been found to work;
line 2 basically repeats this, with the only new information being that this conclusion is supported by two studies. These would be better off combined. Line 3 does
not need to open with "a study": we already know it is describing a study. Line
4 (the findings favored CAM) adds nothing to what follows (a statement of how
CAM had better results than the other treatment). And the first line of the second
paragraph unnecessarily repeats the purpose of the next trial.

The rewrite below brings the word count down from 140 to 100 words with no
loss of meaning.

Revised: Two studies have demonstrated the efficacy of the standard Comprehensive
Anxiety Management (CAM) protocol when the duration is abbreviated from one year
to six months. Masterton et al. (3) compared six months of CAM with a treatment-

as-usual control in patients diagnosed with anxiety disorders. Relative to the control group, CAM participants had significantly lower occurrences of phobias, panic attacks, and irritability episodes. Similarly, Lefarge et al. (4) compared six months of CAM to a matched treatment-as-usual control in patients diagnosed with obsessive compulsive disorder, and found statistically significant differences favoring CAM in terms of reduced repetitive thoughts and compulsive behaviors.

Example 2:

In our survey of pediatricians, nearly all our respondents indicated that their clinical activities should include both diagnosis and subsequent follow-up of child abuse cases. Over 97 percent of those returning the survey said that they believed that they should be detecting and treating this problem.

The second sentence adds little here. The terms *detecting* and *treating* are just restatements of *diagnosing* and *following up* (if there is a distinction, it's a pretty fine one), and *respondents* are obviously the same people as *those returning the survey*. The only actual addition is a specification of what was meant by *nearly all*, and this information is easily incorporated into the first sentence.

Revised: In our survey of pediatricians, nearly all our respondents (over 97 percent) indicated that their clinical activities should include both diagnosis and subsequent follow-up of child abuse cases.

Example 3:

The validity of a test that measures coping traits is restricted to the population for which the test was designed. A measure that is valid when administered to one type of population may not be valid for another, and there are no standardized tests in this field that are appropriate in all situations. It is not possible to develop or refine a test for measuring coping traits that can meet all requirements and perform well in all circumstances. Therefore, researchers must be careful to select a test that is appropriate for their specific situation.

The second-to-last sentence here merely restates what is already clear, so the passage does not lose any information if this sentence is deleted entirely.

Revised: The validity of a test that measures coping traits is restricted to the population for which the test was designed. A measure that is valid when administered to one type of population may not be valid for another, and there are no standardized tests in this field that are appropriate in all situations. Therefore, researchers must be careful to select a test that is appropriate for their specific situation.

SIMPLIFICATION

It is all too common to be so close to your own work that you fail to recognize that an idea that is perfectly clear in your own mind is not coming through to others.

Example 1:

A primary PLD infection is defined as either the first documented, laboratory-confirmed PLD event in the subject's history or a recurrent documented, laboratory-confirmed PLD event that is occurring more than 3 months after a prior event.

This statement defining a medical condition contains two scenarios, an initial PLD event and a recurrent PLD event, but this distinction is obscured because information that is common to both (documented, laboratory-confirmed PLD event) is repeated. That clutters up the sentence and makes it harder to spot what is unique to each scenario. Having the common description appear just once allows for a clearer distinction between what is common and what is unique.

Revised: A primary PLD infection is defined as a documented, laboratory-confirmed PLD event that is either the first in the subject's history or is occurring more than 3 months after a prior event.

Example 2:

A dilemma for clinicians treating suicidal patients with Axis II disorders is how to manage risks in the context of limited knowledge about effective treatment options. Ideally, to effectively manage these situations, clinicians require sound, scientifically derived recommendations upon which to base treatment plans.

This passage illustrates a subtle problem often seen in academic writing: failing to clarify the *purpose* of a statement. Just putting down the statement may not be enough; the reader may get to the end of it and then wonder, "okay, but so what?" The point struggling to express itself above is that it would be good *if* clinicians had more knowledge about effective treatment options, but unfortunately at this time they do not. The references to "dilemma" and "limited knowledge" suggest this only indirectly, and the second sentence does not make it clear that the "sound, scientifically derived recommendations" are a wish list rather than something currently available.

Revised: Ideally, clinicians who treat suicidal patients with Axis II disorders would base their treatment plans on sound, scientifically derived recommendations. At present, however, knowledge about effective treatment options is limited.

Example 3:

Until recently, a prevailing opinion among practitioners was that this disorder was untreatable, largely due to a nonexistent empirical literature providing evidence to counter this belief.

More straightforward wording helps the meaning come through more clearly.

Revised: Until recently, most practitioners believed that this disorder was untreatable, largely because there was no empirical literature providing evidence to the contrary.

READING LEVEL

Reading level is concerned with the number of years of formal education theoretically required by an individual in order for that person to fully comprehend a piece of writing. No matter how well written something is, it will fail in its fundamental task of communication if it is too challenging for its intended audience. On the other hand, if it is written at too junior a level, readers may become bored or feel patronized, and may either put it aside or take its content less seriously.

In some genres of writing, the most obvious being school texts and children's literature, the concept of reading level is critical. Children of the same age of course exhibit a wide range of reading skills, but the averages are known. In the case of adults, reading level is less of an issue but still must be kept in mind. It is self-evident that information on the same topic would be presented very differently in a professional journal and in a popular magazine.

A somewhat rough-and-ready approach to assessing reading level involves determining the average number of letters or syllables per word and the average number of words per sentence in your piece, and using these metrics to come up with an overall readability score. Most word processors provide such a function, and it never hurts to run it just to see what it comes up with. Keep in mind, however, that this approach is simplistic, since such measures do not capture all aspects of reading difficulty. There are many short words with highly sophisticated meanings and many polysyllabic words that are undemanding; similarly, a short sentence can pack in considerable subtlety, while a lengthy one can be straightforward and easy to follow. Reading-level tools can be useful, but ultimately you must rely on common sense and intuition to ensure that you are expressing your ideas in a way that your intended audience will understand.

Apart from age, a factor to keep in mind is the background knowledge of your audience. Specialized terminology that is perfectly appropriate for a readership of, say, engineers, physicians, or scholars of Sumerian cuneiform will need to be replaced or explained for a lay audience. For more detail, see the discussion of jargon on page 322.

Tone

TONE INCLUDES such aspects as the overall flow and character of a piece of writing.

SENTENCE LENGTH

What's an "appropriate" average number of words in a sentence? How long is too long, how short is too short? The extremes are occasionally used for literary effect—think James Joyce at one end and Ernest Hemingway at the other. Long rambling lines can achieve a dreamy or stream-of-consciousness mood, while a series of short, staccato sentences can set an atmosphere of tension or drama. In general, though, neither extreme is advisable, and a strategy that works in the hands of a master may fall very flat in those of a novice. There is of course no defined minimum/maximum range, and it would be improper for any book on style to dictate one. Usually, the most pleasing effect is produced by variation: a majority of sentences of moderate length (say, between fifteen and twenty-five words), the occasional one notably longer or shorter. What you want to avoid is a monotonous uniformity, with every sentence looking as if it came out of the same mold. A special situation, of course, is books for young children, where the reading level (see page 307) requires that all sentences be limited in length.

One interesting strategy is to occasionally throw in very short sentences, which adds a certain punch.

> Do I believe in equality between the sexes? I'm not sure. . . . Women carry the puzzle of family life inside their heads, they just do. . . .
>
> Not long ago, my friend Philippa told me that she and her husband had drawn up a will. Phil said she wanted a clause stipulating that, in the event of her death,

Mark would promise to cut the children's fingernails. He thought she was joking. She wasn't joking.

One Saturday last autumn, I got back from a Boston trip to find Richard in the hall, all set to take our two out to a party. Emily, hair uncombed, appeared to have a dueling scar on one cheek—it was ketchup from lunch. Ben, meanwhile, was bent double, wearing something very small and dotted in apricot that I didn't recognize. On closer inspection, it turned out to be an outfit belonging to one of Emily's dolls.

When I suggested to my husband that our offspring looked as though they were going out to beg in the Underground, Rich said that if I was going to be critical I should do it myself.

I was going to be critical. I would do it myself.

—Allison Pearson, *I Don't Know How She Does It:*
The Life of Kate Reddy, Working Mother

In text where the purpose is to convey information, extremes of length should be avoided, since overly long sentences may come through as verbose and hard to follow and overly short ones as choppy and stilted. To some extent, length is dictated by the genre. For example, in a quick-reference brochure, even moderately long sentences would be inappropriate, while in a scholarly journal, too-short sentences might look simplistic and unprofessional

WORD CHOICES

'You look a little worried, Bunter,' said his lordship kindly to his manservant. 'Is there anything I can do?'

The valet's face brightened as he released his employer's grey trousers from the press.

'Perhaps your lordship could be so good as to think,' he said hopefully, 'of a word in seven letters with S in the middle, meaning two.'

'Also,' suggested Lord Peter thoughtlessly.

'I beg your lordship's pardon. T-w-o. And seven letters.'

'Nonsense! said Lord Peter. 'How about that bath?'

'It should be just about ready, my lord.'

Lord Peter Wimsey swung his mauve silk legs lightly over the edge of the bed and stretched appreciatively. . . .

Mr Bunter had retired to the kitchen to put the coffee on the stove when the bell rang. Surprised, he hastened back to the bedroom. It was empty. With increased surprise, he realized that it must have been the bathroom bell. The words 'heart-attack' formed swiftly in his mind, to be displaced by the still more alarming thought, 'No soap.' He opened the door almost nervously.

'Did you ring, my lord?' he demanded of Lord Peter's head, alone visible.

'Yes,' said his lordship abruptly. 'Ambsace.'

'I beg your lordship's pardon?'

'Ambsace. Word of seven letters. Meaning two. With S in the middle. Two aces. Ambsace.'

Bunter's expression became beautified.

'Undoubtedly correct,' he said, pulling a small sheet of paper from his pocket, and entering the word upon it in pencil. 'I am extremely obliged to your lordship. In that case the "indifferent cook in six letters ending with *red*' must be Alfred.'

Lord Peter waved a dismissive hand.

—Dorothy L. Sayers, *The Fascinating Problem of Uncle Meleager's Will*

One of the joys of English is its bottomless reservoir of vocabulary, with a word to capture pretty well every entity, action, phenomenon, and emotion under the sun. How about *pococurante*, *aposiopesis*, and *palimpsest*? (Look those up if they're not in your repertoire.) A search of a thesaurus will bring up a slew of synonyms on almost everything, some carrying the exact same meaning and others differing just in nuance. No snob, English happily borrows from elsewhere in order to encapsulate a complex description in a single word, if no native term is just right. Think of the German *schadenfreude* (feeling pleasure over the misfortunes of another), the Yiddish *chutzpah* (gall or audacity, carrying an implication of either condemnation or grudging admiration depending on the context), and the Japanese *umami* (the fifth basic taste, along with sweet, sour, salty, and bitter).

Truly, the best way to enrich one's vocabulary is to be a broad reader, so that you absorb new words not through studying lists in reference books but by encountering them in context. It's not a bad idea to keep a dictionary at hand when confronted by an author who is challenging you more than usual.

In your own writing, it is not always advisable to go for a sesquipedalian style. (What, you don't know that one? "Given to or characterized by the use of long words.") Obviously the audience is a factor when choosing your words, and vocabulary must be age-appropriate, with easier words used for younger readers. Even for a mainstream or an educated adult readership, however, putting in a twenty-dollar word where a simpler one would do can come across as "see how clever I am" and cause readers to feel more irritated than impressed. If a particular word is the best fit for the idea you want to capture, though, it should not be avoided. When searching for *le mot juste*, there is a middle ground between dumbing down and being pretentious. If your readers know a word already, good; if not, it will do them no harm to acquire it.

For more on audience appropriateness, see Reading Level on page 307.

WORD VARIATION

Readers can find it annoying to see the same word appear over and over. Sometimes writers are so intent on emphasizing an important term or phrase that they use it to death, to the point where it is more distracting than informative.

Strategies to get around this include using pronouns, synonyms, and elliptical constructions, or dropping unnecessary references altogether. If you are having a hard time coming up with synonyms, remember that a thesaurus can be an invaluable tool.

Example 1:

The family-oriented approach to medical care involves recognizing that an ailment of one family member will have an impact on all family members. A family is continually subject to both the inner pressures coming from its own members and to outer pressures that affect family members. A serious illness of one of its members increases both the internal and external demands placed on the family. Internally, the illness of a family member forces an adaptation by other family members of their roles and expectations. Externally, in this age of specialized medicine, a family member's illness typically demands interaction with multiple health care settings and personnel. Thus, a key focus of family assessment in health-related research and practice must be on family stress and coping.

This passage, just six sentences long, contains the word *family* eleven times and *member* (or *members*) eight times. These counts can easily be reduced to four and three, respectively.

Revised: The family-oriented approach to medical care involves recognizing that an ailment of one family member will have an impact on all. A family is continually subject to both inner and outer pressures, and a serious illness of one of its members increases both these types of pressure. Internally, the illness forces an adaptation by other members of their roles and expectations; externally, in this age of specialized medicine, it typically demands interaction with multiple health care settings and personnel. Thus, a key focus of family assessment in health-related research and practice must be on stress and coping.

Example 2:

The Software Development Manager program provides software development organizations with a mechanism for efficiently managing the components of a software application throughout all development stages of the application. Software Development Manager enables a group of software developers to create and manage multiple versions of a software application. This software manager program also maintains the integrity of the application by not allowing one developer to overwrite another developer's changes to the source.

Here, in three sentences, the word *software* appears seven times, *develop* (or some derivation) seven times, *manage* (or some derivation) five times, and *application* four times. Below, these counts are reduced to three each.

Revised: The Software Development Manager program provides a mechanism for efficiently managing the components of a software application throughout all stages of its development. This program enables a group of software developers to create and manage multiple versions of an application, and maintains the integrity of the application by not allowing one group member to overwrite the source changes of another.

Do not, of course, use different terminology to describe the same concept if this is inappropriate. In many fields, particularly those in science and technology, terms have very precise meanings, and calling the same entity by different names could lead to confusion and misinterpretation. Although it is preferable to avoid using the same word too many times, clarity must always take precedence.

EFFECTIVE REPETITION

The advice about conciseness should hardly be taken to mean that nothing should ever be restated. In many genres of informative writing, summaries or recaps at the end of each chapter are suitable; while in long works, or in books or documents that are not expected to be read from start to finish, it may be appropriate to repeat important details wherever they are relevant. Just be certain that you have a sound rationale for putting down anything that has been explained elsewhere.

The rules are quite different in creative writing, where repetition can be used to literary effect. In the following description of an early twentieth century assembly line, the reiteration of one sentence creates an image that is almost hypnotic:

> On the left stood a man named Wierzbicki; on the right, a man named O'Malley. For a moment, they are three men, waiting together. Then the whistle blows.
>
> Every fourteen seconds Wierzbicki reams a bearing and Stephanides grinds a bearing and O'Malley attaches a bearing to a camshaft. This camshaft travels away on a conveyer, curling around the factory, through its clouds of metal dust, its acid fogs, until another worker fifty yards on reaches up and removes the camshaft, fitting it onto the engine block (twenty seconds). Simultaneously, other men are unhooking parts form adjacent conveyers—the carburetor, the distributor, the intake manifold—and connecting them to the engine block. Above their bent heads, huge spindles pound steam-powered fists. No one says a word. Wierzbicki reams a bearing and Stephanides grinds a bearing and O'Malley attaches a bearing to a camshaft. The camshaft circles the floor until a hand reaches up to take it down and attach it to the engine block, growing increasingly eccentric now with swooshes of pipe and the plumage of fan blades. Wierzbicki reams a bearing and Stephanides grinds a bearing and O'Malley attaches a bearing to a camshaft. While other workers screw in the air filter (seventeen seconds) and attach the starter motor (twenty-six seconds) and put on the flywheel. At which point the engine is finished and the last man sends it soaring away. . . .
>
> —Jeffrey Eugenides, *Middlesex*

AVOIDANCE OF BIAS

> Help the reader focus on the content of your paper by avoiding language that may cause irritation, flights of thought, or even momentary interruptions. Such sources of distraction include linguistic devices and constructions that might imply sexual, ethnic, or other kinds of biases.
>
> —*Publication Manual of the American Psychological Association*

A discussion on how to use language in a way that won't annoy any of your readers—or at least not too many of them—necessarily involves treading on delicate ground, since emotions run rather higher here than on matters such as use of the serial comma. Would you describe someone who uses a wheelchair as disabled or physically challenged? Someone of a race other than Caucasian as nonwhite or a person of color? A member of a municipal government as an alderman or alderperson?

Words that to one reader are simple descriptions may be perceived by another as excluding, dismissive, or stereotyping; on the other hand, what some see as reasonable, thought-out alternatives may be viewed by others as euphemistic, grating, or ridiculous.

Entire volumes have been published on how to steer clear of sexism, racism, ageism, ableism, classism, sizeism, and other 'isms, some of which may seem to demand navigation through a minefield of political correctness. It is, however, important to be attuned to the full significance of the wordings you choose, and assess whether they in any way stereotype or diminish individuals based solely on some demographic trait unrelated to their personal beliefs or actions. Merely alluding to a demographic trait is sometimes justifiably objected to if it has no relevance to whatever is under discussion.

If your intention is to provoke, that is one thing. Some people however are honestly oblivious to biases or irritants in the words they have chosen, or simply feel that there is oversensitivity these days to nuances of language and that others should accept their style without reading too much into it. Yet the APA admonition cited above makes a good point: readers who are alienated by your terms or phrasings will be less receptive to the content of what you are saying—and that, after all, defeats the purpose of writing. It will be in your own interest to choose your words so that they act to convey your message or ideas, not unintentionally distract from them.

Just one issue is addressed below: that of alternatives to using male-only pronouns, in order to avoid excluding the testosterone-challenged half of the population.

* * *

The English language tends to take masculinity as the norm, whereby the basic word for something often connotes maleness while femaleness must be specially elucidated. (Consider the very name of our species: Man.) For writers trying to avoid this type of bias, the most challenging parts of speech to work around are personal pronouns. Grammatically, it is correct to use *he* and *him* to refer to an individual of unspecified sex, yet many people of both sexes see this as inappropriate and excluding. How many men would feel they were being personally included in writing that used only *she* and *her*?

As late as its 1979 revision, the best-selling writer's guide *The Elements of Style* (first published by William Strunk in 1919 and updated by E.B. White in 1959) had this to say on the matter:

> The use of *he* as a pronoun for nouns embracing both genders is a simple, practical convention rooted in the beginnings of the English language. *He* has lost all suggestion of maleness in these circumstances. . . . It has no pejorative connotation; it is never incorrect.

Attitudes have certainly changed on this, in both popular opinion and style guides.[1] An example of the turn in thinking can be found in a 1970s update of Dr. Benjamin Spock's best-selling *Baby and Child Care* (originally published in 1946), where he states in a foreword:

> The main reason for this [revision] is to eliminate the sexist biases of the sort that help to create and perpetuate discrimination against girls and women. Earlier editions referred to the child of indeterminate sex as "he". Though this in one sense is only a literary tradition, it, like many other traditions, implies that the masculine sex has some kind of priority.

Feeling that *he* is inappropriate when applied to both sexes is one thing; finding a graceful alternative is another. *The Elements of Style* raised some valid objections when it went on to say:

> Substituting *he or she* in its place . . . often doesn't work, if only because repetition makes it sound boring or silly. . . . The furor recently raised about *he* would be more impressive if there were a handy substitute for the word. Unfortunately, there isn't—or at least, no one has come up with one yet. If you think *she* is a handy substitute for *he*, try it and see what happens. Alternatively, put all controversial nouns in the plural and avoid the choice of sex altogether, and you may find your prose sounding general and diffuse as a result.

Clearly, the "recently raised" furor hasn't gone away, but neither has anyone come up yet with a handy substitute. The challenge, therefore, is to find less handy substitutes. These sometimes take a bit of ingenuity but, if successful, allow you to work around the problem without your readers even noticing. The pros and cons of various strategies are discussed below.

Using *he/she*, *s/he*, or *they*

The solutions that are the easiest to apply are also the least likely to please: putting down *he/she* or *s/he*, or using *they* as a singular pronoun. The first two are jarring; the third ungrammatical. All three seem like cop-outs, as if you couldn't take the

---

[1] A fourth edition of *The Elements of Style* was produced in 1999, 14 years after the death of E.B. White (Strunk died in 1946). Among the changes was the deletion of this text.

trouble to come up with a more imaginative strategy, and draw attention a bit too loudly to the fact that you're enlightened enough to not use all-male pronouns.

Certainly, there are some contexts where these strategies are appropriate. In speech, everyone uses *they* and *them* when sex is unknown or irrelevant (*if anyone comes by, tell them I'll be back in a few minutes*). It sounds natural and carries no ambiguity. Still, stricter standards must apply in writing, and the fact remains that grammatically, *they* refers to more than one individual. Some authorities argue persuasively for extending its acceptability as a singular pronoun into writing as well, but until this is formalized, you run the risk of having your more fastidious readers thinking you just don't know any better. A sentence such as the following looks outright sloppy:

> To some people, this type of therapy is perceived as very confrontational, so it should not be attempted until the patient feels a degree of security within themselves.

Also keep in mind that the indefinite pronouns *each, every, anybody,* etc., are singular, so cannot be grammatically combined with *they* (although see the discussion of this on page 282). Some—not all—would argue that the following sentences are incorrect:

> Each student must hand in their own lab report.

> Every guest was given a name tag when they arrived.

Finally, with respect to *he/she* and *his/her,* while these strategies are often acceptable in less formal writing, they quickly become tedious if overused. And the non-word *s/he* has little to recommend it other than its efficiency. (How would you *pronounce* it?)

Using *he or she*

The expression *he or she* (along with *him or her* and *his or hers*) is an excellent solution when used sparingly, working its way into sentences in a manner that looks easy and uncontrived. The key word, however, is *sparingly*. It becomes clumsy and annoying with repetition and looks positively dreadful if used more than once within a single sentence. Any reader would find the following distracting:

> The clinician can play an important role on the research team. He or she is invaluable in gathering physical data from his or her patients, and equally useful is his or her role in gathering subjective data based on his or her impressions and feelings.

There isn't a "magic number" of how often is too often for these expressions; certainly, a few appearances in a large document is unobtrusive. If the need arises frequently, however, it is best to vary *he or she* with other strategies.

Alternating *he* and *she*

In some genres of writing, it works well to change about half the occurrences of *he* to *she*. This strategy can be applied to made-up scenarios or case histories, where the reference is to a single individual and a female example would fit in just as naturally as a male one.

It works less well if the reference is to a group or population. For example, in the following, it would be difficult for readers to assume that males are included:

The survey indicated that the average newspaper reader prefers her news in a concise form.

Every worker we spoke to says that she fears for her future and that of her family.

Using the plural form

Going with the plural form instead of the singular is a simple and effective strategy if the context is in fact referring to more than one person. For example:

We asked each participant to speak openly about his feelings.

Alternative: We asked all participants to speak openly about their feelings.

This strategy is popular and often works smoothly and unobtrusively, but it should be avoided if the plural sounds contrived or unlikely. There are many cases where a plural rather than a singular noun simply would not convey the same sense, particularly if you wish to emphasize the individuality of the actors under discussion. Bear in mind the caution about your words coming through as "general and diffuse." And, as discussed above, in more formal genres of writing it is not a good idea to get around the issue by using *they* as a singular pronoun.

Using the indefinite pronoun *one*

In some circumstances, *one* can be substituted for *he*. (This pronoun is also sometimes used as a substitute for the first person, as discussed on page 287.) Use of this pronoun carries an implication that the writer and reader belong to the same group or share some relevant characteristic or interest; in a sense, it conveys the idea of "you or I." For example, in an article aimed at physicians:

> Clinical judgment involves the physician making use of his experience, as well as his knowledge of the particular patient.
>
> *Alternative:* Clinical judgment involves making use of one's experience, as well as one's knowledge of the particular patient.

This approach is probably inappropriate if the intended readers would not self-identify with the group or activity under discussion. Also, overuse of *one* can make writing sound a bit stuffy.

Using the second person

In certain types of writing, you can use *you* in order to avoid the third person—as is done in this sentence. This form is appropriate for genres that address the reader directly, such as instruction manuals and reference books. For example:

> The reader should familiarize himself with these terms before proceeding.
>
> *Alternative:* Familiarize yourself with these terms before proceeding.

Obviously, this strategy can be used only in text that speaks directly to the reader.

Using the passive voice

Consider using the passive voice in order to avoid pronouns altogether. You want to be cautious with this strategy, since the passive voice carries the risk of making sentences clumsy or ambiguous, but it can sometimes work well.

> An advantage to making the surgeon responsible for acquiring the research data is that he often requires it in any case for clinical purposes.
>
> *Alternative:* An advantage to making the surgeon responsible for acquiring the research data is that this information is often required in any case for clinical purposes.

For more on this, see Active Versus Passive Voice on page 289.

Rewording to avoid pronouns

It is often possible to find a way of wording a sentence that eliminates the need for a pronoun without resorting to the passive voice. This may sometimes be the neatest and least jarring solution. Consider the following examples:

> A psychiatrist may ethically obtain research data from his patients, but his main objective must remain that of attending to their needs.

Alternative: A psychiatrist may ethically obtain research data from patients, but must not lose sight of the main objective of attending to their needs.

The bashful writer is reluctant to come right out and state his position firmly.

Alternative: The bashful writer is reluctant to come right out and take a firm position.

Sometimes it may be difficult to capture exactly the meaning you want without using a pronoun. Naturally, your meaning must take precedence over style. Also, do not confuse gracefully recasting a sentence with simply repeating the noun in place of a pronoun:

The writer of technical manuals is cautioned against inserting humorous comments. The writer may feel that such comments liven up a dull topic and make it more readable, but the writer should bear in mind that humor is not universal, and what the writer finds funny, another person may find annoying or offensive.

Readers of such prose would probably wish *its* writer had gone with "he" instead.

In sum, there is no single strategy that will work for all situations, and it is usually best not to use a single strategy throughout. With some effort and imagination, however, you can write around the gender problem in a way that should leave none of your readers alienated.

ACCENTS AND SPEECH PATTERNS

In fiction writing, capturing colloquial accents can add color—although note that a very strong dialect might make things challenging for the reader.

I departed to renew my search; its result was disappointment, and Joseph's quest ended in the same.

"Yon lad gets war un' war!" observed he on re-entering. "He's left th' yate at t' full swing, and miss's pony has trodden dahn two rigs o' corn, and plottered through, raight o'er into t' meadow! Hahnsomdiver, t' maister 'ull play t' devil to-morn, and he'll do weel. He's patience itsseln wi' sich careless, offald craters—patience itsseln he is! Bud he'll not be soa allus—yah's see, all on ye! Yah mun'n't drive him out of his heead for nowt!"

—Emily Brontë, *Wuthering Heights*

If you are creating characters whose first language is not English, don't go overboard in presenting their speech as you think it would sound. The effect may come through as ridiculing of the group the character represents, and may make the dialogue difficult to read. This isn't to say you shouldn't convey foreign accents at all; just use moderation. A dropped letter here and a misused word there will usually be effective enough.

Making fun of the idea of making fun of an accent, of course, is something else:

> The intense, hennaed Solange Renault, who once played Catherine in *Henry V* at our Stratford, was obliged to settle long ago for the continuing role of the French-Canadian settlement nurse in my *McIver of the RCMP* series.
>
> (Private joke: I often request the weekly script that's to be sent to Solange, and rewrite some of her lines for her amusement.
>
> NURSE SIMARD: By Gar, de wind she blow lak 'ell out dere tonight. Be careful de h'ice, everybody.
>
> Or, NURSE SIMARD: Look dere, h'it's Fadder St-Pierre 'oo comes 'ere. Better lock up de alcool and mind your h'arses, guys.)
>
> —Mordecai Richler, *Barney's Version*

If you are quoting a real-life individual who happens to have an accent, either foreign or colloquial, do not to try to reproduce the accent phonetically at all, unless it has some direct relevance to the story. Direct quotes must include the exact words used, but you do not have to carry this to the extent of reproducing intonations.

With regard to style of speech, it is important to make your fictional characters talk realistically. *You* should have a firm handle on the rules of grammar, but you obviously don't want to put perfect diction into the mouths of characters who are meant to be uneducated or rustic.

> Every night now I used to slip ashore toward ten o'clock at some little village, and buy ten or fifteen cents' worth of meal or bacon or other stuff to eat; and sometimes I lifted a chicken that warn't roosting comfortable, and took him along. Pap always said, take a chicken when you get a chance, because if you don't want him yourself you can easy find somebody that does, and a good deed ain't ever forgot. I never see pap when he didn't want the chicken himself, but that is what he used to say, anyway.
>
> —Mark Twain, *The Adventures of Huckleberry Finn*

Do not, however, carry rustic dialect to the point of parody.

JARGON

The term **jargon** can be understood in two ways. In its positive sense, it refers to the vocabulary of a specialized field of knowledge: law, medicine, sports, car mechanics, computer programming, music, publishing, and so on. Every field has terms that may be obscure or unintelligible to outsiders, but serve the purpose of labeling things unambiguously and capturing complex ideas in a concise manner. If such terms weren't available, it would be necessary to use wordy definitions and explanations.

If you are writing on complex topics, you may be faced with a decision as to whether you should use jargonistic words, or substitute terms that would be more generally understood. The answer comes down to the following: know your audience. Some terms may not be appropriate for the layperson; for example, you'd want to avoid obscure medical lingo in a pamphlet aimed at patients (or at least follow the terms with explanations, if the terms are unavoidable). However, to use the simpler words in an article on the same subject aimed at physicians would come through as insulting.

If you feel that you are a reasonable representative of your intended readership, do not include any unexplained terms that you yourself need to look up in order to understand. Conversely, if you are being hired to write something for an audience that is trained in ways you are not, and have been provided with information that includes professional jargon, do not automatically delete or replace terms just because you personally are not familiar with them.

Jargon is without merit when it is used not because no more precise terms exist, but in order to inflate the importance of what's being said—or often, to disguise the fact that nothing very important is being said in the first place. This isn't to say that you should "dumb down" your style: very often a longer or more exotic word does capture a meaning more precisely or effectively. What you ought to avoid is using pretentious words when perfectly good simpler equivalents are available. There is no need to say *utilize* when you mean *use*, to refer to a *facility* when you mean a building, or to *commence dialoguing* when you mean start a conversation.

A particularly absurd use of jargon is when it is applied to soften unwelcome messages. Pupils showing unsatisfactory performance are emerging; employees about to laid off are transitioning; used cars are pre-owned. Put a positive spin on the name, the reasoning seems to go, and the downside will magically not exist.

CLICHÉS

As the language maven William Safire advised in his list of writing rules, avoid clichés like the plague. Clichés are words or phrases that are trite, hackneyed, and irritatingly predictable. How do you know if something qualifies as one? It's a strong contender if the content of a piece of writing leads readers to half-expect a certain term or phrase to appear and sure enough, out it pops in due time. Don't feel compelled to describe every snow-covered landscape as a winter wonderland, or every tropical one as sun-kissed. Medical practitioners don't all need a passing reference as "the good doctor." Not everything of small dimensions must be tiny perfect. And why do gunshots always ring out: what are they, bells?

Another category of cliché consists of words or phrases that are overused to the point of complete banality and have either lost the strength of their original meaning (any term paper containing "awesome" or "incredible" should be docked an automatic five percent) or never had much to begin with (at the end of the day, think outside the box, give a hundred and ten percent. . . .).

A search of the Web will readily yield inventories of vapid phrases to avoid, which spares this author the annoyance of producing a list here.

WHEN LESS IS MORE: THE ART OF SUBTLETY

> Tell all the Truth but tell it slant / Success in Circuit lies.
>
> —Emily Dickinson

In informative writing such as manuals or reports, the goal is naturally to be as clear and straightforward as possible, but this goal does not always hold in every genre. Learn the art of holding back. It isn't needful to name every shade in a sunset or to describe a character's features in photographic detail; good writing leaves something to the reader's imagination. You want to present enough detail to convey an image, but it's not always best to do so with lumbering thoroughness or dedicated realism. For example, qualifying each line of dialogue with descriptive adverbs, such as *"That dress makes you look like a walrus," he said insultingly*, or *"Do you think I should dye my hair purple?" she asked teasingly*, comes through as heavy-handed. As much as possible, make the dialogue and the context convey mood or motivations; spelling things out on every occasion carries an implication that you don't expect your readers to pick up on much themselves. Before you qualify, modify, or elaborate on anything, think about whether your addition is truly having an enhancing effect.

In fiction writing, indirect descriptions are often far more compelling than direct ones. In the following account of a miffed girlfriend dumping her swain for an evening to go out with what proves to be a dull-as-dishwater date, mark how the portrayal of one character is serving equally to convey a picture of another.

> Tall, tanned, solicitous Derek Burton . . . wore a Westminster Old Boy's tie, carried a furled umbrella, and did not instantly sink to the sofa, kicking off his shoes, but remained standing until she had sat down, and lit her cigarette with a slender lighter he kept in a chamois pouch, and raised his glass to say, cheers. He didn't have to be asked how she looked, grudgingly pronouncing her all right, and taking it as an invitation to send his hand flying up her skirts, but immediately volunteered that she looked absolutely fantastic. Outside, he opened his umbrella, and held it over her. Derek drove an Austin-Healey with a leather steering wheel and what seemed, at first glance, like six headlights and a dozen badges riding the grille. There were no apple cores in the ashtray. Or stale bagels in the glove compartment. Instead, there were scented face tissues mounted in a suede container. There was also a coin dispenser, cleverly concealed, filled with sixpences for parking meters. As well as a small, elegant flashlight and a leather-bound log book. Once at the restaurant, Derek tucked the car into the smallest imaginable space, managing it brilliantly, without cursing the car ahead of him, or behind, in Yiddish. Then she waited as he fixed a complicated burglar-proof lock to the steering column. Jake would absolutely hate him, she thought, which made her smile most enticingly and say, "How well you drive."
>
> —Mordecai Richler, *St. Urbain's Horseman*

In the following account of a chess game, note how no moves are actually described. The sense of concentration and excitement is conveyed in a completely intangible way.

> During my first tournament, my mother sat with me in the front row as I waited for my turn. I frequently bounced my legs to unstick them from the cold metal seat of the folding chair. When my name was called, I leapt up. My mother unwrapped something in her lap. It was her *chang*, a small tablet of red jade which held the sun's fire. "Is luck," she whispered, and tucked it into my dress pocket. I turned to my opponent, a fifteen-year-old boy from Oakland. He looked at me, wrinkling his nose.
>
> As I began to play, the boy disappeared, the color ran out of the room, and I saw only my white pieces and his black ones waiting on the other side. A light wind began blowing past my ears. It whispered secrets only I could hear.

"Blow from the South," it murmured. "The wind leaves no trail." I saw a clear path, the traps to avoid. The crowd rustled. "Shhh! Shhh!" said the corners of the room. The wind blew stronger. "Throw sand from the East to distract him." The knight came forward ready for the sacrifice. The wind hissed, louder and louder. "Blow, blow, blow. He cannot see. He is blind now. Make him lean away from the wind so he is easier to knock down."

"Check," I said, as the wind roared with laughter. The wind died down to little puffs, my own breath.

—Amy Tan, *The Joy Luck Club*

In this description of Joseph as a slave in the house of Potiphar, note how his reaction to the instructions of an officious upper servant is conveyed in four words. Adding modifiers such as "disdainfully" or "indignantly," or any verbal response, would only diminish the effect.

". . . The refreshment is here and is written down: the silver bowl, the little gold jug full of pomegranate juice, the little gilt cups, and five sea-shells with grapes, figs, dates, doum fruit, and little almond cakes. You will not steal or even nibble them?"

Joseph looked at him.

"You will not, then," said Khamat, in some confusion. "So much the better for you. I merely asked, though I thought at once you would not like to have your ears and nose cut off—and moreover it is probably not your way. . . ."

—Thomas Mann, *Joseph and His Brothers*
(translated from the German by H.T. Lowe-Porter)

No two writers will have quite the same style, and it cannot be overemphasized that there are no rights and wrongs, no absolutes in this realm. Study what strategies are used by authors whose work you admire, and consider whether your own style might be improved by borrowing or adapting any of these.

Suggestions for Self-Improvement

THIS FINAL SECTION OF THE BOOK describes some techniques for improving your writing style and for assessing how well your efforts are succeeding. Not all these strategies will be right for everyone, but it can't hurt to at least consider them.

Focus on the whole as well as the parts

Any time you add or revise some words, reread what surrounds them to ensure that everything else still fits. Often, a change in one place will necessitate a change in another. Naturally you must focus on each line as you create it, but as soon as you have the first draft in place, back up a few lines and read through the earlier text again. You will sometimes find that the latest addition doesn't fit in quite as it should—perhaps it restates a point already made, or doesn't make a smooth enough transition from what came before. As you form each new sentence, keep going back and rereading it from the start to ensure that all its elements mesh together. As you form each new paragraph, keep rereading it from its first line to see how its sentences fit together: perhaps the topic shifts enough that the paragraph should be broken up, or perhaps a particular word now is repeated too many times within a short space.

Put your work aside for a while and then come back to it

You may be confident that you have polished your words into their final form, only to find that when you look at them a little later, problems jump out: illogical connections, clumsy sentence structures, a strained-sounding tone, subtle grammatical errors. A lapse of time enables you to come back to your work with a more objective eye. A day or more away is ideal, but even a few hours can make a difference.

Have someone else look your work over

Any writer, no matter how skilled, can benefit from getting a second opinion, because by definition one is always too close to one's own work. Given that any writing is ultimately intended for other people's consumption, it only makes sense to find out how other people perceive it. The individual whose opinion you seek need not be a better writer than you, since the goal is not necessarily to have this person correct or revise what you have done. Rather, it is to provide you with feedback on how your points and your tone are coming across. If your critic doesn't get your jokes, or finds a character you meant to be funny and sympathetic merely irritating, or can't follow some instruction because you left out a step you thought would be perfectly obvious to anybody—at least consider the possibility of making changes (and do your best to remain on speaking terms afterward). A professional editor is ideal, but if this is not practical or affordable, select someone whose opinion you respect and who represents your intended readership as nearly as possible.

Look at a hard copy

It's the rare writer today who doesn't work on-screen, and the advantages of word processing can't be overstated. Yet somehow, words can look different when viewed on paper; it's hard to say why. The effect can range from having a typo you'd been staring at all along suddenly pop out, to noticing that your tone is coming through as too brusque, too cautious, too formal, too casual—in sum, you may at this point pick up more clearly on certain intangible aspects of your writing that can make a critical difference to its readability or credibility. Just why such nuances should emerge more clearly on a hard copy is not clear, nor is this effect universal, but some people experience it.

Read your text aloud

This strategy is likeliest to be helpful if your writing is intended for oral presentation, but can be useful for other genres as well. *Hearing* your own words, as opposed to looking at them, may change your impression of them and expose weaknesses such as pretentious-sounding terms, wooden dialogue, or rambling sentences.

And most important of all...

Draft, draft, draft. Write and rewrite. And then rewrite again. This strategy is not an option or a suggestion, but a basic part of the writing process. No professional writer expects to get away without revision; the only question is, how much will be necessary. The act of writing, after all, does not involve simply transcribing ideas inside your head onto a screen or paper: it involves developing and articulating those ideas in the first place. As you write, you can expect to shift your priorities; to change your mind about what information goes with what; to choose a different tack in order to drive some point home. Resist the temptation to hang onto passages that you labored long and lovingly over, if they no longer fit.

Some thoughts to end on:

Writing is thinking on paper. —William Zinsser

How do I know what I think until I see what I say? —E.M. Forster

Je n'ai fait cette lettre-ci plus longue que parce que je n'ai pas eu le loisir de la faire plus courte (*I have made this letter longer than usual, only because I have not had time to make it shorter*). —Blaise Pascal

I was working on the proof of one of my poems all the morning, and took out a comma. In the afternoon I put it back again. —Oscar Wilde

And to sum it up, from U.S. Supreme Court Justice Louis Brandeis:

There is no great writing, only great rewriting.

Credits

Index

Become a
WRITER'S DIGEST
VIP

Fuel your passion for writing with the Writer's Digest VIP Program. You'll have access to the best writing advice, markets, competitions, tips, prompts, and more. The program includes:

- One-year U.S. subscription to *Writer's Digest* magazine

- One-year of online access to WritersMarket.com, with updated listings for more than 8,000 book publishers, magazines, literary agents, contests, scriptwriting markets, and more

- Access to our most important webinar: The Essentials of Online Marketing & Promotion—a 1-hour tutorial on how to promote yourself as a writer, and get the attention of editors and agents

- Discounts on Writer's Online Workshops course registrations and purchases made at the Writer's Digest Shop

- And more!

Become a **WRITER'S DIGEST VIP**
and take your writing career to the next level!

http://www.writersdigestshop.com/product/writers-vip/